HELLENISTIC CULTURE

The late Moses Hadas was, until his death in 1966, Jay Professor of Greek and chairman of the Department of Greek and Latin at Columbia University. He was the author of *A History of Greek Literature, A History of Latin Literature,* and many other books. *The Stoic Philosophy of Seneca: Essays and Letters,* edited by Mr. Hadas, is also published in the Norton Library.

HELLENISTIC CULTURE

Fusion and Diffusion

By MOSES HADAS

Jay Professor of Greek
Columbia University

W · W · NORTON & COMPANY
New York · London

Books That Live
The Norton imprint on a book means that in the publisher's
estimation it is a book not for a single season but for the years.
W. W. Norton & Company, Inc.

W. W. Norton & Company, Inc., 500 Fifth Avenue, New York, N.Y. 10110
W. W. Norton & Company Ltd., 37 Great Russell Street, London WC1B 3NU

SBN   393   00593   3

PRINTED IN THE UNITED STATES OF AMERICA
3 4 5 6 7 8 9 0

PREFACE

IT was in the hellenistic age, after the conquests of Alexander the Great, that disparate cultural traditions interacted upon one another to fix the permanent contours of European civilization, and the processes and products of that interaction, which are the concern of this book, therefore have more than antiquarian interest. Prospective readers who are not students of antiquity must be warned that it is not a text or reference book. It does not pretend to full and even-handed treatment, nor does it limit its views and conclusions, as a reference work must, to a traditional consensus. A period so long, areas so scattered, strands so diverse, cannot indeed be dealt with systematically in a single volume or with a uniform degree of originality by a single investigator. It has therefore seemed best to choose aspects of the whole subject which are obviously essential or particularly useful as specimens and at the same time within the range of the writer's own interests. Of the many omissions the most glaring perhaps is in the realm of the exact sciences, in which interaction between east and west was particularly fruitful and in which the achievements of the hellenistic age eclipsed those of the classical period. For these matters the reader may now be referred, with complete confidence, to the late George Sarton's magnificent *A History of Science: Hellenistic Science and Culture in the Last Three Centuries* B.C. (Harvard University Press, 1959).

My indebtedness to the work of others is acknowledged in the notes. Robert Pfeiffer of Harvard and Avigdor Tcherikover of Jerusalem, whose names recur there frequently and whose friendship I valued, died as my book was being completed. For two

others, Professor Franz Dornseiff of Leipzig and Dr. Marc Rozelaar
of Jerusalem, mere note acknowledgment is inadequate. Professor
Dornseiff very generously gave me permission to reproduce his
arguments showing the connection of Vergil and Horace with the
Sibylline Oracles, and Dr. Rozelaar gave me similar permission to
reproduce his arguments showing the influence of hellenistic erotic
poetry upon Canticles. Other friends who have helped and encouraged me I purposely leave unnamed, because the customary
absolution which accompanies expressions of gratitude in Prefaces
is not enough to dissociate persons named from complicity in
works they may disapprove.

MOSES HADAS

Columbia University
June 25, 1959

CONTENTS

HELLENISTIC CULTURE

Chapter I

GENESIS AND DIFFUSION

THE miracle of Greece is not single but twofold: first the unrivaled rapidity and variety and quality of its achievement, and then its success in permeating and imposing its values upon alien civilizations. What combination of ethnological, geographical, historical, and climatic factors gave rise to the first miracle we can only speculate; for the second we have tangible evidence, and it will be the object of this book to suggest and illustrate some of the less obvious ways in which Greek modes of thought, Greek taste, and Greek ideals became part of the continuing European heritage.

When we first encounter them the Greeks appear to be a mixture of a native Mediterranean element and an aristocracy of Achaean invaders from the North. The Achaean chieftains cherished and propagated the heroic ideal reflected in the Homeric poems. The essence of this ideal is a dynamic conviction of the worth of the individual, which motivated a restless drive for excellence in every department, unhampered by the restraints which blunted other ancient peoples. To safeguard his individual prestige Achilles wills that his own comrades suffer defeat; a good part of the *Odyssey*, which is less heroic, is concerned with the education of Telemachus to the requirements of his aristocratic position. Homer remained the central factor in Greek education, and the outlook characteristic of the heroic ideal which his poems inculcated—individualistic, anthropocentric, essentially aristocratic—persisted throughout the classical period, even when blood had lost its prerogatives. The culmination of the unrestrained drive for

excellence came in the fifth century: between the repulse of the
Persian invasion in 479 B.C. and its subjugation by Sparta in 404
Athens produced the towering masterpieces which have been re-
garded with awe by all succeeding generations.

Later Greeks were themselves the first to regard their glorious
past as classic, and the Romans adopted their view. For subsequent
opinion about the Greeks this is important, because until the last
century Europe accepted the Roman estimate without question.
It is in consequence of the Roman view, and its corollaries that
the main function of antiquarian study is to provide background
for earth-shaking genius and that only a sovereign nation can
possess an individuality worth examining, that the older historians of Greece (and modern purists who share the Olympian
view [1]) look no farther than the death of Demosthenes (322 B.C.).
Even George Grote, who was perhaps the best historian of Greece
and as devoted to democracy as to spiritual greatness, closes his
magnificent twelve-volume history of Greece (1846–56) with this
obituary:

I have now brought down the history of Greece to the close of the
generation contemporary with Alexander, the epoch from which
dates not only the extinction of Grecian political freedom and self-
action but also the decay of productive genius and the debasement
of that consummate literary and rhetorical excellence which the fourth
century B.C. had seen exhibited in Plato and Demosthenes. The contents of this last Volume indicate but too clearly that Greece as a
separate subject of history no longer exists; for one half of it is employed in depicting Alexander and his conquests—that non-Hellenic
conqueror into whose vast possessions the Greeks are absorbed, with
their intellectual brightness bedimmed, their spirit broken, and half
their virtue taken away by Zeus—the melancholy emasculation in-
flicted (according to Homer) upon victims overtaken by the day of
slavery.

But Greece was not emasculated. To say nothing of the intellectual and artistic achievements of the period called hellenistic
(to distinguish it from the earlier "hellenic" period), the energy
which enabled the Greeks to spread their culture over the entire Near East is in itself a demonstration of continuing vitality.

The fusion of cultures which the drive to hellenize achieved marks a major turning point in the history of civilization, for out of the amalgam emerged the civilization of Europe. The processes by which fusion was effected therefore deserve closer examination.

Cultural influences are transmitted in two ways: the past may be exploited for paradigms to be consciously imitated, or the process may be one of unconscious assimilation. The Greek experience does indeed afford a continuously edifying spectacle capable of refining taste, like specimens in a museum; but the models remain exotic and their use may produce such shrieking anomalies as a bowler hat atop a kimono or Gothic fenestration in a skyscraper. The compound of elements in a culture must be chemical rather than physical; the ingredients must coalesce until their separate identities are no longer easily discernible.[2] Indeed the degree of assimilation is in inverse ratio to the ease with which an increment is recognizable, as an etymological example will make clear. *Discus* has been naturalized into English and requires no italics, but it is obviously an alien word, imported to designate a specific novelty and nothing else. *Disc*, an earlier borrowing of the same word, looks strange but not so foreign as *discus*, and its meaning is more general, it designates any round flat object, a phonograph record or part of the spine. The earliest borrowing of the same Latin word is *dish*, which looks thoroughly native; its meaning is so generalized that it may be applied to a vessel of almost any size or shape.

Even if *dish* had not been received into the language the object it represents would still have come into use, and the presence of the word is of no great cultural significance. Some word borrowings may be more meaningful. The adjective *episcopal* is a learned importation whereas its noun *bishop* looks thoroughly English. Both alike derive from *episcopus*, but the noun came in much earlier; its unaccented initial vowel and grammatical ending were soon sloughed off, and the *sc* changed to *sh* and the *p* to *b* according to regular rules of linguistic change. But here the very presence of the word is significant, for without the word we could not imagine the thing. The bishop's cathedral is another case of complete assimilation. We know, as we are meant to know, that an architect who puts a row of columns supporting a gabled pediment on the façade of a public building is exploiting the classical legacy. The nave and aisles and apse and clerestory of a cathedral show that it derives from a Roman basilica, but it and its significance have been thoroughly assimilated.

Not words and buildings alone but literature and all it represents exhibit the same degrees of assimilation, and often in the same work. *Paradise Lost*, for example, has obvious reminiscences of antiquity, such as Greek or Hebrew names and allusions, which are meant to be recognized as such and are therefore no more significant of assimilation than Ajax or Hercules used as trade names. Less easily recognizable as derivative and therefore more fully assimilated are the form and structure—the fact that verse is used for a long and profoundly serious work, that it starts *in medias res* and fills its plot out with a flashback, that it has a great council of chieftains, a virtual battle between gods and giants, an idyllic interlude, and so on; if the *Odyssey* and the *Aeneid* had not existed *Paradise Lost* would never have been written. But the matter of the poem, for which one might suppose the adapted form was only a vehicle, is no more possible to conceive without its antecedents. It is in fact the areas of most thorough assimilation which require, and repay, the closest study.

On the surface Shakespeare looks more independently English, and yet *Hamlet* shows the same degrees of assimilation as *Paradise Lost*. There are, in the most obvious category, names like Horatio and Claudius and their calculated associations. But Shakespeare would not have written his drama in verse, would not have made it a subtle and ingenious work of art worthy of the best attention of intelligent and discriminating audiences, if the Greeks had not written their tragedies. The important lesson the Renaissance learned from the Greeks was not their plots or persons or use of music but the fact that drama could be both artistic and noble.[3] And finally, the issue between man and his fate which is at the heart of *Hamlet* is the product of a complete assimilation of ancient discussions on the subject. Shakespeare is like the fifth-century Greeks but different too, and the difference is largely due to the eastern ingredient.[4]

Where the influence of Greeks upon Englishmen is accepted as a natural development, astonishment is often expressed at the thought that peoples east of the Mediterranean should be similarly affected; it must therefore be emphasized that (as the sequel will attempt to show) they were in fact more deeply affected. The compartmentalization of national characters is a relatively recent phenomenon. Until the development of critical scholarship in the nineteenth century men were content to speak of "the ancients" or of "Greco-Roman antiquity" as an entity, without preferring one half of Plutarch's worthies over the other; and because their interest was human rather than antiquarian they were quite right in so doing. Not until Winckelmann [5] discerned the differences between Greek and Roman works of art in museums and between earlier work and later did students find it important to distinguish between them.

As between the Greco-Roman civilization and the east an even sharper line was drawn, out of religious considerations. Religious history, it was assumed, began with Abraham and secular with Homer, and when the two insulated currents did eventually come into contact there was a natural hostility between them. Fusion took place when the tensions were relaxed by an external force. The notion of hostility goes back to St. Paul's classic characterization of the two parties in I Corinthians 1.22: "For the Jews require a sign and the Greeks seek after wisdom." This dichotomy post-Winckelmann romantics, with their new enthusiasm for the "naturalism" of Greek art and Greek manners, elaborated and crystallized, until the terms hellenism and hebraism have come to conjure up on the one hand an uninhibited and uncompromising naturalism, rationalism, aestheticism, and on the other piety too unworldly to be concerned with logic or beauty or democracy. Needless to say, the picture is enormously distorted on both hands. We shall see that many Greeks required a sign and many

Jews sought after wisdom. The evidences of Greek popular religion show that the average Greek was at least as continuously and intensely aware of the supernatural as the Hebrew; and if the Hebrews were so completely wrapped up in religion they would not need constantly to be chided for worldly backsliding and they could never have won a war. There was certainly enough common ground between the parties to make communication not only possible but attractive.

The constitution of man is reasonably homogeneous, not only in his physical properties but, as we have come to realize, in his psychological characteristics also. The range of his potentialities is large, but not unlimited. They form an arc, in Ruth Benedict's useful image, and cultures adopt a segment as they adopt a segment of the arc of speech sounds men are capable of making in order to fashion language. Here is her image and its application: [6]

We must imagine a great arc on which are ranged the possible interests provided either by the human age-cycle or by the environment or by man's various activities. A culture that capitalized even a considerable proportion of these would be as unintelligible as a language that used all the clicks, all the glottal stops, all the labials, dentals, sibilants and gutturals from voiceless to voiced, and from oral to nasal. Its identity as a culture depends upon the selection of some segments of this arc. Every human society everywhere has made such a selection in its cultural institutions. Each, from the point of view of another, ignores fundamentals and exploits irrelevancies.

It is possible to differ by as much as 180 degrees without getting out of the arc. Actually the civilizations we shall be concerned with occupied contiguous parts of the arc and in many essentials overlapped. We now know that both Abraham and Homer had predecessors, and we have good grounds for suspecting that these predecessors were in some sort of contact with each other. Archaeology shows that there was not a century of the Iron Age during which Greek artifacts, mostly ceramics, were not being brought into Syria and Palestine.[7] Especially significant geographically and chronologically are the contacts with the Ugaritic people; numerous objects of Aegean origin and local imitations of them have been found at Ras Shamra.[8] The new Hittite materials show actual parallels to an important segment of Greek mythology—the castration of Ouranos and the succession of Kronos.[9] Many elements in even the Olympian religion, which is mainly associated with the earliest Achaean invaders of Greece, have eastern affiliations; Apollo himself derives from the east.[10] All of this is a good deal more definite than the vagaries of the "Pan-Babylonians" of a generation ago who forced all myth from Cain to William Tell into the strait jacket of Babylonian astral conceptions or devised esoteric relationships with the Gilgamesh myth. Relationships between Gilgamesh (and other writings of the ancient Near East) and Homer do exist, but they are now argued on more definitely philological grounds, on the basis of specific literary techniques and on the general concept of the epic hero.[11] Indeed there appear to be affinities between the Mesopotamian and Indian civilizations also, as the excavations at Mohenjodaro have tended to show. A relationship between Old Testament and Sanskrit materials and between Sanskrit and New Testament has long been suspected,[12] and now it has been maintained that *Gilgamesh* influenced not only *Iliad* and *Odyssey* but *Ramayana* and *Mahabharata* also.[13] When we reflect on the kinship between Siduri's advice to Gilgamesh, the Egyptian Song of the Harper, Ecclesiastes, and Epicureanism, or between Amenemope, the book of Proverbs, and Hesiod,[14] the world seems a much cozier place.

Community of some degree between the Aegean civilization and the east in high antiquity is an important factor for understanding subsequent interaction. In certain basic outlooks and practices traditions deriving from a common source survived, sometimes in a subliterary existence, among both groups, so that their eventual encounter was rather in the nature of a recognition than of a new experience. We shall notice striking similarities in the matter of cult practices and notions of ritual purity, and, more important, we shall notice them in theological and especially eschatological outlooks also. We shall not then have to debate whether certain basic ideas traveled in one direction or the other or wonder at the susceptibility of one people or another to what had been regarded as an alien importation. A case in point is belief in the dualism of body and soul with all its implications. The older and essentially romantic view of the Greeks as uncompromising rationalists regarded this belief as an alien element which could only be explained as an importation from the east. Actually the complex of Greek beliefs and practices commonly styled Orphic, which premise a dualism of body and soul, derives from the pre-Achaean Mediterranean stock which also spread eastwards.[15] If parallels to eastern thought which are found in Plato necessarily imply fifth- or fourth-century borrowing we should have to include the doctrine of ideas also. Professor Albright points out that "a precursor even of the Platonic idea is found in the Sumerian *gish-khur*, the outline, plan, or pattern of things-which-are-to-be, designed by the gods at the creation of the world and fixed in heaven in order to determine the immutability of this creation." [16]

It is clear, then, that there was never an impervious wall between Greece and the east, and when history becomes articulate there is evidence to show that contacts begun in prehistoric times continued.[17] The word for "Greek" in eastern languages from Hebrew to Sanskrit is something like "Yavan," which is in fact "Ionian." Greek merchants carried their enterprise over Egypt and western Asia from the seventh century on, and by the sixth century the coasts of Syria and Palestine were dotted with Greek cities and trading stations. Naucratis and Daphne in Egypt were important Greek cities and a factor in Athenian foreign policy. There were Greek mercenaries in the armies of Egypt and Babylonia, of Psammetichus II and Nebuchadnezzar. Alcaeus' brother Antimenidas served in Palestine against Jehoiachim in 597–596 or in 586,[18] and one of the oldest bits of Greek we have was scratched on the leg of a colossal statue in Egypt by a Greek soldier serving there. We know from an inscription of Darius Hystaspes that in about 500 B.C. Ionian, Carian, and Lydian artisans were brought to Susa to work on the royal palace. The commercial influence of Greece is indicated by the fact that Asiatic countries began to imitate Greek coinage. Even before Alexander, the Persian satraps and local rulers of Cilicia, Syria, and Palestine were approximating the Attic standard. Even under Persian suzerainty Judaea received permission to mint silver in imitation of Attic coins, adding the inscription *Yahud*.[19]

The Persian Wars, early in the fifth century, gave each party fuller experience of the other. The Ionian refugees from Persian pressure were a leaven for the more sluggish mainland Greeks; we may hazard the paradox that it was the influence from the east that gave Greece the rationalist bent we consider characteristic, and that without it the old Orphic elements would have smothered political and intellectual enlightenment as similar elements did in India. In any case, from the Persian Wars forward relationships with the east continued to be a major and ever present factor in Greek politics. The hostility sharpened the sense of difference between east and west and accentuated the conviction of Greek superiority. This conviction persisted, and after the conquests of Alexander came to be shared by many orientals; their response, as we shall see, was to transform themselves into Greeks.

Even after the pace of hellenization was so enormously accelerated by Alexander the increments were not all added at a single time nor assimilated at an equal rate; nor was the rate equal in different environments. The Middle East was never so thoroughly hellenized as the Near East, and in the Near East a segment (but only a segment) of the Jewish people resisted the hellenism which their near neighbors welcomed. We shall find that the synagogue frescoes at Dura are particularly instructive because they show us the initial stages of fusion. In the third century A.D., in other words, Dura had not yet reached the stage which had been passed at Alexandria in the second century B.C. Moreover individual alien elements may be assimilated without consciousness of surrender, and indeed themselves come to be regarded as part of the tradition which must be protected against encroachment by hellenism. The use of Greek language and literary modes for an apologetic and even polemic "barbarian" literature illustrates the first part of this proposition. The second part is illustrated by the strong antipathy of nascent Christianity to the paganism to which it was itself so heavily and apparently so newly indebted.

The cultural and political situations in which hellenism found the peoples it touched were naturally factors in its progress. In the Seleucid empire, which was an aggregate of diverse people with no unifying tradition and where the rulers encouraged hellenization, progress was easy and rapid. In Egypt, which was unified by an ancient tradition and where the rulers discouraged the spread of hellenization, progress was much slower. The non-Hellenes who had achieved Greek status continued to be proud of their hellenism, as the so-called *Acts of the Pagan Martyrs* show, but the mass of the population was much less affected than in Syria, and remained the Egyptians they had always been, under the Greeks as they would do under Romans, Christians, and Mohammedans.

When intercourse became general, cultural influences naturally moved in both directions, but hellenization of barbarians was far more massive than barbarization of Hellenes. Even in the case of religious doctrine, where it is commonly held that the east was the donor and the west the recipient, the movement was in fact a sort of oscillation, with the pendulum acquiring new color or force at either extreme. Repeatedly, and in matters which appear most characteristically eastern, we find that the initial impulses came from the west, and were then returned to the west with new significance or emphasis. But before we come to examine individual manifestations we must know something of the historical conjuncture which made fusion possible and of the antecedent attitudes of the protagonists. First we shall consider the traditional Greek attitude towards non-Greeks and the ways in which that attitude changed in the hellenistic age.

Chapter II

EXCLUSIVENESS AND INTEGRATION

FOR non-Greek peoples to be admitted to equal participation in Greek civilization, for them to be raised, as it were, from colonial to commonwealth status in the spiritual sense, it was necessary that Greek exclusiveness be relaxed, so that non-Greeks could not only imitate Greek ways but identify themselves with the Greek experience. Military conquest was not enough; for any considerable degree of integration the Greeks themselves and then the natives had to recognize that the outlooks which made the Greeks what they were could in fact be shared by others than racial Greeks. The recognition of at least the potential equality of all men and the consequent conception of all humanity as forming a single society are perhaps the greatest achievement of the hellenistic age, and we must examine the steps which led to the new ecumenical view.

From the beginning the characteristic outlook of the Greeks was aristocratic, and it was therefore inevitable that they should despise lesser breeds. But in the heroic age, at least, before the aristocratic ideal was inherited by a whole democracy, heroes could recognize the high individual worth of their peers among other peoples. In the *Iliad*, at any rate, the Trojans are not despised as such; Trojan language, customs, dress, weapons, and religion are thought of as being like the Greek, and in early vase paintings Trojan warriors are represented as Ionian hoplites. The word *barbaros* ("stuttering, unintelligible, alien") has no pejorative connotation in the *Iliad*. It is applied, in a compound form, to the Carians (2.867), but not to the Trojans or their allies; the reason may be that these, unlike the Carians, were known to the poet only from the saga.

It was the Persian Wars (490–479 B.C.) which gave the Greeks a sense of their unity and crystallized their contempt for barbarians. Among themselves the Greeks were and continued to be truculently particularistic, and rivalry between such states as Athens and Sparta often broke into open hostility, but in the face of the common danger from without they minimized their differences and came to regard all Greeks as a single people—which language and religion prove they in fact were. Similarly the enormous differences between various barbarian peoples were overlooked; their divergence from the Greeks was the paramount characteristic which imposed a unity upon them. After the Persian Wars even the Trojans are made to look effeminate in vase painting and are dressed in barbarian costume when they are represented on the stage. The dichotomy between Hellene and barbarian becomes sharp and decisive. The Hellenes are an elect and the barbarians their inferiors. The Greeks occupy the center of the world, and their usages are the norm by which lesser peoples are judged. Solemn proclamations excluded barbarians, along with criminals, from the celebrations of the mysteries and from the national games. Sacred objects and sites, including the domestic hearth, were rendered unclean by contact with a barbarian. In literature the barbarian is strange and repulsive, uneducated, superstitious, awkward, stupid, unsocial, lawless; he is slavish and cowardly, unrestrained in passion, petulant, cruel, violent, faithless, greedy, and gluttonous.[1]

But despite the contempt for barbarians generally there was always a grudging respect for their nobility, and something like a mythological imperialism to claim them for Greece. From the earliest times Greeks sought to connect foreign peoples with their myths and to invent a Greek genealogy for them, just as later hellenized barbarians claimed kinship with Greeks to enhance their own genealogical credit. In both cases the motive was fre-

quently political.[2] Aegyptus appears in the old myth of the
Danaids, and his reputed father Belus (probably a Greek form of
Baal) is founder of the Babylonian kingdom and ancestor of the
Persian kings. Belus' granddaughter Andromeda was the wife of
Perseus and mother of Perses, the eponymous founder of Persia.
Medus, son of Medea by the Athenian king Aegeus, was the epon-
ymous founder of Media. In the historical period such genealogies
were openly exploited for political reasons and sometimes ancient
authority was claimed for some that were newly invented. Diodorus Siculus (10.61, from Ephorus) reports an amusing case.
The Persian general Datis, who was a Mede, put forward a claim
to rule over Athens on the ground that the Athenians had de-
prived Medus, who was their ancestor as well as his, of his rights.
The claim was rejected by Miltiades on the grounds that whereas
an Athenian had founded the kingdom of the Medes, a Mede had
never ruled Athens.

The tradition of barbarian inferiority seems to have been first
questioned, but only by indirection, in the work of a medical man.
In his *On Airs, Waters, Places* Hippocrates attributes human differences to geographic and climatic conditions; he implies, though
he does not state, the principle that diverse races are fundamen-
tally equal. The implication was made explicit in the rising sophistic enlightenment. In the papyrus fragments of Antiphon's *On
Truth* the plain statement is made that "all men are created alike
by nature in all respects, both barbarians and Greeks."[3] The
proof is that all men breathe through their mouths and nostrils;
they are therefore alike in *physis* ("nature") and different only
in *nomos* ("convention"). *Physis* is immutable; *nomos* is an artificial creation and so subject to change.[4] It should be changed
when the conditions for which it was created no longer obtain, or
when the powerful who manipulate it for their own advantage
can be overcome.

The *nomos-physis* argument conditioned subsequent attitudes
toward the barbarian. Euripides' attack on Greek assumptions of
superiority vis-à-vis women, in the *Medea* and elsewhere, and the

"cosmopolitanism" of Diogenes, which we shall consider presently, were based upon it. Even the more aristocratic philosophers acknowledged its validity when they exculpated class distinctions by insisting that slaves were such *by nature*. Plato recognizes the influence of geography and climate in the formation of a people's character and makes a place for the influence of education— which his rival Isocrates recognized as the great leveler; like Thucydides he deduces the character of the ancestors of the Greeks from that of contemporary barbarians. Plato goes beyond Hippocrates, then, in acknowledging the fundamental equality of humanity; but his theory does not prevent him from making the commonplace differentiation between Greeks and barbarians.[5] Plato's chauvinism appears most clearly in his discussion of the state. The ideal state is thought of as a Greek *polis*, with its traditional attitude towards barbarians. Strife among Greek cities is really civil war and should be avoided or carried on humanely; real war is against barbarians and should be carried on energetically. A story told of both Socrates and Plato is true probably of neither but characteristic nevertheless: the Greek is reported to have rendered thanks that he was born a man and not an animal, a man and not a woman, a Greek and not a barbarian.

Aristotle is direct and unequivocal in his assertion of the superiority of the Greek—which he significantly asserts is *natural*. At the beginning of the *Politics* he declares that slaves are such by nature and that barbarians are naturally slaves. Apparently he regards the position as self-evident, for he offers no logical proof. Perhaps Aristotle is curt and positive because the opposite current was gaining strength. Isocrates, whose alumni were far more numerous and influential than those of the rival Academy, had declared that "Greek" denoted a man's education rather than his race. His statement (*Panegyricus* 50) is in effect a rationale and a program for hellenization: "So far has Athens left the rest of mankind behind in thought and expression that her pupils have become the teachers of the world, and she has made the name of Hellas distinctive no longer of race but of intellect, and the title of Hellene a badge of education rather than of common descent."

The program could work both ways: if racial barbarians could be honorary Greeks, then their own cultural attainments could be appreciated. Eventually Babylonian astrology, Persian magic, Egyptian and Jewish thought were studied; translations of Zoroaster, Mago, the Bible, were made; curiosity about foreign peoples was aroused and accounts of them (which we shall glance at in another connection) were written.

In his political and social views Aristotle represents an order that was dying. His own pupil Alexander was so to change the world that the concept of the *polis* and even of Hellas would be transcended in a larger concept and the traditional distinctions between Greek and barbarian be obliterated. And Aristotle's own successor as head of the Lyceum, Theophrastus, applied the school's biological approach to justify the change philosophically. A fragment of his [6] declares that all men are related, either because of an ultimate common ancestry, or because of their common sustenance, habits, and character. The scientific approach of the Peripatetics was propagated by the scholars of Alexandria, and Eratosthenes, who was the greatest of them, is reported (Strabo 1.66) to have said that men should not be classified as Greeks or barbarians but rather as good or bad.

The arguments for human equality on the basis of a common *physis* received much wider dissemination through the Cynics and their street-corner preachers. When the Cynic Diogenes, who became the legendary exemplar for flouting convention, was asked of what city he came he pronounced the classic utterance, "I am a *cosmopolites*—a citizen of the world" (Diogenes Laertius 6.22). The meaning here is negative rather than positive; Diogenes is really saying, "I am not a citizen of any of your Greek cities." His is the proud assertion of a ragged exile's consciousness of his own worth in the face of a bourgeois society which scorned him, a rebellious reaction against every kind of coercion imposed by the community upon the individual.[7] A positive, philanthropic turn was given to cosmopolitanism by Crates of Thebes, Diogenes' well-born disciple who renounced wealth and position and took up his master's scrip and staff and ragged cloak. "I am a citizen of the lands of Obscurity and Poverty, impregnable to Fortune, a fellow-citizen of Diogenes," he said (Diogenes Laertius 6.93), but in his case it was evident that he had become naturalized in the larger community out of choice, and he preached its advantages over the smaller community out of love.

The Cynics were concerned with the happiness of the individual, not the well-being of the community, large or small. It was the Stoics who thought primarily in terms of the community, insisting that nothing could be injurious to the individual if it was good for the community of which the individual was part. The crucial point is the understanding of "community." Relationships of blood or race or country are meaningless, political and social stratifications are rejected. All good men, whatever their social or geographic position may be, are equally citizens of the larger *polis* which embraces the entire *cosmos;* they are in fact *cosmopolitai*, citizens of the world.[8]

Zeno had sat under Crates, but unlike the Cynic's cosmopolitanism Zeno's involved expansion and assimilation rather than contraction and limitation. "Zeno's earliest work," writes W. W. Tarn,[9] "his *Republic*, exhibited a resplendent hope which has never quite left men since; he dreamt of a world which should no longer be separate states, but one great City under one divine law, where all were citizens and members one of another, bound together not by human laws but by their own willing consent, or (as he phrased it) by Love." Nor were Zeno's followers the impractical perfectionists their austere doctrine would make them. Their theory recognized no degrees in virtue and assumed the equality of all men, but they did in fact recognize that, as Chrysippus put it, nothing could prevent some seats in the theater being better than others. They soon realized that the revolutionary world order their system envisaged was impossible of immediate realization, and devoted themselves to ameliorating the world as it was with a view to the gradual realization of their ideal. It was the Stoic Sphairos of Borysthenes, for example, a disciple of Zeno himself, who seems to have been the directing force behind Cleomenes' social revolution in third-century Sparta; and a century later the Stoic Blossius of Cumae seems to have been responsible for much of the liberal program of the Gracchi. The outlines of the Augustan principate seem to have been drawn by Stoic theorists; what actually resulted was an autocracy, but we know of other cases where liberal theory has been subverted in execution. Nor did human dignity and equality remain an esoteric doctrine of the educated; it was carried to the multitudes who were most nearly concerned by Cynic-Stoic popularizers who preached their "diatribes" in the highways and byways. Stoicism, then, was an important factor for facilitating fusion; as members of a single community all men were duty bound to promote the political realization of the egalitarian doctrine. But the rival school of the Epicureans, which was a more revolutionary and probably a more influential force in the hellenistic world, was at least as effective in breaking down barriers between peoples.[10]

It was one of the principal charges against the Epicureans that they were indifferent to the state, and indeed they advocated an "open" in opposition to Plato's "closed" society, with a minimum of government. But this made Epicureanism exportable. As Cicero scornfully put it (*Tusculan Disputations* 5.37.108), "Those who guide their lives by pleasure can be happy wherever pleasure is available—as Teucer remarked: 'My country is wherever things go well with me.' " The Epicureans made it part of their code to proselytize and even wrote pamphlets for the purpose, and we know that their campaigns were successful. Cicero, again, says with some bitterness (*De finibus* 2.15.49), "Not only Greece and Italy but all barbary seethes with that philosophy." Epicureanism was the court philosophy of Antiochus IV and his son, the opponents of the Maccabees, and we shall see from our examination of Ecclesiastes how deeply the enemy doctrine penetrated among the Jews. The reason that Cicero (and the rival schools) hated Epicureanism was because it questioned the supernatural basis of authority. Actually it anticipated the Jews and Christians in divorcing doctrine from local sovereignties. It was for reasons analogous to Cicero's, because it questioned the authority of govern-

ment and religion, and not because it was Greek, that Epicureanism is condemned in the Wisdom of Solomon and IV Maccabees
and similar writings.[11] On the contrary, these condemnations, and
the fact that *epikoros* became the Hebrew word for "infidel,"
show how deeply Epicureanism affected the thought of the east.
Actually, the condemnation of Epicureanism in the two deeply
religious works cited is offered not so much in defense of Judaism
as of a Platonized Judaism.

Whether as cause or symptom the hellenistic philosophies
marked a relaxation of the old exclusiveness, and so promoted intercourse between Greek immigrants and the part of the population with which they came into contact. In such a significant
matter as intermarriage there had never been prejudice outside
mainland Greece; the original Greek settlers of Cyrene, for example, had taken Libyan wives, and we know that the Greek women
of Cyrene continued to observe certain Libyan religious usages.[12]
In the east the position seems to have been that Greeks would
intermarry readily where hellenization had proceeded so far that
their Greekhood was not imperiled. It was only in remoter areas
where a Greek minority could not assert itself against a strong
existing civilization and where intermarriage must therefore eventually result in a surrender of Greekhood that intermarriage was
avoided.[13]

It is the Romans, significantly, rather than the later Greeks
who are exercised over the dilution of hellenism. A conscious effort to preserve Greek values is suggested, and applauded, in a
passage in Livy (37.54, from Polybius, referring to 190 B.C.):
"The cities in the old country are no more Greek than their settlers who have gone into Asia; the change of terrain has not
changed their breed or habits." And of Seleucia Tacitus says
(*Annals* 6.42): that "it did not lapse into barbarism but retained
the standards of its founder Seleucus." [14] Now it was the Roman's
turn to disparage the barbarians. Livy speaks of "Syrians and
Asiatic Greeks, the vilest breed of men, and born for slavery"—

the last phrase obviously an echo of Aristotle; and again (38.17, 189 B.C.), "The Macedonians who inhabit Alexandria in Egypt, who inhabit Seleucia and Babylon, and who inhabit other settlements scattered over the world, have degenerated into Syrians and Parthians and Egyptians."

Sophists and Stoics may have proven the oneness of mankind and Isocrates may have redefined Hellene and barbarian in terms of education rather than race, but literature could not be censored to correspond to new notions of integration any more than it can in our time. Yet if the ideological lesson did not abolish the old exclusiveness it relaxed it. When their Greekhood was not imperiled Greeks could mingle with non-Greeks without feeling that they had compromised their principles. We shall next look at the spiritual and political climate which made a certain degree of mingling inevitable.

Chapter III

ALEXANDER AND THE *OIKOUMENE;* THE SUCCESSORS

THE various currents which promoted cosmopolitanism were in part the cause and certainly in their accelerated pace the effect of the conquests of Alexander the Great. The movement of philosophy toward the practical and the ethical, of art toward the literal and sensational, of literature toward the familiar and the bourgeois—phenomena which we shall presently glance at more narrowly—had begun early in the fourth century and would doubtless have gone forward without revolutionary change in government and without enormous geographical expansion. It may be, indeed, that the new social and intellectual climate in itself contributed to the revolution and expansion; Alexander may be thought of as a somewhat premature secular arm for both Stoic and Epicurean doctrine. In any case, the relaxed hellenism of the late third century was more capable of export and more accessible to non-Greeks than the hellenism of the classical period could have been. Alexander's achievement stimulated the Greeks to export wholesale and the eastern peoples to accept with eagerness. Whether, as his detractors assert, Alexander was merely an opportunist who coveted the wealth and power of Darius, or whether he was a visionary who from the first made it his goal to unify mankind, there can be little doubt that after his conquest of the Persians was assured he was in fact impelled by a drive, perhaps motivated only by self-aggrandizement, to unite the *oikoumene* into a single body.[1] So much is indicated by his making the Persians equal to the Macedonians, giving them Macedonian dress and the Macedonians Persian dress, encouraging and leading the way in intermarriage, and especially by his solemn sacrifice to Homonia ("Concord") at far-off Opis, where he offered special prayer for community of heart between the two peoples.[2]

Alexander's own Macedonians, it must be noted, were very far from sharing his ecumenical ideal. To give the Persians equality was, in their sight, to violate all precedents for the relationship between conquering Hellenes and subjugated barbarians, and they resented, to the point of armed mutiny, the diminution in their own status which Alexander's program implied. Needless to say, it was the attitude of the Macedonians and not Alexander's ideal which motivated his Successors. They not only justified their rule by the right of conquest but enhanced their authoritarianism, as indeed Alexander himself had done, by claiming divinity. When they did promote hellenization it was for reasons of military expediency, not humanitarianism.

In any case, whatever Alexander's personal motivations may have been, he is the great catalyst for the hellenistic melting pot. Intercourse between east and west had antecedents, as we have noticed, but what had been a trickle now swelled into a flood. Thousands of Greeks were attracted by the opportunities offered by the new countries, and everywhere there was a new awareness of regions and peoples hitherto but dimly known. With the enormous and sudden expansion of geographical horizons whole populations which had been insulated by obscurity were enabled to participate in a new movement of ideas, and, perhaps most significant of all, Greeks and barbarians alike were stripped of the shelter of the minuscule political organisms which had enveloped them and were compelled to devise a new spiritual shelter in an overwhelmingly large universe. The Athenian of the Periclean age was as certain of his preeminence as the Florentine of Dante's.

The Athenian merged his individuality and fulfilled himself in the small city-state of which he was an important and conscious part. He actually owned it, as a member owns his clubhouse or a voting stockholder his corporation, and received dividends in the form of grain and other bounties; that is why citizenship rights were so jealously guarded. Tragic poets and artists were his agents and must satisfy his taste; he could be proud of his city's cultural achievements in a way impossible for citizens of nation states. Excavations of Greek cities show temples and council chambers and theaters, but rarely a private residence; the meaningful part of life was as a member of the *polis*.

And now the *polis* lost its exclusiveness and became in effect another provincial town. The changes in men's outlook are easy to sense, in art and literature and philosophy. Each shows a turning away from what is too colossal for the individual to comprehend, and too indifferent to him, to the only thing he can know and elicit a response from—himself. In sculpture,[3] for example, eloquently as the classical masters could make marble speak, they were curiously reticent in portraiture. Their figures are all idealized, as if they were only a step removed from the gods to whom the ideal was appropriate; there are only the slightest suggestions of the individuality of the specific statesman or poet represented. In the hellenistic age portraiture becomes painfully realistic, almost to the point of caricature. Great virtuosity is displayed in showing the distortions of pain or anger and other passions, the ravages of age or disease.

In literature [4] too the move is from the general to the particular, from the heroic to the bourgeois. Tragedy gives way to New Comedy, probings into the conflicts of generalized man and fate to concern with establishing identity and marrying; men wish to live happily ever after, not to achieve heroism by a glorious death. Because bourgeois ideals are universal New Comedy could find audiences in many places, even in Rome in Plautus' adaptations. But tragedy, which had depended upon being a communal enterprise of a homogeneous population, could survive only as a *tour de force*. Now literary men were the personal dependents of royal patrons, and addressed themselves not to an audience of fellow citizens but to other literary men whom they sought to impress with their erudition and virtuosity. The characteristic of Alexandrian art, literary and other, is the highly polished miniature. The content is no matter. One needs but to compare one of the so-called Homeric Hymns with a hymn of Callimachus to realize that the one is genuine religious utterance and the other an ingenious literary exercise. Callimachus himself was probably not aware of the difference but thought that he was doing with more recondite materials and greater sophistication precisely what the older poets were doing naively and with obvious materials. The walls of the Alexandrian Library seem actually to have closed off the view of the larger world without. That is what Timon, called the Misanthrope, meant when he called the Library the bird cage of the Muses.

But when formal literature had become wholly estranged from life a new literature arose to answer the needs of ordinary people. Instead of the affairs of the heroes of myth, which no one longer took seriously except as a subject for literary composition, men now invented love stories of a more immediate kind, and instead of tales of gods in whom no one believed men celebrated the careers of latter-day saints for actual religious edification. These and other motifs were combined in works like the Greek Romances, which were at first despised by the educated but which eventually achieved a respectability of their own.

In philosophy too the same phenomenon of turning from the general to man's individual self is apparent. Men turned from first philosophies and speculations on the ideal state, which they could never conceivably do anything to make real, to systems which would help them endure life in a terrifyingly large world which reduced them to ciphers. We have seen that the Stoics and Epicureans severally set themselves to redress the new imbalance between man and his world. Both had their physics and cosmologies, to be sure, but only as scaffoldings for their ethical teaching, not as part of the general quest for truth for its own sake.

Nor were the Greeks alone stripped of their insulation and constrained to devise new attitudes towards the world. The eastern peoples underwent much the same experience. Behind national boundaries they could accept their own polities, their own beliefs, their own manners, without question. They were forced to question when they saw amongst themselves gay and witty and attractive people who had superior technology, and who—most exigent argument of all—had proved victorious. Their response, as we shall see, was not to resist the new but rather to imitate it, and to satisfy the requirements of loyalty to native tradition in ways that would not prevent participation in the new ways.

The complicated political history of the hellenistic monarchies need not detain us, but we shall wish to know something of the relations of the Macedonian ruling dynasties and their native subjects. After Alexander's death in 323 B.C. his principal generals held the areas to which he had assigned them nominally as satraps, but one after another declared himself king, and each was ambitious to succeed to Alexander's own empire. The only one who could hope to unite the fragments was Antigonus, who held the west, but his defeat and death at Ipsus (301 B.C.) left three distinct and fairly stable dynasties in a balance of power. The actualization of the ecumenical ideal now seemed an impossibility, until the Romans virtually realized it, apparently without intending to do so.

The two dynasties which concern us are the Seleucids (usually named Antiochus) in Asia and the Ptolemies in Egypt.[5] The ruling houses were themselves Macedonian, and at first seem to have sought to maintain the Macedonian (which is essentially the Homeric or ancient Germanic) system—a king who is "first among equals," free peers who are his "kin," and free men in arms who constitute an assembly. But neither in Egypt nor in Asia, as we have seen, could the fiction be maintained. In Egypt Ptolemies could rule only as legitimate successors to the Pharaohs, and their rule was as autocratic as the Pharaohs' had been. For their army and administration they absolutely required Greeks, and they encouraged large-scale Greek immigration. But the object of Ptolemaic as of Pharaonic rule was in effect the exploitation of the country; they were not interested in enlightening the native population, and maintained a barrier between them and the Greeks. As Professor Rostovtzeff put it,[6] "On the Egyptian foundation they built their edifice in which all the upper storeys were for the dwelling of strangers and the cellars reserved for the natives."

The Seleucids had nothing like the Egyptian foundation to build upon. Their empire was a conglomerate of diverse nations and civilizations, roughly constituting three large complexes. The eastern third included Persia, which was highly civilized, and its appanages in the region of the Indus and the Ganges on the one side and Armenia and the foothills of the Caucasus on the other. The central portion included the relics of Babylonia and Assyria, Syria with its caravan cities, Phoenicia, and Palestine. The third portion was Asia Minor, with Greek cities on the coast and a great variety of peoples in the interior. The eastern portion was predominantly Iranian, the central portion predominantly Semitic, and the third too varied a mixture to be categorized. The Seleucids might conceivably have made themselves kings of Persia, in succession to the native Persian royalty, and ruled their empire from Persia as Darius had done, but this would have entailed orientalizing their establishment. Instead they relied upon the stronger community of interest between themselves and the Greeks in the east, both alike aliens. That is why they spent much effort and wealth to encourage Greek immigration, and why, when the Romans cut off the source of supply, they tried to produce surrogate Greeks.

In Asia as in Egypt, then, the Macedonians soon became a minority in an army of mercenaries, and the king's council of "Friends" only honorific and advisory. Monarchy was orientalized, and the kings became as autocratic as the Pharaohs or Babylonian kings had been. In the Greek world philosophers of all schools wrote treatises *Peri basileias* ("On Kingship") to provide a rationale for the unexampled concentration of authority in the person of the king.[7] The usual solution, based ultimately on Plato, was that the king was *nomos empsychos*, "law incarnate." Gradually the kings first accepted and then engineered deification of themselves in their own lifetime. This was only a natural development of the heroization of benefactors, and its meaning was almost purely political. It implies no such blasphemy as it would if the notion of deity were transcendental. The political implications of deification become clear in the Roman adaptation. Rome itself was deified, and temples to Rome were erected in all parts of the empire, in order to give a religious basis and sanction to patriotism.

But the hellenistic theory of empire was not Roman; there was not even a pretext of serving humanity such as was proclaimed in Vergil's magnificent *Tu Romane memento* at the end of the sixth *Aeneid*. The Athenian empire itself, during the Peloponnesian War, was frankly based on the right of the stronger, as we see from the Melian dialogue at the end of Thucydides' fifth book. Of the gods we suppose and of men we know, the Athenians say, that they rule where they can—not because they have a mission to carry the white man's burden. In the eastern tradition, of course, the proposition did not even have to be stated.

From the constitutional point of view the thousands of Greeks and Macedonians (now indistinguishable from Greeks) who came to the east as officials or businessmen or settlers were not a separate element, but like the natives subjects of the king; yet measures were taken to make them preserve their national and cultural identity. In Egypt and probably in the Seleucid realm also foreigners always had to give the country of their origin in official documents and could not shift even from one foreign group to another. Individuals belonging to the same foreign group formed officially recognized associations which enjoyed a measure of self-government. The cohesive force among the Greeks in a given community was the gymnasium and its alumni. The role of the gymnasium in maintaining the cultural level and the unity of Greek-speaking groups was, as we shall see, very great. And it was these groups which provided the king with administrative personnel.

In effect the Seleucid like the Ptolemaic rule was essentially exploitation by a thin alien crust which had only an official connection with the exploited. Our histories of Ptolemaic Egypt are very full, because of the abundance of papyrological evidence; we learn much about the administration, political and especially economic, which was managed by Greek-speaking officials, but the preponderant part of the population which worked the fields and paid the taxes and clung to their ancient ways remains a vague undifferentiated mass. For purposes of administration, and chiefly of tax collection, there were divisions into satrapies and smaller local units largely preserving existing arrangements. During the third century, when the Ptolemies held Palestine, they seem to have introduced the more elaborate Egyptian system there also. There was a large number of small temple states, controlled by hereditary high priests, who exercised secular as well as religious authority.[8] In hellenistic terminology Jerusalem was such a temple state. There was a constant effort on the part of the central government to whittle down the secular power of these temple states (as of all feudalisms) and limit their function to collecting and transmitting taxes to the royal exchequer.

The most widely used and most effective device for implementing the rule of the central government was the establishment of cities of the Greek pattern.[9] These might be new foundations, perhaps originally military colonies, but were usually reorganizations superimposed on a native village or a combination of villages. In Greek terminology any collection of houses, no matter how large, was only a village unless it possessed certain organs of political life which made it a *polis*. Among the essentials were a council, an assembly, duly elected magistrates, a fiscal system, and certain cultural institutions. It was obviously easier to deal with a functioning organism with defined and universally recognized procedures and obligations, with ideals which harmonized with the ideals of the central government, than to deal with an amorphous and capricious mass. That is why the new foundations were so numerous; there is a baffling proliferation of Alexandrias, Antiochs, and the like all over the Near East, though most that survived reverted to their original names. Jerusalem itself was for a time officially an Antioch. These cities were the single most important factor in the spread of hellenization. Naturally there were no Egyptian or Syrian "cities" in Greece proper, which is one explanation for the fact that the cultural flow from west to east was much greater than the flow in the other direction.

The most striking feature of the hellenistic world as compared with what went before is its approximation to uniformity in the daily habits and outward surroundings of life.[10] Travel was easier and more frequent, and there were many guide books to enable a businessman or colonist to choose his route and learn about his destination. The Greek *koine* rapidly became the lingua franca of the Near East and the language of business. Business increased vastly and its practices were standardized, and coinages, though varying slightly from monarchy to monarchy, all followed a Greek standard and so were virtually uniform. Educational curricula, goals, and techniques all followed the same Greek pattern. Actors and musicians were organized into professional groups as "craftsmen of Dionysus" and received important privileges; these groups maintained connections with their fellow-craftsmen in other countries, and so promoted cultural uniformity in important areas. Private law in such matters as marriage and inheritance followed Greek models and so was virtually uniform. Even the physical appearance of cities in plan and architecture took on a degree of uniformity. Cities laid out by hellenistic rulers as far afield as Mesopotamia followed the scheme prescribed by the Greek architect and town-planner Hippodamus.

Anywhere in the hellenistic world, then, a Greek or a hellenized native would find reasonably familiar scenes, institutions, and outlooks; but it is important to remember that among the great masses of the people native habits and institutions persisted. Even those who were hellenized had to use the vernacular in their contacts with their less enlightened fellow-countrymen; and the fact that the vernaculars survived after centuries of hellenistic domination while Greek was eventually forgotten proves that native usages as well as native language were never wholly overwhelmed. But the marks which hellenism left have remained ineffaceable.

Chapter IV

BARBARIAN RECEPTIVITY

WHEN imperialist historians speak of their nation's armies "liberating" the regions they conquer and bringing them the blessings of civilization we are entitled to remain skeptical. Even the vaunted Pax Romana was not regarded as a blessing by those upon whom it was first imposed: "They make a solitude," the Briton in Tacitus (*Agricola* 30) says, "and they call it peace." But of the peoples newly subjected to hellenization it may be said that they welcomed the innovations, despite, or it may be because of, the fact that they were themselves heirs to venerable civilizations. Because they were they had much to give the Greeks in return, but by far the stronger current ran from west to east. The western influences affected the upper classes directly, whereas the slighter influence from the east touched mainly the lower classes, whence it forced its way up into respectable Greek society only gradually. And so far from resisting hellenism the upper classes, in the Near if not the Middle East, welcomed it with open arms.

In view of the relative positions of the peoples involved, politically and culturally, it was inevitable that this should be so. The Greeks were the conquerors, and their military and administrative personnel and their numerous settlers lived and worked in the eastern lands, not the other way about. Business was in the hands of the Greeks. The language of business, of administration, and of fashion was Greek. And not only were the Greeks efficient but they were quick-witted and buoyant and lived gayer and brighter lives; it is easy to see that upper-class youth would be attracted by the newcomers and strive to emulate them. But it was also expedient that they adopt the new ways, for unless they did they would surely be marooned in the backwash of civilization, like modern Egyptians or Japanese before they were Europeanized, and remain barbarians indeed. With one important exception their position was analogous to that of the Far East today. Proud and tenacious of their native culture as Chinese or Indians or Japanese may be, they must, to survive in the modern world, adopt western technologies, and with them must come a degree of westernization in manners and dress and even in modes of thought. And the current in the other direction is similarly slight: how many westerners study the Upanishads or are connoisseurs of Ming pottery?

In one important aspect westernization was easier in the hellenistic world. Modern peoples of the Far East have sovereignties which are identified with and so foster their respective cultures; the peoples of the Near East had long been under Persian domination and the advent of the Greeks was in some sense a liberation. The cities which Alexander and his successors established as units of administration enjoyed a considerable degree of autonomy, and these cities were also prime agents of hellenization. An indispensable feature of the Greek city was its gymnasium, whose function it was to inculcate the manners and outlook of a Greek gentleman in those who were privileged to attend it. It was the upper classes who came into contact with the products of the gymnasium, and the upper classes who were most rapidly hellenized and most eagerly promoted the hellenization of their people. That is why, as we read in the First and Second Books of the Maccabees, it was the priesthood and the urban aristocracy who were the most ardent hellenizers in Jerusalem. Inevitably, and with justification according to the dictum of Isocrates, upper-class natives came to look upon themselves as Hellenes, and at the same time (by an intelligible paradox) to despise themselves as barbarians. It was this feeling which gave rise to the considerable apologetic and polemic literature we shall examine in the sequel.

The benefits which accrued to the barbarians, at least as the Greeks saw the situation, is indicated in Plutarch's youthful essay

On the Fortune of Alexander 328 f.; the context is part of an argument that Alexander was a more effective teacher than the philosophers:

When Alexander civilized Asia Homer became common reading, and the sons of Persians, Susianians, and Gedrosians learned to intone the tragedies of Sophocles and Euripides. And although Socrates when tried on the charge of introducing foreign deities lost his cause to the informers who infested Athens, yet through Alexander Bactria and the Caucasus learned to revere the gods of the Greeks. Plato wrote a book on the ideal state, but because of its forbidding character he could not persuade anyone to adopt it; but Alexander established more than seventy cities among savage tribes, and sowed all Asia with Grecian magistracies, and thus overcame its uncivilized and brutish manner of living. Although few of us read Plato's *Laws*, yet hundreds of thousands have made use of Alexander's laws and continue to use them. Those who were vanquished by Alexander are happier than those who escaped his hand; for these had no one to put an end to the wretchedness of their existence, while the victor compelled those others to lead a happy life. . . . Alexander's new subjects would not have been civilized had they not been vanquished; Egypt would not have its Alexandria, nor Mesopotamia its Seleuceia, nor Sogdiana its Prophthasia, nor India its Bucephalia, nor the Caucasus the Greek City; for by the founding of cities in these places savagery was extinguished and the worse element, gaining familiarity with the better, changed under its influence. If, then, philosophers take the greatest pride in civilizing and rendering adaptable the intractable and untutored elements in human character, and if Alexander has been shown to have changed the savage natures of countless tribes, it is with good reason that he should be regarded as a very great philosopher.[1]

Plutarch is not writing as the apologist for an imperial power (though he may have learned something from Roman justification of its imperial rule), for in his day Greece itself was ruled by Rome. For Plutarch the idea of hellenism was something like a cult which recognized no national boundaries. In this sense his encomium of Alexander, overblown as it is, has essential truth. The generality of "barbarians" did in fact welcome hellenization, and those who did not resisted it, significantly, for the sake of an opposing cult.

As Plutarch saw, and as has been remarked above, it was the newly organized cities which served as the chief agents of hellenization. Their very names created a new climate. Seleucus I Nicator (358–280 B.C.) made northern Syria and Mesopotamia a new Macedonia not only by naming settlements after towns in the old country—Pella, Aegae, Edessa, Cyrrhus, Beroea, Arethusa, Anthemus, Ichnae, Europus, Amphipolis, Chalcis, Larissa—but by giving Macedonian names even to the physical features of the countryside, calling the Orontes the Axius, the mountainous coastline Pieria, and the plains around Nisibis Mygdonia.[2] His motive, like that of Constantine six hundred years later when he named sites in his new capital after sites in old Rome, or that of American colonists who named their settlements after the places they emigrated from, was to create a sense of continuity and make the new immigrants feel at home. The proportions of the proliferation of new cities is indicated by the fact that this same Seleucus established, among numerous other settlements, sixteen Antiochs, nine Seleucias, six Laodiceas, and three Apameas.[3]

So far from resenting their new names and status the indigenous peoples coveted them, and a needy king like Antiochus IV could make a good thing of selling the privilege. Sometimes a native city took the name by which the Greeks had before been accustomed to call it; thus Phoenician Gebal had long been known to the Greeks as Byblus—just as the English choose to call Livorno Leghorn. Sometimes, as we shall see was the case with personal names, the native name was assimilated to a similar-sounding Greek name, and sometimes it was translated. In the former category belong such names as Pella for Syrian Pehel, Orthosia for Phoenician Ardata, and probably Anthedon for 'Ain Teda. Where a native name was theophoric the corresponding Greek divinity was used, as in Apollonia, Heraclea, Diospolis, and the like. In Egypt, where the language was especially difficult for Greeks to pronounce, names were frequently descriptive, sometimes using the name of the appropriate totem animal, as Crocodilopolis or Oxyrhynchus—a kind of fish. There is evidence that the natives were very willing to use these names.[4] Even in their classical period the Greeks themselves had adapted myths, for political reasons, to establish a connection with one or another non-Greek people;[5] in the hellenistic age this practice was eagerly followed by non-Greek peoples who claimed that their founder was some figure out of Greek legend.[6] These tendencies are indicative of the eagerness of native peoples to emulate Greek ways and to aspire to the dignity of citizenship in the Greek sense and the measure of autonomy which civic status implied.

The language of the Greek city, and the official language in all the dominions of the Successors, was Greek. In the beginning natives may have learned it out of necessity, for the uses of commerce or government, or by the compulsion of snobbery, but they continued to use it out of choice, and it soon became at least a second vernacular among a considerable proportion of the population.[7] Upper-class natives must of course have known their native vernaculars, but they spoke to each other in Greek and were literate only in Greek. The use of a new language is not only a sign manifest that a new culture is being accepted but a key to the culture as a whole. We shall see that even books written by natives as propaganda for native values and intended mainly for a native audience were written in Greek,[8] and that even books written in native languages were affected, in form and content, by Greek models.[9]

Some native languages did of course survive, to become the basis for vernaculars in the Near East today, and it is interesting to see to what degree religion was a factor in the survival. The clearest case is hieroglyphic, which Egyptian priests continued to use though they understood it very imperfectly. On the other hand, Egypt was traditionally literate as well as conservative, and there continued to be lower-class Egyptians who could write demotic. In a remote place like Palmyra Aramaic continued to be an official language. But Syriac was able to produce a religious literature in the early centuries of Christianity because it had served as a sub-literary vehicle for religion in the preceding period. Neither would Hebrew have survived but for religious motivations. Aramaic, not Hebrew, was the vernacular, and even before the coming of the Greeks Hebrew had something of the position of Latin in the Middle Ages as the language of Scripture and religion. That position it could retain even if Greek became the vernacular; it was only after the fall of Jerusalem in A.D. 70 and the rise of Christianity that the study of Greek was frowned upon on religious grounds.

In the pre-Christian period literary and other remains of the Jews afford abundant, and for our purposes highly relevant, evidence for the spread of Greek. The Bible was translated into Greek not, as Aristeas [10] alleges in the beginning of his book, as a literary curiosity to be deposited in Ptolemy Philadelphus' library, but, as the end of the book indicates, for the use of a Jewish community who could receive their Scriptures in no other way. It is very doubtful that so devout a man as Philo knew any Hebrew or even Aramaic at all; certainly he makes the phrasing of the Septuagint the basis for his exegesis. Passages of prayer or psalmody which occur in such Greek books as III and IV Maccabees and the Wisdom of Solomon shows similarities with Septuagint phraseology even when they are not quotations, and it has been thought that such passages are therefore translations of Hebrew originals. A more probable explanation is that "Septuagint Greek" had become normal for devotional compositions and that they were written in that language—just as a twentieth-century minister will use the style of the King James Bible for a prayer of his own composition. St. Paul did not receive Greek as part of his enlightenment on the road to Damascus; he must have learned the Greek poets he quotes (and expected his Jewish auditors to know) when he was a faithful Jew.

For the diaspora, then, which came to be more numerous than the population of Palestine,[11] it is plain that Greek was the vernacular and that public worship was conducted in that language. But we know that Greek was a familiar language in Palestine itself. At a relatively early period we find evidence that classical Greek literature was known in Palestine, and the rabbinic writings of the later period contain a high proportion of Greek loan words.[12] When the anti-humanist trend was at its strongest a new and more literal Greek version of the Bible was made, that called Aquila's, in order to reduce the possibilities of latitudinarian interpretation. When Paul addressed a Jerusalem crowd in Hebrew (Acts 22.2) they were pleased; apparently they expected him to speak in Greek and would have understood him if he had done so; in the diaspora Paul did address Jewish congregations in Greek. It would be very strange if the Jewish literature written in Greek in Alexandria and Antioch were not read and even emulated in Palestine.

The most forcible evidence that Greek had become the vernacular comes from epigraphy. Inscriptions in languages other than Greek are extremely rare in hellenized areas, and this is true not only of official inscriptions but even of grave inscriptions, and even in the case of quite humble burials. And it is fully as true of Jewish as of other burials, not only in Alexandria and Rome but in Palestine itself, and during the entire span of Greek and Roman sway. A city like Tiberias, which was a great center for rabbinic study, has yielded very numerous Greek inscriptions and very few Hebrew.[13] Greek inscriptions, along with Greek decoration, appear in the ruins of synagogues,[14] and the directional signs in the temple were in Greek.

An important index to hellenization is the adoption of Greek personal names. At first, doubtless, the Greek was only a collateral name, to be used in documents and intercourse with Greeks, while the native name was used at home; but as hellenization proceeded and easterners wished to forget their "barbarian" origins and become thorough Greeks the old name was dropped altogether and only the Greek was used. Where native names were retained, alone or together with a Greek name, the motive was frequently religious. But as in the case of place names, even personal names which contained a reference to a deity could be hellenized, and even among the Jews; that is why hellenized regions show a preponderance of such names as Apollonius, Dionysius, Demetrius, or Theodorus, Metrodorus, Isidorus.[15]

The use of Greek names began early and spread far. Personages who are important enough to go on embassies or to be mentioned in history can be expected to have Greek names; but of a total of fifteen thousand names recorded in hellenistic Egypt some eight thousand are Greek, though the hinterland furnishes a larger number than does Alexandria.[16] The evidence of clay tablets from hellenistic Babylonia points in the same direction.[17] Even the Jews adopted Greek names as freely as did other non-Hellenes.[18] At least as early as the beginning of the second century B.C., as we learn from the books of the Maccabees, the upper priesthood in Jerusalem bore Greek names, and the nationalist reaction that followed the uprising did nothing to discourage the practice. If the Greek name was initially adopted only for official reasons, later the native name was retained along with it only for official reasons. Such was probably the case at Uruk-Warka in Babylonia and elsewhere,[19] and as late as the third century the son of Zenobia of Palmyra was called both Athenodorus and Vaballath. The practice was common in Palestine, as it is among conservative Jews today, and we find it illustrated in the New Testament. We may surmise that Mark and Peter and Didymus were called John and Simon and Thomas by their intimates and where religion was involved.

The basis upon which a particular name might be chosen shows an interesting progression. At first there was an effort to approximate the sound of the original. Before Alexander's day Abdastart of Sidon had called himself Strato, and in the early second century the Jewish high priests Joshua and Eliakim were called Jason and Alcimus. Saul into Paul is another instance of the same practice. Simon was a great favorite because it was a Greek name and at the same time very like the Biblical Simeon. The next step was translation. In a bilingual Greek-Phoenician inscription of the third century B.C. Samabaal is equated with Diopeithes, Abdtanit with Artemidorus, Abdshemesh with Heliodorus, and so forth.[20] Among the Jews the practice of making the Greek name translate the Hebrew was common; we have such examples as Thomas-Didymus, Tanhum-Paragorios, Isaac-Gelasios, Gad-Eutyches, Zadok-Justus. Soon there was no perceptible connection between the two names, either in sound or meaning. From Egyptian papyri and inscriptions we know of such combinations as Samuel-Theodore, Jose-Theophilos, Johanna-Euphrosyne, and the like.[21] The evidence from Rome, mainly from Jewish catacombs, exhibits similar phenomena; of five hundred persons commemorated the great majority bore Greek names.[22] The next step, as among children of enfranchised Romans or of less conservative Jews today, was to use only one name, and that Greek. At first the colorless theophoric name was favored; Theodoros, Dorotheos, Theophilos, Theodotos, and Dositheos (which is commonest of all) were very usual. But non-theophoric names were also usual, and some with plainly pagan elements, using combinations of Athena, Dionysus, Ammon, Sarapis, and the like, were not excluded. It is quite possible that such names were adopted without their bearers being aware of their significance.

One curious aspect of the distribution of names is that the Hebrew, at least as a collateral name, seems to have been retained more tenaciously in Egypt and Italy than among the hellenized population of Palestine. This may be explained by the circumstance that many of the immigrants had come as prisoners of war or refugees and had a special motivation to show their loyalty. The movement into Egypt continued from the sixth century B.C., perhaps a consequence of the fall of Jerusalem in 586, fairly steadily until well into the Roman period;[23] Claudius' famous letter to the Alexandrians[24] reproves the Jews for continuing to bring their countrymen down into Egypt from Syria. There were many refugees from the Maccabean disturbances: Onias IV went down to Egypt with numerous followers and built a replica of the temple there. And there were refugees for conscience's sake from the excesses of the Hasmonean rulers. In Rome many of the numerous Jewish colony were sons of prisoners of war who were likely to cherish a loyalist tradition.[25] The Greeks in their diaspora behaved similarly; they were most careful to assert their Greekhood in areas where it might be dissipated.

If hellenization, in language and nomenclature, had gone so far among the Jews it went even further among the Syrians, at home and abroad. Only a fraction of the great number of persons

in Rome who bore Greek names or even who were referred to
as Greeks were actually Greek. The satirist Juvenal does make a
distinction. "I cannot abide, good Romans," he cries (3.360 f.),
"a Rome of Greeks; and yet what fraction of our dregs comes
from Greece? The Syrian Orontes has long poured into the
Tiber." But the lines following show that he means newly come
immigrants conspicuous for their religious rites. A Syrian who
wished to pass for a Greek could, and many doubtless did. Even
in the east hellenized natives might be called Greeks; the "Greek"
soldiers who garrisoned Jerusalem were undoubtedly Syrian—
and the "Zeus Olympius" who was the "abomination of desolation" which defiled the altar was actually the Syrian Baal Shamayin
in Greek dress.[26] The woman who besought Jesus to cast the devil
forth out of her daughter is described (Mark 7.26) as "a Greek,
a Syrophoenician by birth (*genei*)."

Along with language, or even preceding it as a sign of accultura-
tion, is dress. So certain is the evidence of dress that a torso in
the Metropolitan Museum can confidently be labeled "barbarian"
on the basis of a scrap of costume. In the matter of dress all our
evidence suggests that Greek forms were universally adopted, at
least by persons important enough to be portrayed in sculpture or
coins or mummy paintings. The aristocratic youth of Jerusalem
flaunted their hellenism by wearing the broad-brimmed hat and
jaunty cape (*petasos* and *chlamys*) which identified the ephebe
(II Maccabees 4.10–15). The fact that the names for various garments in rabbinic literature are Greek loan words proves that
Greek costume was usual.[27] On the reliefs of Gandhara the women
present at a birth of the Buddha are dressed like Greek ladies, and
even Isis eventually came to be represented in Greek dress. Along
with dress came the manners and amusements appropriate to the
style. Western etiquette was adopted in dining and other forms
of social intercourse, and in particular Greek athletic sports,
which were wholly new to the east, were received with the
greatest enthusiasm and enjoyed an enormous vogue in all parts of
the hellenized world. The enthusiasm is reflected in II Maccabees,

and the novelty in the outraged feelings of the conservative onlookers.

In the gymnasium, which was a regular appurtenance in every
Greek settlement, young men learned a great deal more than
calisthenics. In old Greece the gymnasium was the principal
instrument for fashioning Greek gentlemen, and in the hellenized
east this function was even more important.[28] A man bred in
the gymnasium required colonnades to stroll in, monumental public
buildings of the Greek pattern, and most of all a theater; and even
such a site as that of the Biblical Ramoth Gilead provided him
with all these facilities. If the first thing any group of Greek settlers did was to establish a gymnasium, the next thing they did
was to provide a theater; ruins of Greek theaters have been found
in all parts of the hellenized world, in Baalbek and Gerasa and
Amman, and as far afield as Babylon.[29] Not only gymnasia but
theater and other arts received official encouragement; the actors'
and musicians' associations enjoyed special immunities and could
even cross boundaries in time of war. References to these associations show that they were almost as widely scattered as the theaters, and prove, as do incidental statements in Plutarch and other
authors, that Greek drama enjoyed a great vogue.[30] The great
auditoria could not have been filled by Greeks alone, and there
is literary evidence that others attended and knew the classic
repertory; Pausanias (1.22.1) remarks that "the veriest barbarian
who has a smattering of Greek knows the story of Phaedra." At
Miletus a special section of the theater was reserved for Jews.[31]
Philo freely admits his fondness for the theater, and the author
of IV Maccabees models his whole work on the pattern of
tragedy.[32] The rabbis (and Tertullian) would not call attending
theater "sitting in the seat of the scornful" if those they reproved
never sat there.

Even natives who had little to do with gymnasium or theater
must have been affected by the stately and graceful architecture
of the Greek temples. The surviving examples in hellenized countries are, to be sure, of later date, but it is certain that they had
temples in the Greek form from early in the hellenistic period.

Frequently the adoption of the Greek form involved a syncretization in cult,[33] and it is again significant that only where religious tradition was very strong was any resistance offered to Greek temple architecture. In Egypt temples to the native gods continued to be built in the traditional form all through the hellenistic and Roman periods, and Herod built the new temple at Jerusalem according to the prescriptions in Kings and Chronicles; even so the courts and colonnades surrounding the temple, as we learn from Josephus, were in the Greek style. This mixture, like the temples at Baalbek and Palmyra, illustrates fusion in several aspects. Baalbek and Palmyra may be far too imposing and too ornate for sound Greek taste, and modern critics find a stronger oriental strain in them than had previously been noted,[34] but they are obviously adaptations of Greek architecture.

Adoption of Greek architectural forms certainly caused a revision in ritual practices to approach Greek modes of worship, and even among the Jews. Mosaic and other Greek decoration, sometimes with distinctly pagan themes, has been discovered in synagogues, significantly in such as came to some catastrophic end, like those in Galilee or in Dura-Europus.[35] On the basis of rabbinic literature it had been firmly believed that such decoration was impossible; but the literature was crystallized after the anti-humanist tendency had become a condition of survival. It is easy to imagine that before the crises which called forth official prohibitions the Jews, like other native peoples, would be attracted by the pomp and elegance of the Greek temples and forms of worship and so far as possible emulate them. It is not unlikely that Greek music was also influential.[36] Certainly the Church adapted Greek musical forms; the best key for studying ancient Greek music today are the chants of the Russian Orthodox Church.

Along with other branches of administration the courts were hellenized, and the law was another instrument for popularizing Greek ways. The codes promulgated by the Successors were taken directly from Greek patterns. In some details these were adapted to local usages, but there is evidence that in inheritance,

degrees of consanguinity, validity of testimony, and the like hellenistic law tended to shape practice.[37] The rationale of the Maccabean administration and much of its detail was adapted from
Greek models,[38] and this was doubtless the case with other prin-
cipalities. An interesting example of fusion of native and Greco-
Roman legal concepts is afforded by the massive legalistic literature
of the rabbis. The principles of deducing and adapting law and
formulating decisions there employed are frequently adaptations
of the principles and practices of the ruling power, and in certain areas show striking similarities.[39]

To be sure public institutions and buildings were imposed from
above rather than (as in the Athenian democracy) being an expression of the popular will, but they must have influenced wide
reaches of the population nevertheless. To begin with, there were
very considerable numbers of Greek settlers in the east. We know
that the official class was very large and that there were many rich
individuals who were not officials.[40] Soldiers received allotments
in scattered areas, though they may have exploited them in ab-
sentia. The ruling house maintained cordial relations with upper-
class natives, whose influence must have affected their humbler
countrymen. We have little data on intermarriage, but it must
have been common in the central portion of the Seleucid realm.
We know, moreover, that during its first century, at least, the
Seleucid empire enjoyed a high degree of economic prosperity,
and thus must have influenced the population in favor of the
new order.

But this is not to imply that hellenization was total, or that
there was no organized opposition to its progress. Native languages
and with them native outlooks survived even in the most thoroughly hellenized areas. Among peoples culturally advanced and
articulate, like Egyptians, Babylonians, and Jews, there were
writers who advertised the worth of native tradition, as we shall
see when we come to examine their apologetic literature, but
they were willing to accept the advantages of hellenization nevertheless, as their use of the Greek language shows. Organized

opposition, where it occurred, was motivated not by antipathy to hellenism but by normal desire for independence or by the ambition of rivals for power. The Egyptian probably always regarded the Ptolemies as foreign tyrants, but the regime was so completely totalitarian that there was no possibility of organized opposition. There were indeed insurrections after Philopator (244–205 B.C.) had experimented with using natives in his army, but these were quickly silenced. The proud and highly civilized peoples on the eastern marches of the Seleucid empire might be expected to shake foreign suzerainty off at the first opportunity.

The one rebellion which has been recorded in history as directed against hellenism, that of the Maccabees in Judaea, was not, in its origin, a reaction against hellenism.[41] From the contemporary or almost contemporary accounts in I and II Maccabees it is clear that hellenism had proceeded very far indeed, and apparently without protest, before the insurrection began. Violence started in consequence of rivalry between equally hellenized contenders for the high priesthood, and religion was not an issue. The standard of religion was raised in the countryside, and then served to rally the people to the cause. It was only after religion had become the battle cry of the rebels that Antiochus IV issued his decrees against the observance of central religious rites, and it is highly significant that as soon as the anti-religious decrees were rescinded the pietist group withdrew from the fighting. The object of the Hasmonaean rulers was not to protect religion—their bitterest opponents were pietists—but to maintain a sovereignty which should be able to hold its head up among others which were being carved out of the weakened Seleucid empire. They were permitted to do so as the price of their support of one or another rival to the Seleucid succession. Neither the nationalists nor even their opposition objected to hellenism as such; both parties, as we shall see, borrowed freely from Greek political and literary models. Among the Jews as among the other self-conscious peoples in the Seleucid empire the controlling principle was something like "Accept the largest possible measure of hellenization *and* retain the greatest possible measure of loyalty to native tradition." Obviously the simultaneous pursuit of discrepant objectives necessitated compromise or self-deception. Both of these responses appear in the reactions to the various effects of hellenism which we shall examine. Our next task is to consider the implications of compromise in language.

Chapter V

LANGUAGE AND ETHOS

THE basic meaning of *hellenizein* ("to hellenize") is "to *speak* Greek," and its proper use is with reference to people who would not normally be expected to do so. In its wider sense "hellenization" is the adoption of Greek modes of behavior in general by people not themselves Greek. The extension of meaning is legitimate, for the adoption of a new language is a sign manifest that its culture has been accepted and the language in turn provides the fullest introduction to the traditions and spirit of the new culture. It is a measure of the hellenization of the east that Greek came to be so widely used. As we shall see, even natives concerned to perpetuate their own traditions used Greek for the purpose, even when addressing a native audience, and even when using the native language they frequently adapted Greek forms and motifs. The outstanding example of the presentation of native tradition in Greek dress is of course the translation of the Bible called the Septuagint. We know of no case where a Greek work was translated into an oriental language.

The markedly different Roman reaction is an index of the greater readiness of the east to embrace hellenization. Culturally Rome was as much a province of Greece as Syria of Egypt, and indeed more dependent because the Romans were cultural parvenus as compared with the heirs of ancient Babylon, and in the end Rome entered most fully of all into the legacy of Greece. Roman literature is unthinkable without its Greek models; to be the first to introduce a given Greek form into Latin was originality enough for Horace (*Odes* 3.30) and other Roman writers. And yet Romans insisted that their literature be Latin. While Jews were translating their Bible into Greek in Alexandria, in Rome Livius Andronicus was translating the *Odyssey* into Latin. The language itself, though the forms and even the mythology of the literature were Greek, was a means of preserving national character. Among the Jews a dictated return to Hebrew, after Greek had come into common use, served a similar end. But the penetration of Greek left ineffaceable traces; the dynamics of a language in themselves affect modes of thought. In the paragraphs which follow we shall consider the nature of the Greek penetration and the ethical consequences of its interaction with other habits of speech.

The Greek which was spoken and written (except by conscious archaizers) in the hellenistic age is called *koine*, or "common language." Koine is a natural development of Attic, with little traces from other Greek dialects except the kindred Ionic.[1] Grammarians fix the lower limit of koine at the reign of Justinian; "middle" is applied to the Greek language from the sixth century to the fall of Constantinople in 1453, at which point "modern" begins. The variations between one stage and the next are relatively slight; in the eighth century, for example, Slavic invaders were so numerous that Greece was called Slavonia on maps, but they left no detectable traces in language.[2]

Neither was Greek much influenced by non-Greek vernaculars in the hellenistic age. Certain ordinary Greek words (*chiton* for a garment, *canon* for a measuring rod, and others) had been taken from the east at a very early stage, and the new acquisitions in the hellenistic age were similarly the names of unfamiliar objects (various stones, for example) or other things outside the Greek experience (*amen, pascha, sabbath*). Pronunciations were inevitably affected by regional peculiarities, as transliterations of names and of Latin words show. An Egyptian Greek, for example, would not distinguish between the pronunciation of *hegoumenos* and *oikoumenos*. Illiterate papyri and inscriptions show that many changes from classical Greek which are found in modern Greek had already begun to be felt in the hellenistic period (*i* for *e*, *ai, oi, ui, ei; v* for *b; th* for *d; o* for *ō;* the disappearance of the initial aspirate; *u* as a consonant); but these variations are due to normal processes, not to the influence of other languages.

If Greek was little affected by competing languages, the effect it exerted upon them was very great. As is the case with the naturalization of Latin in the Romance languages, the nature of the Greek element in the languages it affected depends on the duration and intensity of the exposure. Aside from geographical nomenclature (*kom*, from the Greek word for village, is as common on Egyptian maps as *chester* is on English), and aside from learned borrowings and artificial coinages based on Greek such as are found in all European languages, the heaviest and most fully naturalized Greek precipitate, aside from Latin, is to be found in Coptic and Ethiopic, in Armenian and in Syriac (the Christian successor to Aramaic), and in Hebrew. In each of these cases, as in the French element in English, the presence of so large a body of foreign words proves that the language from which they derive must once have been widely understood.

Latin is in a special case. On the one hand it is related to Greek in the Indo-European family of languages, and on the other it was maintained with tenacity by a people able to enforce its will. The Greek books which Romans wished to circulate they translated or adapted into Latin. And yet all cultured Romans, throughout their history, seem to have known Greek. Before the second century B.C. and after the second century A.D. even Roman writers frequently used Greek, and even in the classical period Cicero says (*Pro Archia* 23), "Graeca leguntur in omnibus fere gentibus"—virtually every nation reads Greek. Even in the west and in the fourth century Ausonius says that his father knew Greek well, but not Latin. As the language not only of books but of business and diplomacy Greek was carried almost over the whole *oikoumene*. In Asia Minor it took so firm a hold that that region could remain the heart of the Byzantine Empire, though elsewhere its tenure was more transitory. From the days of the republic Romans negotiated wih Phoenicians, Carthaginians, and Jews in Greek, and during all the centuries of the empire Greek was the official language (except in the army) for the eastern half of the empire. Augustus' testament, known as the *Monumentum Ancyranum* from the first specimen of it found in modern times, was inscribed on many temples of Rome and Augustus in the east. The private inner walls of the temple carried the original Latin text; on the outer walls, where the public could read it, was a Greek version.

The great monument of translation, and an eloquent testimonial of the relative position of the cultures in the east, is the Septuagint. It has been argued with some plausibility (and as plausibly refuted) that this translation was made not from Hebrew manuscripts but from a text already transliterated into Greek characters;[3] apparently, then, even in the third century B.C. (when the early portions of the Bible were translated) ability to read Hebrew was not common, and as in modern cases where liturgy is not in the vernacular, some could pronounce the words without knowing the meaning. So at a period when Hebrew characters were more familiar a modern Greek version of the Bible was printed in Hebrew characters—at Constantinople in 1547,[4] and so was Moses Mendelssohn's German version in the nineteenth century. It was long thought that the Septuagint was a hybrid Greek whose Hebraisms would make it unintelligible to Gentile readers. Actually the Hebraisms are no more marked than they are in the King James version, and its other deviations from classical idiom can be paralleled in other Greek writings of the period.[5] The Septuagint differs from contemporary secular works only as a translation of a sacred text might be expected to do; significantly, the least idiomatic is the Pentateuch, where there was special reason for literalness, and where the art of translating was still new. It was also long thought that the strangeness of the Septuagint would repel any but Jewish and Christian readers; in the sequel we shall see that others may well have looked into it.[6]

The effect of Greek upon native languages can best be studied from its effects upon Hebrew, which has left a large body of literature and is at the same time most relevant to our central concern. What happened in Hebrew happened in other languages also. Rabbinic literature, which dates largely from a period when humanistic study was not encouraged, contains so large a proportion

of words naturalized from the Greek (and so not easily recognizable) that a reader who knows only Biblical Hebrew finds
many passages unintelligible.[7] The borrowings are not confined to
novelties for which the ancient language had no word but extend
through the whole range of speech. And in addition to assimilated
words there is frequent use of a Greek expression so to speak in
italics, as an English writer might employ an unassimilated French
expression, of Greek adages and apophthegms and even of brief
allusions to Greek stories which the audience is expected to recognize and fill out.[8] These writings were not composed by or addressed to the upper classes exclusively, and hence imply a familiarity with Greek on the part of the general population. Even
after the loss of sovereignty and the rise of Christianity made for
official discouragement by the rabbis of the study of Greek it
was impossible to eliminate the language. At the end of the first
century A.D. we hear that the patriarch Gamaliel II had five hundred of the thousand children in the school which he maintained
study Greek (*Sotah* 49 b). When Procopius preached Christian
sermons at Scythopolis (Beth She'an) he had to employ a translator
for the benefit of the Aramaic-speaking congregation.[9] And when
rabbinic preachers addressed ordinary congregations in Hebrew
or Aramaic they used Greek analogies to explain passages of Scripture, and even cited texts in Greek.[10] It was natural, for example,
to find in Hieremias, the Greek transliteration of "Jeremiah," the
sense of *eremia* or "desolation."

Interpreting Jeremiah by its Greek form is probably a conscious
homiletical device, the interpreter being aware that Jeremiah
does not in fact bear the meaning he chooses to give it. But even
the most literal translations must import new connotations. *Savoir
faire* and "know-how" look like equivalents, and an apprentice
translator would be pleased to be able to remember the one when
he encountered the other; actually the substitution of one for the
other introduces a totally new realm of feeling. In precisely the
same way familiar Hebrew expressions sometime acquire new
connotations when transposed to a Greek equivalent, and this
is particularly true when the Greek words had been given a

specialized meaning by the philosophical writers.[11] When the
Septuagint translates the enigmatic *ehyeh asher ehyeh* ("I am that
I am") in Exodus 3.14 by *ho ōn* ("the being") it is surely if in-
advertently introducing a Platonic element. It is inevitable that
nephesh should be rendered by *psyche*, but *psyche* carries with it
a whole complex of ideas elaborated by the philosophers which
nephesh did not. Such terms as providence, conscience, virtue,
had similarly been given quasi-technical meaning by the Greeks.
Writers or speakers who first employed these superficially equivalent substitutes for a Hebrew original did not intend to introduce
Greek philosophical ideas and were doubtless unaware that they
were pioneering a new realm of thought. And their successors
who worked exclusively from the Greek could not imagine that
they were departing from the original at all. This second stage is
obvious in Philo, and to a lesser degree in IV Maccabees and
Wisdom of Solomon; but it surely affected, if it did not initiate, a
whole trend of philosophic speculation, even in Hebrew writings.
Once it had been equated with *psyche, nephesh* itself was endowed
with all the significations of *psyche*.

Psyche, in turn, came to carry, in later religious writings, connotations which may have been peculiar to *nephesh*. The reverse
process is illustrated by the words for "spirit," which is itself from
a Latin word meaning basically "blast of wind." That is the basic
meaning of *ruah*, which is translated by the Greek *pneuma*, which
also means "blast of wind." The developed meaning which
pneuma (and *spiritus*) carry in religious terminology is an increment due to its acceptance as an equivalent for *ruah*, which admitted such an extension.

One other possible influence from east to west in the realm
of language is in the introduction of rhythmic verse into later
Latin and the vernaculars of Europe. One view of the history of
accentual verse is that it was native to republican Rome, was then
eclipsed by quantitative verse borrowed from Greece, and came
back in force at the end of the classical period. Another is that
the new verse developed out of quantitative verse by substituting

accented for long and unaccented for short syllables. The trouble
with both theories is that rhythmical verse in the west was entirely a Christian possession and was never employed by pagan
writers. It cannot then have been a natural development in Latin
but must have been borrowed from elsewhere.[12] The source has
been plausibly identified as the versification of Syriac hymns,
which are known to have influenced western hymnody. "Syriac
verse," Mr. Beare writes,[13] "seems to have been based on the num-
bering of syllables; and the ornaments of acrostic and alphabetical
arrangement, strophic grouping and rhyme, were also present.
If, then, we find these features suddenly appearing in Greek versions from Syriac hymns, and later in Latin hymns; if the use
of song was one of Christianity's chief weapons; and if, as Augustine states (*Confessions* 9.7), the singing of hymns was introduced
into the west 'after the manner of the eastern churches,' we seem
to have a *prima facie* case for regarding Latin rhythmic verse as
of Syriac and therefore of Semitic origin." As in the case of
other influences, the channel of transmission was religion, but the
innovation was soon naturalized in the secular realm.

"There is a petrified philosophy in language," Max Müller
has said, and many writers have sought to reconstruct the ethos
of Semites and Greeks on the basis of vocabulary and syntax.[14]
The Semitic languages do not have the particles, the auxiliaries, the
array of tenses, and the elaborate subordinating syntax which
makes a wide variety of logical and temporal relationships explicit.
Hebrew syntax is atomistic; the reader himself supplies the relationships, as a passage like the following (Isaiah 5.1–2) will
show:

My well-beloved hath a vineyard in a very fruitful hill, and he fenced
it, and gathered out the stones thereof, and planted it with the choicest
vine, and built a tower in the midst of it, and also made a wine-press
therein, and he looked that it should bring forth grapes, and it brought
forth wild grapes.

The individual passes from one picture to another, and only
juxtaposition determines relationships. Of tenses the Hebrew has

only a past and a future, and must use an awkward participial phrase to express the present. The thought does not proceed step by step, nor is it detached or objective. There is too much earnestness for logic or detachment; the writer or reader must identify himself with the reaction. There are no half-tones; as in the code of Hammurabi things are either right or wrong. Its disconnectedness and its love of bold imagery makes Semitic writing lyrical rather than rational, concrete rather than abstract, sublime rather than elegant. Hebrew possesses very few abstract nouns.[15]

Even the mechanics of a language reflect an attitude towards the external world, and on the basis of syntax and semantics a number of scholars have extrapolated modes of thought characteristic of the peoples who used the languages with which we are here concerned.[16] Those upon which there is a measure of agreement may be listed as follows. The Hebrew mode of thought is dynamic, the Greek static. "To sit" or "to stand" in Hebrew are actually "to move into a sitting or standing position," and "it was" must frequently be rendered, as it correctly is in our versions, by "it came to pass." In descriptions the Greek is concerned with the contours of a building or a person, the Hebrew with the process of construction (as notably in Noah's Ark, the tabernacle in the wilderness, Solomon's temple) or the essential trait. When a physical detail is given, such as Saul's height, it is only to emphasize a trait. For the Greek the prime sense is seeing, for the Hebrew hearing. The Greeks are concerned with space, the Hebrews with time. In objects the Greek concern is with symbols, the Hebrew with instrumentality. The Greeks, in sum, sought objective truth, the Hebrew inner conviction.

Like all formulations in an area where precision is impossible these require qualification, but they have enough of truth to give them a certain usefulness. How they may reveal themselves in actual works of literature has been shown by Erich Auerbach, in the opening chapter of his *Mimesis*,[17] by a comparison of Homer's account of the recognition of Odysseus by the aged Eurycleia when he returns to his home in the guise of a beggar, and the story of Abraham's prevented sacrifice of Isaac as told in Genesis. Homer, Auerbach shows, leaves nothing "half in darkness and unexternalized"; every object, every psychological process, every allusion to a past event receives its sharp outline and color. The Biblical story, by contrast, takes place as in a vacuum. There is no background, no description of the personages or implements engaged. We are told only so much as is essential for understanding the point of the story. The sentences and clauses are coordinate and at the farthest possible remove from the elaborate subordinating syntax of the Greek which is capable of expressing the subtlest relationships. Such relationships as are essential the adult reader does not need to have spelled out; to finger them for their own sake would dilute the impact of the story. Contrast the visit of Hermes to Calypso, where every detail of motivation and circumstances and appearance is made explicit, with the starkness of the beginning of the Abraham story (Genesis 22.1): "And it came to pass after these things, that God did tempt Abraham and said to him, Abraham! and he said, Behold, here I am."

It would be difficult [Auerbach remarks] to imagine styles more contrasted than those of these two equally ancient and equally epic texts. On the one hand, externalized, uniformly illuminated phenomena, at a definite time and in a definite place, connected together without lacunae in a perpetual foreground; thoughts and feeling completely expressed; events taking place in leisurely fashion and with very little of suspense. On the other hand, the externalization of only so much of the phenomena as is necessary for the purpose of the narrative, all else left in obscurity; the decisive points of the narrative alone are emphasized, what lies between is nonexistent; time and place are undefined and call for interpretation; thoughts and feeling remain unexpressed, are only suggested by the silence and the fragmentary speeches; the whole, permeated with the most unrelieved suspense and directed toward a single goal (and to that extent far more of a unity), remains mysterious and "fraught with background."

An essential corollary of this dichotomy is the quality of belief demanded by the respective stories. The Biblical author believed his story passionately, and expected his audience to do likewise; if he did not, then he was not a poet who asked merely for sus-

pension of disbelief, but a conscious liar who for political reasons
wished to make people believe what he knew was not true. The
Greek writer, by contrast, was licensed to create so long as he
created well and truly; if he did, then, as Aristotle says, his poetry
is truer than history.[18] It is interesting to see that the question of
the poet's truth was said to have been debated (but we know the
story, significantly, only from late writers) as early as Thespis'
time. Solon, as Plutarch (*Solon* 29) tells the story, went out of
curiosity to see Thespis act, and after the play was over "asked
him if he was not ashamed to tell so many lies before such a large
number of people; and Thespis replying that it was no harm to
say or do so in a play, Solon vehemently struck his staff against
the ground: 'Ah,' said he, 'if we honor and commend such play
as this we shall find it some day in our serious business.' "

The interview is probably a retrojection from a later age. In
the classical period there seems to have been no question of the
ethical propriety of what the tragic poets were doing. The conception of truth in the Old Testament narratives is of a different
order. If there are things which strain belief we may write the
narrator down as simple but not as a knave. It is not a question
of the reader's faith; a reader outside the religious tradition receives
the same impression, and senses a different conception of the
writer's function in such essentially imaginative works as Job or
Judith. It is because the ancient books of the Bible communicate
the sense of literal truth that the devout have been troubled by
later narrative works, such as Judith, whose association with the
older works would seem to imply the same standard of veracity.[19]
Because our Bible is a selection made from a specific point of
view we cannot say with assurance that avowed literary fiction
did not exist in Israel, but the probability is that it did not; and
if that is the case the conception of the poet's license to create is
a result of Greek influence.

One of the differences between Greek and Hebrew modes of
thought which has been noted has to do with the concept of time.
The presence in Greek of the timeless aorist tense, which leaves
time unspecified,[20] and the absence of any tense except past and

future in the Hebrew are indices of a significant difference in outlooks upon the world. At an obvious level the difference expresses itself in the respective uses of history. The Greeks seem
almost to have lacked a sense of history: everything, whenever
it happened, is conceived of as present. Homer may be cited for
wisdom or decoration but not as an authoritative record of a
past which defines the aspirations and destiny of the future. Thucydides is a political analyst who uses contemporary history for
illustration; when he speaks of the remote past, as in his introduction, he despises its barbarism, and Homer he deflates as mere
poetic exaggeration. Herodotus has many kinds of curiosity,
among them a curiosity about the past; but his work may be
more accurately described as a guidebook with useful sociological
and anthropological data than a work of history. The lack of
historical sense appears most clearly perhaps in Alexandrian
criticism of Homer, which makes no allowances for a social and
material world different from the Alexandrians' own.[21]

The difference in outlook in the Biblical tradition is enormous.
All of history is the unfolding of a grand scheme, single and unified, with such clearly defined stages as the Creation, the revela-
lation at Sinai, the conquest of the Promised Land, the Exile, the
Crucifixion. Into this scheme every occurrence in the world or
above it must find its place, and every individual fulfills his function in the scheme. The view of history as the unfolding of a
grand scheme with its corollary of man's responsibility to his
history, and not the momentariness of the Greeks, has prevailed in
Europe. Its unquestioned acceptance was due not only to the
Judeo-Christian tradition but also to that of Rome, which had a
sense of history and of national destiny like that of the Hebrews
and demanded a similar surrender to national aspirations. As
we shall presently see, there are grounds for thinking that this
Roman emphasis was itself inspired, if indirectly, by the Biblical
tradition.

The differences in the sense of time find expression in less obvious ways. A Greek tragedy, like the aorist tense, is timeless.[22]
It exists at the moment, or rather it exists always. What happens

may be the result of what had gone before, and so much as is needed for the comprehension of the action before us we are told, but merely as the data for a geometrical problem; we are not invited to speculate about it, or about what will happen in the future. Even within a play factors of time are virtually ignored, as when, in Aeschylus, Agamemnon arrives immediately after the telegraphed news of his victory in distant Troy. Shakespeare's plays, even when they are not historical, are infinitely more careful in their internal time economy, and we are shown how the events of a play are the consequences of what went before and what they portend for the future. The procession of time is enormously important.

Shakespeare regarded time as he did because that was the European climate of belief. But it is remarkable that Seneca, who is the intermediary between Greek tragedy and Elizabethan, stands with Shakespeare rather than with the Greeks in regard to the conception of time and all that it implies. In Greek tragedy there are no villains: Clytemnestra and Aegisthus may not have sufficient justification for compassing the death of Agamemnon, but they have some, if only as the leaders of a political opposition, and so it is throughout Greek tragedy. The Senecan villains are sinful, for they know the better and do the worse. And their sins are not a thing destined in the order of the universe but in defiance of that order: that is why the very elements are disturbed when Oedipus sins, why the sun stops still and then retreats to its rising when Thyestes commits his crime. The sense of treason to a world order is not to be found among the Greeks: the question is whether it is native to the Roman tradition.

It can be strongly urged that it is not, that it was a by-product of the Augustan program for raising patriotism to a religion. Pride in their heritage and a sense of obligation to it the Romans had apparently always had, but the conceptions of the Romans as an elect destined to bring peace and civilization to the world, of all history as a divine scheme to enable the Romans to rise to their high destiny, and of the duty of the individual Roman to serve this destiny seems to be a deliberate construction of the men who shaped the Augustan principate. The sense of irresistible destiny which the phrase *senatus populusque Romanus* still evokes seems to have been created under Augustus and retrojected to the very beginnings of Rome. All antecedent history was a preparation for the foundation of Rome, which would embrace all subsequent history under its heaven-directed leadership. It was the conviction of Rome's destiny as an elect that Vergil's epic and Livy's history were designed to propagate, and Augustus' building program and religious innovations were calculated to inculcate a sense of responsibility to this destiny.

If the conception was, if not newly contrived, at least crystallized and given shape and direction under Augustus, we may legitimately look about for antecedents. The only valid pattern for the idea and its literary vehicles is Biblical tradition. Similar situations may indeed evoke similar challenges, and every people seeks to aggrandize its own history and aspirations. In the case of the Romans, moreover, there was the historical example of Alexander the Great and the ecumenical teachings of the Stoics to give example and precept. But, as we shall notice when we come to consider the conceptions of law and authority at Rome,[23] Vergil and Livy parallel the Biblical tradition not only in the general concept but in details and even in points of technique, and it is easier to assume that there was some actual connection between the two traditions than to assume that there was none.

It is curious and perhaps significant that the two pagans whom the Church took most warmly to its bosom were Vergil and Seneca. Seneca is commended highly by the Latin Fathers and came to be regarded as virtually one of them. This distinction is in part due to the apocryphal correspondence with St. Paul, and his reputation as an ethical teacher rests on his philosophical writings. But the premise of a divinely ordered universe which underlies his tragedies and the sense that his wrongdoers are sinners would make his tragedies (thought by the Middle Ages, to be sure, to belong to a different Seneca) acceptable to Christians, as uncompromising pagan writings—unless, like Ovid, they were allegorized—could not be. Vergil is even more markedly an *anima naturaliter Christiana*—not only in his sense of destiny and lessons of obedience to the divine will, but in his brooding pity and most of all in the hopes he holds out for a better world. St. Paul is said to have wept at Vergil's tomb because he died before the light had come into the world. The legend is embodied in a touching hymn in the service for St. Paul's day at Mantua. The readiest explanation for Christendom's finding these spirits kindred is that they were inspired from sources from which Christendom was itself inspired. Rome was the first beneficiary of the amalgam formed by the hellenization of the east and its prime transmitter, with its own ingredient added, to the subsequent history of Europe.

Chapter VI

EDUCATION: GENTLEMEN, SCRIBES, SAINTS

THE most significant characteristic of the Greeks is that no group of them settled anywhere without at once establishing a school, and organized education was the most important single factor in the process of hellenization and also in the resistance to that process.

The American experience offers enlightening analogies. Generations of children of the foreign-born have been so rapidly Americanized by public schools that communication with their own parents became difficult. On the other hand, where loyalty to native traditions, usually reinforced by considerations of religion, is strong the parents establish schools of their own to preserve their traditions. So in New York children who attend public schools may also attend schools where Hebrew or Yiddish or Greek or Chinese is taught. Where no marked physical traits or religious loyalties hamper the process and (an important point) where the native tradition is in no such danger of perishing that indifference amounts to defection, the process of assimilation is as rapid as it is easy. Statistics of the steady decline in circulation of the foreign-language press in proportion to the number of persons whose parentage might make them readers of foreign-language newspapers are sufficient demonstration.[1]

An obvious objection to the analogy is that in the hellenistic world it was the Greeks who were the immigrants and the natives who were subjected to hellenization. The objection clearly applies to the first surge of immigration, but, as we have seen, there were special considerations which quickly gave hellenism the upper hand and made Greek the preferred language. To compare the relationship between the Greeks and the peoples of the Near East to that between the English immigrants and the Indians and Spanish, French, or Dutch they found in America is manifestly unfair on the basis of the enormous differences in cultural levels and population density. But the important index to cultural dominance is language, and though native languages persisted in the Near East to an enormously greater degree than they have in America, in the metropolitan centers Greek was the language of government and of fashionable society.

In areas where their numbers were fewer and where (as in the Middle East) they were confronted by a culture too advanced and too vigorous for them to dominate, the Greeks behaved as we should expect of a minority tenacious of its traditions in the face of danger of being submerged. Here too the American scene offers an analogy. A foreign group isolated in a remote area is especially concerned to safeguard its traditions. Individuals who might not participate in the cohesive activities of their group in a metropolis where its survival seems assured are now more likely to manifest their identity with the group—not only by communal worship and social activities, but by subscribing to a newspaper in the old language and seeing that their children receive instruction in it. So in the remoter stretches of their diaspora the Greeks were more conscious of their Greekhood and made strenuous efforts to preserve it. And the central institution for this purpose was the gymnasium, which was to be found wherever Greeks were settled.

The gymnasium was the strongest cohesive force in the community, its leaders persons of the highest authority, and affiliation with it an absolute prerequisite to participation in the affairs of the community. So much we know from our hellenistic sources, but on the highly important questions of curriculum and program, and most of all, of the special outlooks it sought to inculcate we are less well informed. Its over-all object was to fashion Greek gentlemen, and since emulation of the ideal of a Greek gentleman is what gave hellenization its character it is important to know what the ideal was and how it was implemented. For this we must look briefly at education in the classical period and see how its practice was modified in the hellenistic age.[2]

In all the countries with which we are here concerned education seems to have moved from a knightly to a scribal ideal. What the scribal ideal was we shall consider when we come to speak of the educational systems which the Greeks encountered. They themselves eventually reached it, certainly with the rise of Christianity, but in Greece the knightly ideal, however modified, persisted through the hellenistic age whereas the scribal ideal was in full force among the people they hellenized. It is the difference in educational ideals, in fact, which is the central distinction between the two groups, for from it all other distinctions flow.

The conception of *paideia*[3] (which is education as opposed to training) like that of Olympian religion came with the Achaean invaders, and like the Olympian religion it is reflected in Homer. The Homeric heroes were conscious of noblesse oblige and saw that knightly attitudes as well as accomplishments had to be learned. Phoenix had been assigned to make Achilles a proper speaker of words and doer of deeds (*Iliad* 9.442); the first four books of the *Odyssey* are concerned with the education of Telemachus to be a responsible aristocrat. It is in the sense that the Homeric ideal of accomplishment and courtesy pervaded Greek education that Homer may be spoken of as the Bible of the Greeks. A character in Xenophon says (*Symposium* 3.5): "Because my father wished me to become a gentleman he made me learn the whole of Homer, so that to this day I can recite the whole *Iliad* and *Odyssey* by heart." Plato acknowledged that Homer had educated Greece (*Republic* 10, 606d) but would exclude him from the ideal state nevertheless.

In Sparta the heroic ideal was trimmed down to military usefulness, though the famous Spartan *agoge* still included some literature and music. In Athens it was democratized, to the great distress of conservatives like Aristophanes, as we can readily see

in the *Clouds;* but it was still a gentleman's education. Its aim was
to create a "harmonious" soul, and its means were "music," which
included literature and indeed all the provinces presided over by
the nine daughters of Memory, as well as athletics. The sophists
pioneered in making education professional, from the point of
view both of expert teachers and utilitarian objectives. Even so
they protested that they taught "for culture, not a craft" (Plato
Protagoras 312b) and regularly used the poets as texts. Nevertheless specialization did set in. Musicians became virtuosi, athletes
professional performers, and literary men philologians. We can
see the trends in the first institutions of higher learning recogniza-
bly like our own, founded early in the fourth century respectively
by Plato and Isocrates. Plato believed in special training for every
function, even voting, and relied on mathematics rather than
words for developing the intellect, and Isocrates glorified the
word. As a man is to animal, he said, so is Greek to barbarian
(which for Isocrates meant merely uneducated), and the object
of Isocrates' education was humanistic or what we should call
liberal arts education. It was the Isocratean, not the Platonic,
ideal which prevailed, both in the hellenistic age and in the education of Europe. At times it might degenerate to empty word-
mongering, but it did preserve and propagate the best that had
been thought and said and it did make participation in the legacy
available to large numbers.

We get a sense of the character of liberal education from Plato's
famous description (*Protagoras* 325d):

They send the boy to teachers, and enjoin them to see to his manners
even more than to his reading and music; and the teachers do as they
are desired. And when the boy has learned his letters and is beginning
to understand what is written, as before he understood only what was
spoken, they put into his hands the works of great poets, which he
reads sitting on a bench at school; in these are contained many admonitions, and many tales, and praises, and encomia of ancient famous men,
which he is required to learn by heart, in order that he may imitate or
emulate them and desire to become like them. Then, again, the teachers
of the lyre take similar care that their young disciple is temperate and
gets into no mischief; and when they have taught him the use of the

lyre, they introduce him to the poems of other excellent poets, who are the lyric poets; and these they set to music, and make their harmonies and rhythms quite familiar to the children's souls, in order that they may learn to be more gentle, and harmonious, and rhythmical, and so more fitted for speech and action; for the life of man in every part has need of harmony and rhythm. Then they send them to the master of gymnastic, in order that their bodies may better minister to the virtuous mind, and that they may not be compelled through bodily weakness to play the coward in war or on any other occasion.[4]

This kind of education, Plato says, is limited to those who can afford it and is directed by the parents. Aristotle says that "education should be regulated by law and should be a concern of the state." The rationale and something of the program of this education he sets forth in his *Politics* (1337b):

There can be no doubt that children should be taught those useful things which are really necessary, but not all useful things; for occupations are divided into liberal and illiberal; and to young children should be imparted only such kinds of knowledge as will be useful to them without vulgarizing them. And any occupation, art, or science, which makes the body or soul or mind of the freeman less fit for the practice or exercise of virtue, is vulgar; wherefore we call those arts vulgar which tend to deform the body, and likewise all paid employments, for they absorb and degrade the mind. There are also some liberal arts quite proper for a freeman to acquire, but only in a certain degree, and if he attend to them too closely, in order to attain perfection in them, the same evil effects will follow. The object also which a man sets before him makes a great difference; if he does or learns anything for his own sake or for the sake of his friends, or with a view to excellence, the action will not appear illiberal; but if done for the sake of others, the very same action will be thought menial and servile. The received subjects of instruction, as I have already remarked, are partly of a liberal and partly of an illiberal character.

The customary branches of education are in number four; they are— (1) reading and writing, (2) gymnastic exercises, (3) music, to which is sometimes added (4) drawing. Of these, reading and writing and drawing are regarded as useful for the purposes of life in a variety of ways, and gymnastic exercises are thought to infuse courage. Concerning music a doubt may be raised—in our days most men cultivate it for the sake of pleasure, but originally it was included in education, because nature herself, as has often been said, requires that we should be able not only to work well but to use leisure well; for as I must repeat once again, the first principle of all action is leisure.[5]

In keeping with the program of education for leisure, reading was the chief subject, from the time the child started school at the age of seven. The word for teacher unqualified (*didaskalos*) means teacher of reading. We have reading texts and fragments of school anthologies from Egypt which are not unlike *McGuffey's Readers* or *Stepping Stones to Literature*. A provincial town like Oxyrhynchus apparently had a considerable school library. Egypt has also preserved exercises in writing, where pupils copy a model line written by the teacher. There were no specially designed buildings or trained teachers, and the schoolmaster was not much regarded. When Demosthenes wishes to insult Aeschines he says (*On the Crown* 258): "In your childhood you were reared in abject poverty. You helped your father in the drudgery of a grammar school, grinding the ink, sponging the benches, and sweeping the schoolroom." The third Mime of Herondas represents an irate mother ordering a schoolmaster to whip her naughty son until the fur flies.

From these and other indications it is clear that schooling was a private, not a state, enterprise, though there may have been some sort of state supervision, as there certainly was in hellenistic times. Nevertheless literacy was general from an early date. Cleisthenes' law on ostracism (507 B.C.) assumed that any citizen could scratch a name on a potsherd. From disasters that befell them we know that schools were well attended. In 494 B.C. the roof of a schoolhouse on Chios collapsed and nearly all of the 120 children who were learning their letters were killed (Herodotus 6.27). At about the same time a disappointed athlete went berserk and pulled down the pillars of a schoolhouse, killing sixty children (Pausanias 6.9.6 ff.). In 423 B.C. a company of demobilized Thracians ravaged the town of Mycalessus in Boeotia and butchered the children in their school; the disaster was so great that Thucydides, who tells the story (7.29), refuses to give the number.

After the primary years the curriculum included not only literature but physical education, drawing, music, and dancing; but these subjects progressively diminished in importance in the hellenistic age and interest was centered on what we should call the humanities—a unified collection of masterpieces as the foundation of all educational values. The classic texts which were the basis of study naturally afforded openings for what we should call the social sciences, and indeed for everything that is contained in books as well as for the study of literature in the narrower sense. Secondary schools too were privately owned, except in a handful of cases where we know of large legacies of public-spirited individuals which provided for maintenance and salary of teachers. But there was careful state supervision. As Professor Marrou puts it,[6] "At the risk of a certain anachronism we could define the hellenistic system as one of independent schools plus state examinations."

A central factor in education, paramount in the hellenistic age, was the gymnasium and the institution of the ephebate connected with it. Originally gymnasia were merely places for physical exercise, but eventually they became centers for social and intellectual life also and were housed in elaborate installations provided by the state.[7] In the hellenistic and Roman period the buildings of the gymnasia had become so standardized that the architect Vitruvius (5.11) could describe them in detail, and the remains that have been found (most fully at Priene) conform to his pattern. The pattern itself points up a significant difference between our educational practices and the Greek: where we shut our school off from the public gaze, the educational activities in the gymnasium were carried on in full view of an interested and critical gallery.[8]

Based on the gymnasium was the institution of the ephebate, which was the most important single factor in the process of hellenization; we know that it existed in more than a hundred hellenistic cities. The ephebate started in Athens as a select military draft, perhaps in the fifth century, and its program was centered on military training and induction of future citizens into their political and religious duties, but it always included cultural sub-

jects. When the military became professionalized, and when
Athens could no longer have an independent foreign policy and
therefore needed no army, the institution continued as a kind of
college, and even drew students from abroad; but there was still a
relic of the past in a heavy emphasis on athletics. The fact that the
Macedonian overlords countenanced it is proof that it was not
primarily a military institution. It is interesting to note that state
support for higher education in Athens was a reverse influence
from the hellenized east. There it was essential for cultural survival and unable to function without state support; and the example carried to Athens itself.[9] From the account given by Aristotle in his *Constitution of Athens* (42) we learn of the discipline
and ideals which continued to characterize the institution wherever it spread:

> The present constitutional order is as follows: the right of citizen-
> ship belongs to those whose parents have been citizens. They are en-
> registered on the rolls of the demes at the age of eighteen. When they
> come up for enrollment, their fellow demesmen decide by vote under
> oath . . . whether the candidate is freeborn and of such parents as the
> law requires. . . . When the young men (*epheboi*) have passed this
> examination, their fathers assemble by tribes and, after having taken an
> oath, elect three of their fellow tribesmen over forty years of age whom
> they consider the best and the most suitable to supervise the young
> men. Then out of these men the people elect by vote one from every
> tribe as guardian (*sophronistes*), and, from the other Athenians, they
> elect a superintendent (*kosmetes*) for all of them. These men then call
> the young men together and first make the circuit of the temples. Then
> they proceed to the Piraeus, and one part takes garrison at Munichia,
> the other at Acte. The Assembly also elects two trainers for them
> and special instructors who teach them to fight in full armor and to use
> the bow, the javelin, and the catapult. They [the people] pay the
> guardians one drachma each for their keep and the young men four
> obols each. Each guardian receives the allowance for all those of his
> tribe, buys all the necessary provisions for their common upkeep (they
> have their meals together by tribes), and also takes care of all other
> matters. This is what they do in the first year. In the following year,
> when there is an Assembly of the People in the theatre, the young men
> give a public display of their military drill before the people. Then
> they receive shield and spear from the state, and from then on they

HUMANISTIC EDUCATION TO SHAPE ATTITUDES SUPPORTING GREEK REALITY CULTURAL IDEAL

NOT INFORMATION UNTIL EUCLID'S GEOMETRY TEXT.

patrol the country and are stationed at the guardposts. While they are in service for their two years, their uniform is a military cloak, and they are free from taxes. And, so that they will have no pretext for requesting a leave, they cannot be sued at law or bring suit against someone else.[10]

Even in the Athenian system the directors of the ephebes were men of high standing; in the hellenistic diaspora they were the most important individuals in the community. The object was clearly to initiate the new generation of leading citizens into the traditions and the outlook and the manners of Greekhood. *Hoi apo tou gymnasiou*, "those from the gymnasium," or in our terminology "the alumni," constituted the center of gravity of a community, politically and socially. These men were bound together by the common experience of a special kind of education; they had studied the same books and imbibed the same ideals, and they set the tone for what a Greek was expected to be.

The educational practices and objectives so far considered are of the type we should call liberal arts—the type best calculated to perpetuate a cultural ideal and therefore most germane to our purposes. In the field of specialized education the hellenistic age departed more markedly from antecedent usages, and their innovations reacted upon general education also. The tenor of the innovations is indicated by a new use of textbooks. Plato had insisted, in his *Seventh Epistle*, that his doctrine could not be acquired from his writings but only from long-continued personal contact with the master. Isocrates had written and encouraged others to write treatises, but these were pamphlets intended to shape an attitude rather than to communicate knowledge. Aristotle's school produced numerous technical treatises on a variety of specialties; but though these belong to his exoteric rather than his esoteric productions they still envisage mature, almost professional, scholars. The first man to write textbooks such as are used in secondary schools today was apparently Euclid—whose geometry continued in use in such schools until this century.

The significant step of adapting Euclid's appliance to other fields seems to have been taken by Epicurus.[11] For spreading his doctrine abroad Epicurus prepared not handbooks but graded texts, the smaller Epitome and the greater. The presentation of doctrine in such a form is essentially a step in the direction of democratization and makes wide diffusion possible. As has been noticed above, the Epicurean belief in an open society with a minimum of governmental control facilitated universalism, and the eager evangelists of Epicureanism did in fact propagate their doctrine far and wide in the hellenistic world. The Epicurean texts came near to becoming a scripture and the founder a prophet; the tendency to transform a doctrine into a cult was, as we shall see,[12] characteristic of hellenistic religious life. But though its central teaching prevented Epicureanism from becoming a cult and its founder from being deified, it nevertheless illustrates a new attitude toward learning and the learned which was the result of the interaction of Greek and non-Greek approaches to education.

The ancient civilizations of the Near East which the Greeks encountered naturally had educational traditions of their own, and in the case of the Egyptians a considerable proportion of the population was literate. But the objectives and ideals were different. The most telling distinction is that whereas Greek education was designed to produce gentlemen amateurs, eastern education was designed to perpetuate a guild of professional scribes. In Egypt where different types of writing, and in Mesopotamia where different languages were used simultaneously, great technical proficiency was demanded of the scribe and his services were indispensable; it was possible for him to achieve a high position in the government.[13] He functioned not only in the bureaucracy, but part of his duty was the guardianship of specialized tradition, and this included such codified prudential wisdom as we find in Egypt from the teachings of Ptahhotep in the twenty-sixth century to those of Amenemope in the eighth, and in the Biblical book of Proverbs which drew from the Egyptian. In Israel the independent currency of the narratives of J and E before they were edited to become part of a canonical book proves the existence of nonprofessional literacy analogous to that in

Greece. The scribal stage came much later than in other countries of the east, but it was the prevailing form after Ezra, who is himself called a scribe.[14]

Where learning is a mystery shared only by specialists who have undergone a hard apprenticeship the scribe-scholar comes to enjoy special prestige, and where the mystery involves religion he may be entitled to something like a superhuman state and even immortality. When a Roman poet who professes to be a minister of the Muses declares *non omnis moriar*, "I shall not wholly die," it is merely an assertion of the artist's pride; he will not die because the monument he has builded is more enduring than bronze. But when a Hesiod or a Pindar claimed to be the special wards of the Muses they meant it literally.[15] A poem addressed to "a woman of no education" by Sappho reads (71): "When you are dead you will lie unremembered for evermore; for you have no part in the roses that come from Pieria; nay, obscure here, you will move obscure in the house of Death, and flit to and fro among such of the dead as have no fame." It may be that Sappho too is merely asserting the artist's pride, and that the immortality she implies for herself is, like Horace's, an immortality of reputation. But the lines do not give the impression of hyperbole. There is a strong likelihood that Sappho had a special connection with Orphism, and this may be the basis of her assurance of immortality.[16] At any rate we can see the origin of the curious epithet *doctus* or *docta* ("learned") applied to a poet as high praise; and we can also see that the poet's claim to immortality has a long history, however thinned down the conception of his immortality may have become.

Actually, in the eastern parts of the hellenistic world the notion that erudition was a key to immortality gained special strength. "Of all our qualities," said Plutarch (*On Educating Children* 8e), "learning alone is immortal and divine." This was no hyperbole, for it appears that education came actually to be regarded as a guarantee of immortality. A remarkable number of inscriptions and tomb decorations represent the deceased as a *mousikos aner*, a protégé of the Muses.[17] In the *Axiochus*, in the Platonic corpus but actually a work of the first century B.C., the chief delights of the Elysian Fields are represented (371 cd) as "discussions for the philosophers, theaters for the poets, dancing, concerts, intelligent conversation round the banquet table." Those capable of such rare delights, it was believed, would be vouchsafed them. Education is endowed with a mystic quality which makes of it an object of religion.

Preoccupation with a classic literature of such high authority that it is canonized into a scripture must eventually introduce a scribal form of education. We can see the tendency in the *Axiochus* and in Plutarch, though it is only by metaphor that the Greek classics can be called canonical, we can see the tendency consummated in Judaism; and the scribal form of education with its concomitant of special status for the scholar was inevitably adopted in Christianity. Our fullest picture of the process is in the book of Ecclesiasticus, written in Hebrew in Palestine at the beginning of the second century B.C. and translated into Greek in Alexandria towards the middle of the century. The relevant passage (38.24–39.11) starts with a picturesque and detailed description of the work of the ploughman, the carpenter, the graver, the smith, and the potter, and praises their skill and usefulness. "Without these cannot a city be inhabited; and they shall not dwell where they will nor go up and down. . . . They will maintain the state of the world" (38.32). But the scholar seeks out the wisdom of all the ancients, and is occupied with prophecies, and keeps the sayings of the renowned, and searches out the secrets of grave sentences. He "shall serve among great men and appear before princes. . . . Many shall commend his understanding; and so long as the world endureth it shall not be blotted out; his memorial shall not depart away, and his name shall live from generation to generation. Nations shall show forth his wisdom, and the congregation shall declare his praise."

The position of the scribe is exalted indeed, and Ecclesiasticus gives him as full an immortality as he could conceive of. Presently, when a more literal kind of immortality was envisioned, the scholar was assured of that also. This development came, significantly, in the hellenistic period, after scholars ceased calling themselves scribes. In the chapter following we shall notice that certain usages of the rabbis—the dialectic method, the explication of ancient texts, the expansion of ancient stories, the system of "difficulties and solutions," the relationship between teacher and taught —were parallel to Greek usages, and shall suggest that since they were introduced after the spread of hellenism they might actually have been inspired by Greek practice. The extraordinary reverence paid to learning may be part and parcel of this same influence. Usually the learning so honored was religious in character, which might explain the high regard in which it was held, but this was not necessarily the case. At the end of each tractate of the Talmud, even where the subject is torts or contracts, there is a formula to be recited by those who have finished studying it. In part it runs as follows:

I thank thee my God and God of my Fathers that thou hast set my lot among those that sit in the house of study and hast not set my lot among those that sit at the street corners: for I rise early and they rise early, but I rise early for things of study and they rise early for things of vanity; I toil and they toil, but I toil and receive reward and they toil and do not receive reward; I hasten and they hasten, but they hasten to the pit of destruction and I hasten to life in the world to come.

Chapter VII

PLATO THE HELLENIZER

IF education was indeed the chief factor in hellenization it becomes important to know what books were studied in the gymnasia of the Greek diaspora and what authors shaped the outlook and the political attitudes of people newly hellenized. We have no school syllabi, unfortunately, but we know that the end of education was *paideia*, the fashioning of a Greek gentleman, and that the means was the body of recognized literary classics. In a non-hellenic environment the humanistic program was more essential for maintaining traditional values than in a hellenic. What the recognized classics were we do know. The primacy of Homer was undisputed; one could not be a Greek without knowing *Iliad* and *Odyssey*. Next came the other poets, tragic and lyric; and these too doubtless did their part in supplying a cultural background for the sons of prominent "barbarians." But though we know that even barbarians knew the Phaedra story and that Christians later cited Pentheus to show the danger of flouting an unfamiliar deity these books must have remained essentially school classics; from the hellenistic point of view their language is archaic and difficult, their mythology remote, their moral teachings irrelevant. Of the historians and orators the same might be said: they supplied knowledge of the Greek past and served to refine style but had little relevance as a guide to the present. The Greek author who was at once an indubitable classic, a spiritual guide whose teachings were sympathetic to non-Hellenes, and a political theorist of high usefulness in the movement to reshape eastern polities in what was fancied to be the Greek mold was Plato. On this basis alone we should surmise that Plato was a force for the spread of Greek ideas; actually there is a strong probability that he was the most important single intellectual factor in the process of hellenization and that his is the major responsibility for shaping the east's eventual contribution to the west.[1]

The evidence for this is largely inferential, but its cumulative effect is impressive. As a preliminary we must know whether copies of Plato's works were available, and evidence shows that they were abundant in hellenistic and Roman times. For Egypt the range of reading is indicated by statistics of papyrus finds, and these may be projected over other hellenized areas—with allowance made for the fact that Egypt was exceptionally bookish and therefore apt to show more technical scholarship. In number of papyrus fragments, then, Homer stands far ahead of any other Greek author, but Plato figures prominently among the half dozen authors in the second place.[2] Another indication of the vogue of Plato is that in his case, as in Homer's, every writing ascribed to him in antiquity has come down to us.

More cogent evidence is to be deduced from the circumstance that Plato in particular is declared by ancient authorities to have had special connections with the east. For one thing, he is said to have made extensive journeys to consult the sages of one or another eastern country and receive their doctrine. The evidence that he did so is highly questionable. The conviction that Plato must be indebted to eastern teaching has indeed persisted among modern writers, but only among such as cherish the essentially romantic view of the ancient Greeks as thoroughgoing rationalists and who must therefore explain Plato as "an alien drop in the Greek bloodstream."[3] The highly improbable travels which still survive in some modern biographies of Plato were plainly invented to afford the alien drop a means of entry. Actually, there is nothing anywhere in the Platonic corpus for which a source outside Greek tradition needs to be posited, as a series of highly competent studies has demonstrated.[4] The nonrational elements in Plato, and in particular the so-called Orphic matter with its tendencies towards dualism, do show affinities with eastern teachings, but these are to be explained as a common heritage from prehellenic antiquity.

Why then were certain authorities in later antiquity concerned to record that Plato did travel in the east and learn from eastern sages? The story originated in the east, and it gained currency because it would save the pride of native peoples and enhance their prestige in their own and Greek eyes if they could show that the most respected of the Greeks learned the doctrines they accepted from the Greeks from their own sages. Nor need we charge disingenuousness. "Borrowings in religion," George Foote Moore has sagely remarked,[5] "at least in the field of ideas, are usually in the nature of the appropriation of things in the possession of another which the borrower recognizes in all good faith as belonging to himself, ideas which, when once they become known to him, are seen to be the necessary implications or complements of his own." The Greek-speaking Jews in Alexandria claimed not only that Pythagoras and Plato had adopted Jewish doctrine but asserted that "Musaeus," the reputed teacher of Orpheus and so the founder of Greek culture, was in fact a distorted spelling of Moses,[6] and the Christian Fathers accepted this view. Josephus (*Against Apion* 1.6–7) is astonished at the Greek reputation for antiquity and originality when in fact "in the Greek world everything will be found to be modern, dating, so to speak, from yesterday or the day before." At the outset of his book Diogenes Laertius finds it necessary to refute Persian, Babylonian, Assyrian, Indian, and other claims to higher originality in philosophy before he can proceed with his account of the doctrines of the Greek philosophers.

Nor was face-saving the only motive; if Plato's doctrine was ultimately eastern, then eastern leaders could claim that they were only following native tradition when they introduced administrative innovations for which the authority of Plato might be cited. The system of the Maccabean rulers, in theory and practice, clearly owes more to Greek patterns than to ancient Hebrew precedent.[7] The textbook out of which Greek patterns were learned would seem to be Plato, whose ideal was Sparta. The

ancient kings of Israel had been political and military leaders who
submitted to the prophets in religious matters; Plato advised that
every phase of human conduct be subjected to religious sanctions
(the most striking feature of the Lycurgan system was that it
claimed the direct authority of Apollo) which are in fact to be
manipulated by the ruler. One specifically Spartan feature in the
Maccabean polity is the council of elders or Sanhedrin, for which
our sources (e.g., Acts 5.21) use the Spartan term *gerousia*. Later
this body became a kind of high court, with some independent
authority, but in origin it was equivalent to the Spartan institution. The Hebrew monarchy had no such institution; the only
connection with the Hebrew past is the number seventy, which
Exodus tells us was the number of elders in Moses' day. It is in
this light that books like Aristeas [8] and the puzzling correspondence between the Maccabee Jonathan and the contemporary king
of Sparta [9] are to be read. The object is not merely to enhance
the credit of the Jews by showing that they were well received
by Ptolemy Philadelphus or that they shared a common descent
with the noble Spartans, but to establish a justification for adopt-
ing certain usages of Greece and especially of Sparta—of which
Plato was the herald.[10]

But it is in the realm of thought rather than politics that the
Platonic influence would be most meaningful, and for this we
turn to literature. The literature which is fullest and the vehicle
of the thought most relevant to our interest is that of the Jews.
Two distinct categories come into consideration, an older literature in Greek, which contains palpable Platonic material but
which has been thought to lie outside the mainstream of Jewish
tradition, and a later literature in Hebrew, in which Greek elements are minimized by design and must mainly be inferred.
Even from the point of view of Jewish tradition the first category
is not as negligible as has been alleged; it is true that by the end of
the first century A.D. this literature was excluded from the body of
tradition, but in its own day it had a wide audience not only in
Alexandria and Antioch and other diaspora centers, but, as we
have noticed above, in Palestine itself. From the general European

point of view the first category is immeasurably the more important, for it not only entered but significantly influenced the mainstream of thought. Its traces are perceptible in the New Testament and it is much cited by the Church Fathers.

The first Jewish writer who comes to mind in connection with Plato is of course Philo of Alexandria, of whom it was said, "Either Plato philonizes or Philo platonizes." [11] Philo's adaptations may force the meaning of Plato unduly (but not nearly so much as he forces the meaning of Scripture) yet he never takes open issue with Plato, as he does with the Stoics, and is plainly unaware that he may be doing violence to Plato.[12] The nature of his Platonism may be illustrated by a single instance: the Scriptural passage which speaks of God creating man "in the image of God" he declares must apply to the whole of the sensible world.[13] And Philo is the principal mediator between Plato and the Christian tradition; Professor Wolfson has shown that the entire system of patristic philosophy, even on themes like the Trinity and the Incarnation which are not touched by Philo, is built upon the framework of the Philonian system.[14]

But Philo may be too late, too individual, and too academic a writer to illustrate the earlier and more pervasive influence of Platonism. The Apocryphal Wisdom of Solomon, perhaps a generation older than Philo, is a more popular and representative kind of work.[15] Unlike earlier Greek-Jewish writings (Aristeas and the fragments from Alexander Polyhistor preserved in Clement of Alexandria and Eusebius) whose main object was to relieve Greek-speaking Jews of the stigma of barbarism, Wisdom is a deeply felt call to traditional piety, and its easy use of the philosophic clichés is therefore the more significant. At 8.7, for example, the author enumerates the cardinal virtues, and at 11.7 he speaks of creation *ex amorphou hyles* ("out of shapeless matter"). The Greek words in which familiar Hebrew ideas are expressed inevitably, and perhaps without conscious design, give these ideas new connotations. Words like *soul, providence, conscience, virtue* have new precision because the philosophers had made quasi-technical terms of them. Greek modes of thought are obvious in such notions as that wisdom is an *emanation* of God, that wisdom *initiates* into its secrets, that God *loves* humanity, that God is omniscient, omnipotent, universally active, that wisdom has specific attributes. The definite personification of wisdom (as contrasted with the vaguer personification in Proverbs) is Greek; here wisdom possesses not only moral and religious virtue but all the secular knowledge the Greeks had acquired. The virtual hypostatization of wisdom has special importance as a stage in the development of the doctrine of the *logos*.

The principal innovation of the Wisdom of Solomon which may be attributable to the kind of Greek influence of which Plato was the chief vehicle, and which in turn had a major influence upon subsequent religious development, is the explicit doctrine of the immortality of the soul and of rewards and punishments after death. God is cognizant of good and evil done in the world and will make due requital, but not necessarily in terms of temporal awards. "The souls of the righteous are in the hands of God . . . their hope full of immortality. . . . The hope of the ungodly is like dust that is blown away with the wind" (3.1–4; 5.14). No previous Jewish writer of whom we know made *individual* immortality (not the survival of the nation) so specific, or righteous conduct so definitely a condition of salvation. And since the doctrine makes its appearance in a book written in Greek and manifestly influenced by Greek modes of thought and expression it is natural to infer that the source was Plato.

This brings up the question of the numerous apocalyptic writings produced in the intertestamentary period. The traditional explanation of apocalyptic is that it is a natural growth out of Old Testament prophecy, with deviations due to changed political and social conditions and imaginative framework influenced by Persian and Babylonian contacts during the period of the Exile. The little apocalypse in Zechariah is enough to justify a connection with Old Testament prophecy, but even here the possibility of Greek and specifically Platonic influence must not be eliminated. A reader who has familiarized himself with various pagan treatments of eschatological themes [16] does not feel transported to a

different world, either in respect to ideas or imagery, when he
moves to the eastern apocalypses. The Testament of Abraham,
which is incidentally one of the plainest links between pre-
Christian and Christian eschatology, shows very clear traces of
Platonic Orphism.[17] In its structure and in certain details of its
setting (for example, the locale on the banks of a river) the vision
of Er at the end of the *Republic* is a complete apocalypse. With
the new evidence of the penetration of hellenism even in Palestine
it is hard to imagine that any writer, even one who used Hebrew
or Aramaic, would not know of the most striking passage in
Plato's most celebrated work. The doctrinal point in which the
Semitic eschatologies differ significantly from Plato's is that they
are concerned with the destiny of a nation whereas Plato is concerned with the destiny of individuals. Whether or not they
learned from Plato, then, it seems certain that Wisdom did. In the
stress upon individual salvation which we find in Wisdom and its
successors, Christian and Jewish, we may see an example of a
western importation returned to the west with fresh emphasis
and urgency.

The Fourth Book of the Maccabees so called is, like the Wisdom of Solomon, a Greek diatribe in form, but it is written with
greater sophistication, addresses itself to a more cultivated audience, and makes more expert use of Greek, and especially Platonic, tradition.[18] This book affords us perhaps our best example
of an amalgam, rather than a mere collocation, of Greek and
Hebrew ideas. The story it tells is of the martyrdoms of the aged
Eleazar and of Hannah. The persecuting king is represented as
pleading with the sage to save himself by ostensible compliance;
he assumes that his interlocutor is a Stoic and uses Stoic arguments
to reenforce his plea. Eleazar's position is consistently Platonist;
Plato is not merely an armory of adventitious arguments to con-
fute the pagans with their own weapons but a way of thought
espoused by the author and presumably by his audience. From
Plato comes such specific doctrine as the four cardinal virtues,
the two parts of the soul, the destiny of human beings after death,
the question of the animality of the stars; and from Plato comes

the personality and the moral posture of the protagonists. The model for the disputation between the sage and the tyrant is quite clearly the *Gorgias;* the arguments they use are essentially those of Socrates and Callicles. When Callicles declares that justice is the power of the strong, Socrates insists that it is better to suffer than to do wrong, and better for a wrongdoer to be punished than to escape. When Callicles objects that the tyrant can torture his victim, Socrates replies that the wrong is the tyrant's; a good man fares well however he fares and is blessed and happy, while the wicked man is wretched. True judgment will take place in the future, when men are stripped of their bodies and their bare souls can be examined. It is through the Judeo-Christian tradition rather than Plato's own writings that this doctrine has become part of European civilization; IV Maccabees shows how that tradition received and disseminated that doctrine.

In contrast to the Greek books we have glanced at, the Hebrew writings to which we now turn had only a minor role. They reached their present form only after Christianity was firmly established and in position to propagate its inheritance from the Greek-Jewish writings, and part of their purpose was to make survival without participation in that inheritance possible. Not only is there no mention of Philo, for example, anywhere in rabbinic literature, but from that literature alone it would be reasonable to infer that no such figure as Philo could ever have existed. But though the rabbinic traditions were reduced to writing only after the second century, some are of much earlier date and may therefore yield evidence germane to our inquiry. Hellenism has left its traces even in the Talmud, which contains a considerable proportion of Greek loan words and even some dicta whose origin may have been forgotten.[19] But the clearest bases for assuming an ingrained Platonic influence are the modes of argumentation and certain societal objectives.

The method that the rabbis used for reaching truth can only be described as a species of Socratic dialectic. The method of the prophets had been to exhort, upon the authority of direct revelation; in the rabbinic as in the Socratic dialectic questions are raised and solutions proposed and rejected until a satisfactory conclusion is reached. Even the use of a revered text as a theme for fruitful exegesis has its analogues in Plato, as when a "canonical" poem of Simonides is analyzed for authoritative doctrine in the *Protagoras*. The technique of "difficulties and solutions" (*aporiai kai luseis*) which the hellenistic schools learned from the Academy is a regular procedure in the Talmud, and the relation of pupil and teacher is precisely like that in the philosophical schools, not that of prophet and disciple. The connotations of the Hebrew *talmid* are exactly equivalent to those of the Greek *mathetes*. There is, of course, no direct evidence of causal relationship, but it is to be noticed that the dialectic method makes its appearance only after the Platonic writings became known.

Greek affinities are suggested by another technique of the rabbis, found in *midrash*, or homiletic texts, rather than in *halakhah*, or legal texts. An episode briefly recounted in the Bible will be expanded and given an ethical interpretation, or some new episode for which there is no basis in the Bible will be attached to some well-known Biblical figure. Both of these procedures are familiar enough in Greek literature but have no known antecedents in Hebrew. Tragedians regularly expanded brief episodes out of what was in effect a scripture into ethically meaningful compositions. Most of the creative literature of the hellenistic age is expansion and reinterpretation of ancient myth. Aside from such things as Aesopic fables, stories newly created for edification are few and late. The one exception is the "myths" in Plato, which were surely the most widely known as they were the oldest. There are of course too many yawning gaps in our knowledge for anyone to argue seriously that the techniques of *midrash* are based on Greek models, but the analogy at least is worth noticing.

Aside from techniques of argumentation and presentation there is a larger sense in which Platonic doctrine may be a factor. It is possible that the system which the Talmud constructs is consciously calculated to achieve a goal which Plato specifically prescribes, and further that that system was then adopted by forces which did shape European civilization. We shall look first at Plato's prescription. The teachings which lend themselves most easily to direct application in giving shape to the organization of society are detailed in his final, fullest, and most outspoken work, the *Laws*. His program is briefly and correctly summarized by E. R. Dodds [20] as follows:

1. He would provide religious faith with a logical foundation by *proving* certain basic propositions.
2. He would give it a legal foundation by incorporating these propositions in an unalterable legal code, and imposing legal penalties on any person propagating disbelief in them.
3. He would give it an educational foundation by making the basic propositions a compulsory subject of instruction for all children.
4. He would give it a social foundation by promoting an intimate union of religious and civic life at all levels—as we should phrase it, a union of Church and State.

Except for the first item, where revelation obviated any need for logical proof of basic principles, this summary is a fair description of the objectives and devices which govern Talmudic legislation. Morally the acceptance of revelation in good faith, as the rabbis accepted it, makes an enormous difference; Plato's Nocturnal Council was to impose religious penalties on civic infringements by consciously *pretending* to have divine authorization. But whether by religious conviction or expediency, the complete control of civic as well as religious life by the established authorities is common to the Platonic and the Talmudic program, as is the significant prescription that all children be educated to accept that control. Plato himself summarized the objective of his program in unequivocal terms (*Laws* 942 ab):

The principal thing is that none, man or woman, should ever be without an officer set over him, and that none should get the mental habit of taking any step, whether in earnest or in jest, on his individual responsibility. In peace as in war he must live always with his eye on his superior officer, following his lead and guided by him in his smallest actions. . . . In a word, we must train the mind not even to consider acting as an individual or know how to do it.

The shocking thing here is that the alleged religious authority for the program is confessedly a contrivance and its object merely to ensure well-disciplined subjects. The rabbis were men of faith, and their object was the service of religion, but their method for securing discipline was, like Plato's, to provide authority for men's smallest actions. The program succeeded so well that with no secular power at their disposal the Talmudic authorities were able to direct the lives of their communicants all over the Roman Empire, to enforce compliance by the instrument of excommunication, and to collect fixed contributions. One may wonder whether the Church might not have been influenced by this pattern in developing its very similar organizational program. If that is the case we should have the final and most telling example of Greek doctrine set forth by Plato, naturalized in the east, and returned to the west with new power.

Chapter VIII

BARBARIAN APOLOGETICS

THE outstanding philosopher was not the only eminent Greek for whom the barbarians claimed credit. They asserted that the outstanding Greek poet and the outstanding Greek conqueror belonged to them. And presently, with growing assurance, they sought to demonstrate that personages in their own tradition were fully equal to any the Greeks might produce.

Homer was claimed to be both a Syrian and an Egyptian. Meleager argued that he was a fellow-Syrian by a rather curious inference (Athenaeus 157a):

Meleager of Gadara in the work entitled "The Graces" declared that Homer was a Syrian by birth, and accordingly represented the Achaeans as abstaining from fish, in keeping with the Syrian practice, though there is a great abundance of fish in the region of the Hellespont.[1]

And in the *Ethiopica* the sage Calasiris asserts that Homer was an Egyptian (Book 3):

Different authors have ascribed different countries to Homer, and indeed the sage is at home everywhere; but it is certain that Homer was an Egyptian and that his city was Thebes of the Hundred Gates, as he himself declares. His father, men think, was a priest of Hermes, but in fact it was Hermes himself. When the priest's wife had completed a certain traditional ceremony and had gone to sleep in the temple, the god consorted with her and begot Homer. The mark of his ill-assorted parentage Homer bore from his birth—a long strip of hair growing on one of his thighs. That is how he got the name Homer (or "The Thigh") when he wandered over Greece and other countries chanting his poems. His true name he never told, nor his city or family . . . because he was ashamed of being an exile [i.e., *not* because he was ashamed of being an Egyptian].[2]

Some who did not venture to claim Homer sought at least to lower his pedestal. So Josephus (*Against Apion* 1.12):

Throughout the whole range of Greek literature no undisputed work is found more ancient than the poetry of Homer. His date, however, is clearly later than the Trojan War, and even he, they say, did not leave his poems in writing. At first transmitted by memory, the scattered songs were not united until later; to this circumstance the numerous inconsistencies of the work are attributable.[3]

A claim of Egyptian origin is also put forward for Alexander the Great. The intriguing and exasperating *Alexander Romance* ascribed to Pseudo-Callisthenes,[4] starting with a circumstantial account of Alexander's origins, solemnly declares that an Egyptian personage crossed the sea to consort with Olympias for the specific purpose of ensuring that the great conqueror should be an Egyptian. Later legend made Alexander the national hero of virtually every people he conquered. And Egypt claimed credit for the wisdom of Aesop. The longer version of Aesop's life in the Morgan Library, edited by Professor Ben Perry, states that Aesop received his instruction from Isis and was suspicious of Apollo. Professor Perry suggests that the Life is the work of a hellenized Egyptian who was irritated by Greek claims to superiority and convinced of the priority of his own people in matters of wisdom.[5]

Another mode used by non-Hellenes to establish a place for themselves within the hellenic tradition was to claim blood kinship with some indubitably Greek people on the basis of common descent. It was the Greeks themselves who set up the precedent; their ancient genealogies, as we have noted above,[6] made a place for the founders of various eastern nations, including Egypt and Persia, and in the historical period they were not above inventing such genealogies when it suited their political ambitions. In the hellenistic age a connection with an authentic Greek people would enhance the standing of a hellenized people and might even be made the basis of a request for assistance. An interesting illustration is afforded by a letter reputedly written by the Maccabee Jonathan about 142 B.C. and recorded in I Maccabees 12:

This is the copy of the letter which Jonathan wrote to the Spartans: "Jonathan the High Priest, the Council of the Nation, the priests and the rest of the Jewish people, to their Spartan brothers, greetings! Even before this a letter was sent to Onias the High Priest from Areius who was then king among you, to the effect that you are our kinsmen, as the copy herewith submitted sets forth. Onias received the man who was sent honorably, and accepted the letter, in which declaration was made about alliance and friendship. Although we are not in need of these pledges, since we find encouragement in the holy books which we possess, we have undertaken to send to you to renew the pact of brotherhood and friendship, that we may not become estranged from you, for much time has gone by since you sent word to us. So we remember you at every opportunity, incessantly on the festivals and other appropriate days, in the sacrifices which we offer and in our prayers, as it is right and fitting to recall our kinsmen. Moreover we rejoice in your glory. But many hardships and many wars surrounded us, and the kings around us made war on us. We did not wish, therefore, to trouble you nor the rest of our allies and friends with these wars; for ours is the aid which comes to us from Heaven. We have been preserved from our enemies, while our enemies have been brought low. We have selected Numenios son of Antiochus and Antipater son of Jason and have sent them to the Romans to renew our former friendly alliance with them. We have ordered them to go to you also, to greet you and to deliver a letter from us concerning the renewal of our pledge of brotherhood. Now will you please answer us about this."

This is the copy of the letter which they sent to Onias: "Areius king of the Spartans to Onias the High Priest, greetings! It has been found in a writing concerning the Spartans and Jews that they are related, and that they are of the family of Abraham. Since we have learned this will you please write us about your welfare. We are writing in turn to you that your cattle and property are ours, and ours are yours. We give charge, therefore, that this be reported to you." [7]

The implication of Jonathan's letter, if it is genuine, is that in the middle of the second century B.C. people could be expected to believe (whether or not the writer did) that Jews and Spartans were blood kin; and if the letter quoted as from Areius is genuine, that the same situation obtained at the beginning of the third century B.C. The notion of peoples so disparate being related seems so absurd that many scholars have dismissed the whole correspondence as forgery.[8] The only external corroboration is a virtual transcription in Josephus (*Antiquities* 12.225 ff.); but the fact that a writer with considerable knowledge of eastern Medi-

terranean politics and traditions did not find the story absurd is
itself significant. II Maccabees 5.9 suggests that people believed
that Jews and Spartans were related, and in *Jewish War* 1.515
Josephus shows that the belief existed at least as late as the time of
Herod. Moreover, fuller knowledge of hellenistic epistolography
suggests that the letters may well have been written at the date
purported.

As for Jonathan's own letter, then, there is no reason to doubt
its genuineness, and most scholars accept it at face value. It was
perfectly natural for a state which had newly regained its sovereignty to seek diplomatic status abroad if only to enhance its
prestige, and it was a regular practice for peoples on the periphery
of the Greek world to claim relationship with states of greater
power or of unquestioned hellenic lineage. Rome itself, as soon
as it became aware of Greek civilization, claimed one or another
Homeric hero as the founder of this or that Italian city, and documented its own antiquity as well as independence by asserting that
it was founded by the other party to the Trojan War. As late as
the fourth century A.D. Synesius, who was bishop in Cyrene,
proudly refers to his descent from the Spartan Heraclids.

For more immediate political reasons and at an age close to
Jonathan's we have numerous examples of similar claims. In 197
B.C. the Lampsacenes, whose country was in the Troad, used that
circumstance to argue that they were kin to the Romans and
hence could legitimately ask for Roman help against Antiochus
III. Perhaps a closer parallel, since it involves a Semitic people, is
the claim of kinship with Delphi put forward by Tyre in 146 B.C.
Sparta was claimed as mother city, most implausibly, by a congeries of eastern cities, especially in southwest Asia Minor.[9] Sparta
itself was a broken reed in the middle of the second century, and
Jonathan disclaims any desire for material assistance; it is plain
that his objective was prestige for his people and perhaps their
acquiescence in accepting governmental and other usages like
their "cousins'."

The appended letter of Areius is on a different footing and has
a different kind of interest for us. Though the names are right

enough—Areius did reign in Sparta 309–265 B.C., and Onias was high priest in Jerusalem 320–290—it is hard to imagine the Spartan taking the initiative and claiming descent from Abraham. Claims of relationship between hellenic and non-hellenic peoples were proffered not by the Hellenes but by the non-Hellenes, as we saw in the instances cited above, and the practice seems to have been initiated at a date later than the Areius-Onias synchronization would suggest. If Areius' letter is supposititious it was fabricated in Jonathan's chancellery. But "the writing concerning the Spartans and the Jews that they are related" which the spurious letter mentions probably did exist, and was probably what suggested the composition not only of the spurious letter but even of Jonathan's own genuine letter.

The substantive existence of a writing of which we hear only in a document admittedly spurious is naturally not susceptible of positive proof. All that can be shown is that there did exist a class of writings in which the work here envisaged would belong, that there were sufficient motivations for this particular work, and that its effects are discernible. In our consideration of historiography we shall find that hellenistic practice recognized three categories: "true history," "false history," and "history such as might likely have happened." [10] The requirements for the third species, which was by far the most important, were that it must be essentially true, that its elaborations must have verisimilitude, and that it must be edifying. Essentially these are the rules which governed the early tragic poets also, as Aristotle saw when he said that poetry is truer than history. If there was a pre-existing "writing" which furnished Jonathan's chancellery with incentive and text for their Spartan correspondence, it was a hellenistic *plasma*, tricked out for verisimilitude with historical names and other appropriate background, and of a piece with Aristeas and kindred works to which we shall come presently.

Tragedy was the source from which the conception of useful and plausible fictional treatment of essential truth ultimately derived, and tragedy continued to influence hellenistic literature. We shall see that the *Hippolytus* of Euripides affected all subse-

quent love stories; a much older play, the *Suppliants* of Aeschylus,
supplies a connection with the literature of barbarian apologetics.
An important issue in the *Suppliants* is whether or not Danaus,
the father of the ostensibly Egyptian maidens, is of Argive descent; only if he is can their petition for asylum be heeded at the
risk of war. In the hellenistic age Danaus' departure from Egypt
is made to figure in a story in which Jews are involved and in
which their connection with Sparta is adumbrated. Early in the
third century B.C. Hecataeus of Abdera or of Teos (not to be
confused with the Hecataeus of Miletus whose work Herodotus
used) wrote an *Aegyptiaca* intended to glorify Egypt as the
source of all civilization; this was the basis of Manetho's doubtless
superior and certainly better known work.[11] A fragment of this
Hecataeus tells how the Jews together with other foreigners,
among them Danaus and Cadmus, were ejected from Egypt during an epidemic.[12] Apparently this represents Egyptian reaction
to claims of superiority on the part of both Greeks and Jews.
Egyptians doubtless smarted at the story of the Exodus as advertised in the Septuagint and other Jewish-Greek works, and it
pleased their pride to lump with the Jews such revered Greek
heroes as Cadmus and Danaus.[13] It is to be noticed that for the
premise of his story, that is, the presence of Jews and Greeks in
Egypt, Hecataeus had the authority of the ancient literature of
both peoples. Hecataeus' fictitious elaborations of his historical
kernel included an account of the hardships the exiles suffered in
common during their wanderings, and this, in view of Danaus'
position as progenitor of the Spartan kings, may have been the
basis of the story of the relationship between Jews and Spartans.

If Hecataeus was an apologist for the Egyptians it becomes
difficult to explain his remarks favorable to the Jews cited in
Josephus and elsewhere and his apparently laudatory *On Abraham*. The difficulty was felt in antiquity; Origen says: "The
author is so attached to this nation because of its wisdom that
Herennius Philo [a hellenized Phoenician of the late first century]
in his work *On the Jews* in the first place expressed doubt whether
the work is by the historian, and in the second place says, if it

really is his work, that he has been ravished by Jewish persuasive-
ness and won over by their doctrines." The doubts are surely justified. Though some recent scholars have maintained that the author of *On Abraham* is the same Hecataeus who wrote the
Aegyptiaca, it is much more probable that he was a Jewish writer
who lived a century later and sought to give his work credit by
attaching to it the name of a respectable author of the past. The
practice was by no means without precedent. Not only was the
name of Solomon attached to a wisdom book and to psalms
written in the hellenistic age in order to give them standing, but
the names of classical Greek authors were similarly used. The
230-line poem attributed to Phocylides (actually a gnomic poet
of the sixth century B.C.), Books 3–5 of the Sibylline Oracles [14]
which are manifestly of Jewish or Christian authorship, sundry
Orphic poems, and lines ascribed to Sophocles and others belong
to this category.

Whether Hecataeus was one man or more, the works ascribed
to him illustrate a phenomenon common to the hellenistic world.
After the conquests of Alexander proud peoples on the eastern
periphery of the Greek world found themselves degraded to the
position of "natives" and their ancient cultures despised as barbarian. Despite the external uniformity of the hellenistic *oikou
mene*, pride in native traditions persisted, and among peoples
whose political independence had been suppressed there was felt
a need, usually bound up with motives of religion, to assert the
antiquity and dignity of individual national traditions in the face
of the dominant Greek environment. Very early in the hellenistic
period the Babylonian Berossus, priest of Bel, dedicated his *Baby-
loniaca* to Antiochus I Soter, and Manetho, high priest at
Heliopolis, his *Aegyptiaca* to Ptolemy Philadelphus. Berossus'
history was divided into three books: from the origins to the
flood; thence to Nabonassar (747 B.C.); and thence to the death of
Alexander. Manetho's book similarly reached from the beginnings
to the death of Alexander. The dynastic lists which modern historians follow are from Manetho, who claims to have consulted

the sacred records for them. Manetho's standing and the direction of his thought are indicated by the fact that he was one of the architects of the Sarapis cult, which was calculated to fuse Egyptian and Greek religious interests.[15] The remains of these books are too fragmentary to provide a basis for judgment, but the fact that their design was clearly apologetic makes it certain that they used all the liberties which hellenistic historiography allowed.[16] By modern canons they would be classed probably as historical fiction rather than as history.

Later apologetics based on the remote past move farther in the direction of fiction. The next step after the chronological scheme was apparently to center a story upon the eponymous or national hero of a people, its founder or lawgiver. It is apparently to such works that Plutarch alludes (*Isis and Osiris* 360b) when he speaks of the Assyrians celebrating Semiramis, the Egyptians Sesostris, and the Phrygians Manes. We shall see that the Babylonians celebrated Ninus similarly, in the *Ninus Romance*, and the Jews Moses, in Artapanus' "history." To judge from these two, each hero was made the protagonist of a story which permitted him to display great prowess and wisdom, and was also provided with a love story, to suit contemporary hellenistic taste.

Accommodation to Greek taste, indeed, is a highly significant aspect of all the apologetic works. Though the object was to raise the esteem of the native peoples, in their own sight and in the sight of the world, it was the Greek, not the native, standard that was paramount. Where native material would be creditable in Greek eyes and adaptable to Greek forms it was used; unassimilable elements were glossed over. The voluminous exegetical writings of Philo illustrate the point perfectly. Where Scripture in its plain sense is admirable or acceptable to the Greek view Philo presents it in its plain sense; where it would seem coarse or primitive he resorts to allegorical interpretation to assimilate it to Greek sensibilities. It is true that hellenized peoples adapted Greek forms and motifs, in literature as well as art, for use in native mediums, but the Greek mode was the unquestioned standard. Only in

Rome was there wholesale translation and adaptation of Greek works, and only in Rome could the naturalized forms claim to vie with the Greek on its own terms.

It is entirely possible that the histories written to promote cultural survival, and particularly the glorifications of national heroes, are the source of the novel. In the *Ninus Romance*, and also in the *Moses Romance* if we may call it so, we have an "historical" element to display the hero's virtue and prowess, and an erotic element to engage the reader's attention. Now these two elements are present in our extant Greek Romances, and in their probable chronological order the historical element is progressively reduced to a vestigial background and the erotic becomes central. Yet even when their sole purpose seems entertainment the romances have a propagandist aim, if only to show that, appearances to the contrary notwithstanding, gods watch over their special charges and contrive a happy ending for those who prove loyal.[17]

Defense of a cultural minority is at least a collateral objective of Heliodorus' *Ethiopica*, which is so well written that this motivation escapes notice. The heroine Chariclea is discovered to be the daughter of an Ethiopian queen, who exposed her in infancy to escape imputations on her character for having given birth to a white child. Chariclea's foster father, Calasiris, is a Gymnosophist priest, upright, sagacious, and benevolent; at the end of the story he introduces significant moral reforms. The scene is laid in the fifth century B.C., and an important part of the action takes place at Delphi. The authorities at Delphi, which is the central hearth of Hellenism, receive Calasiris with high marks of respect, and no less a person than a descendant of Achilles himself falls madly in love with the Ethiopian girl, who is regarded, even before her royal birth is known, as fully his social equal. One is tempted to guess that the author of this book was dark-skinned and attached to the Gymnosophist cult. Surely it was no small part of his purpose to show that at the most brilliant period of Greek history a people and a cult currently despised was highly regarded; and if he wrote at a time when foreign pressure or disdain heightened the nationalist feelings of his own people, his book would show them that the Greeks had many admirable traits and could be lived with and in some respects emulated.

In its propaganda aims and in its means of implementing them the so-called *Letter of Aristeas* [18] is remarkably similar. This book was written in Egypt, probably during the Maccabean uprising; it is not yet a romance, but it follows the hellenistic rules for narrative prose in the form of an epistle. The substance amounts to this: Ptolemy Philadelphus (who lived more than a century before the book was written) is reminded by Demetrius of Phalerum (who is also a historical personage) that he must procure a Greek translation of the Hebrew Scriptures to make his famous library complete, and sends an embassy to the high priest in Jerusalem to request that he supply a company of translators. The king addresses the high priest as a full equal, and his embassy is much impressed with the beauty and stateliness of Jerusalem and the temple service. (It is quite clear from the descriptions that the writer had never seen Jerusalem.) When the company of seventy-two translators arrive in Alexandria they are welcomed with the greatest respect and entertained at a series of dinners at which they astonish the philosophers present by their sagacity and courtliness. No difficulty is made of their dietary habits: the king realizes that different peoples have different usages and his staff has had experience in catering to different requirements. When the translation is completed the king shows reverence for the work and respectful gratitude to the translators. Now one obvious purpose of the book is to give authority to the Septuagint and perhaps to a festival which annually celebrated its completion. Another purpose, equally obvious, is to show, at a period when Jews were suffering certain disabilities, that in an earlier day the Grand Monarque of the hellenistic world was eager to accept the Jews as equals. This much is quite parallel to the treatment of Calasiris and Chariclea at Delphi. But there was probably a third purpose, perhaps even more central to the author's mind than the other two. He was, after all, addressing his fellow Jews, though he himself assumes a pagan mask; it is extremely unlikely that a book like Aristeas ever found its way into the regular book trade, and there is no evidence that any but Jews and Christians read it. The audience he had in mind is indicated by his effort to give authority to the Septuagint and to a Jewish religious celebration. When we realize that it was to his fellow Jews that he addressed his book, the other motive becomes clear. What this book is seeking above all to do is not to win the respect of the Greeks for the Jews, but the respect of the Jews for the Greeks. What it is saying is that it is perfectly possible for Jews to share Greek ways without compromising the essentials of their religion, to engage in dialectic with Greek philosophers, to dine with them, even to have no thought or hope of a return to Palestine. We shall see in the sequel that III Maccabees, written more than a century later, is a refutation, probably intentional, of the position of Aristeas. III Maccabees will say that rapprochement with Greeks is impossible; Aristeas urges Jews to cultivate rapprochement.

Aristeas survived because it was an important witness to the Bible; there were other books advertising the merits of other non-hellenic peoples which no one was concerned to preserve. We know of the existence of many such from Alexander Polyhistor, who made it his business to make excerpts of the romanticized histories of eastern peoples written in Greek. Alexander was a Milesian Greek who was brought to Rome as a prisoner in the course of the Mithridatic Wars and there given his liberty by Sulla in 82 B.C.[19] Among his works (which Suidas describes as "beyond number") we find such titles as *Aegyptiaca, Libyca, Indica, Cretica, On Caria, On Lycia, On Phrygia, On Syria, On Bithynia, On the Euxine Sea, On Cilicia, On Paphlagonia, On Illyria, On Lycoreia, On the Jews, Chaldaica.* He has been called the most important single intermediary bringing information about the east to the west. His technique was merely to weave excerpts from local historians, with no shred of critical selectivity, into a chronological mosaic. Alexander's work is lost except for scattered citations. By far the greater number of these are from his *On the Jews,* and these have survived only because they were cited by the Christian apologist Clement of Alexandria (c. A.D. 150–215) and the Church historian Eusebius (c. A.D. 260–340).[20] How faithfully the citations represent the original texts it is difficult to say. We do not know how much of his sources Alexander cut away and how far he went in regularizing their style. And though Eusebius was a careful workman, the text of Alexander which he used was faulty, and his own text is in an unsatisfactory state. Despite the complicated history of the fragments which concern us, however, their texts still reveal the individual character of their authors and offer admirable illustrations of the stages of hellenization applicable, surely, to other eastern peoples as well as to the Jews. The clearest gradation is shown by the historians, to whom we turn first.

The oldest of these is Demetrius, who wrote his *On the Kings in Judaea* toward the end of the third century B.C.[21] His fragments amount to some six printed pages. The first and longest deals with Jacob's flight to Haran, his marriages and begettings, his return to Canaan, and the sojourn in Egypt up to the birth of Moses. The second describes Moses' flight to Midian and his marriage to Zipporah. The third and fourth are brief notes on the sweetening of the waters of Marah and on the captivity of Judah, Benjamin, and Levi. Demetrius uses the Septuagint and adheres closely to the Biblical narrative; there are touches of midrashic exegesis but no such fanciful additions of romantic details as we find in later authors. For example, Demetrius resists the temptation, to which his successors succumbed, of embroidering the stories of Joseph or Moses. But there is an effort to give an atmosphere of Alexandrian scholarship. The chronology is so meticulously worked out that we are told the intervals between the births of Jacob's children to the month, and the age of each, to the month, when they came to Egypt; where no dating is specified in the Bible Demetrius reconstructs a chronology, indicating how he arrives at it. The methods of Alexandrian research, furthermore, are suggested by posing problems and offering solutions (*aporiai kai luseis*); Demetrius will say, "One might be at a loss," or "one might ask," and then supply the answer. So far, then, there is an effort to make the

Biblical narrative acceptable to Greek readers, but with no marked departure from native tradition, no claims for superiority over paganism, and no romantic elaborations of a purely hellenistic character. These elements will become increasingly prominent in Demetrius' successors.

Eupolemus,[22] who wrote his *On the Kings in Judaea* towards the middle of the second century B.C., is much more the panegyrist and apologist; he adorns, exaggerates, and invents additions for his Biblical materials. The extant fragments amount to six or seven pages. The first is: "Eupolemus says that Moses was the first wise man (*sophos*), and the first to give the Jews letters, that the Phoenicians received them from the Jews and the Greeks from the Phoenicians, and that Moses was the first to give written laws, and to the Jews." Another fragment gives the succession of prophets from Moses to Joshua to Samuel, the establishment and the expansion of the kingdom under David, the divine disapproval (through the epiphany of an angel) of his premature attempt to build a temple, and the succession of Solomon. There follow "copies" of exchanges of courteous letters between Solomon and Vaphres, king of Egypt, and Solomon and Suron (Hiram), king of Tyre. Finally, there is a detailed description of the structure and furnishings of the temple.

The hellenistic influence is marked. The claim for priority in cultural inventions (*heuremata*) is characteristic. Foreign potentates recognize the god whom Solomon calls "the greatest." When King Vaphres speaks of Solomon as "a man approved by so great a god," and Hiram blesses the god "who has chosen so worthy a ruler," their expressions of formal courtesy are very like those of the Rosetta Stone (dated at 196 B.C.).[23] The name "Jerusalem" is derived from *hieron Solomonos*, "temple of Solomon"; this is in keeping with the Greek habit of finding Greek etymologies for foreign names, and incidentally what one would expect from a writer who uses the Septuagint (as Eupolemus does) rather than the Hebrew Bible. Considerable latitudinarianism, or perhaps a tendency towards syncretism, is indicated by Solomon's sending Hiram "a golden pillar which is dedicated in the temple of Zeus

at Tyre." Fictive letters are a commonplace in hellenistic literature; they are much used in the romances and sometimes themselves constitute a romance, and they are used to give verisimilitude to history. An exchange of letters between Solomon and
Hiram is cited at II Chronicles 2; Eupolemus conforms these to
Greek usage and invents the exchange with Vaphres to match
them. These letters, incidentally, which Alexander Polyhistor obviously copied without alteration, show the poverty of Eupolemus' Greek style and suggest that Alexander smoothed over the
remaining fragments.

Each of the traits noticed in Eupolemus is further accentuated
in Artapanus: [24] claims for Jewish priority in cultural advances
are exaggerated to the point of absurdity, wild deviations from
native tradition are countenanced, and hellenistic literary conventions distort the Biblical narrative out of all recognition. The
two shorter fragments of Artapanus are not too startling. The
first states that Abraham in a twenty-year sojourn in Egypt
taught the Egyptian king astrology, and that when he returned to
Syria many of his followers remained in Egypt. The second deals
with Joseph's administration of Egypt, where his services in or-
ganizing land tenure and inventing measures won him the affection of the Egyptians.

Artapanus' third and longest fragment, which deals with Moses,
is as baffling as it is intriguing; here is a summary: Merris, daughter of a king hostile to the Jews and wife of Chenephres king of
Memphis, being childless took up a Jewish child whom she called
Moüsos, but whom, when he was grown, the Greeks called
Musaios. Moses was the teacher of Orpheus, and invented a variety of machines for peace and war and also philosophy. He
divided the country into thirty-six nomes and assigned each its
gods—cats, dogs, ibises; he invented hieroglyphs and apportioned
a special district for the priests. These things he did to ensure
Chenephres' sovereignty, and he was beloved by the people and
honored as a god by the priests; they named him Hermes because of his invention (*hermeneia*) of hieroglyphs. Out of envy
Chenephres sent him against the Ethiopians with inadequate

forces, but Moses collected a hundred thousand peasants, built a city which he called Hermopolis to accommodate them during a ten-years campaign, and established a cult of the ibis because that bird destroys noxious reptiles.

The Ethiopians so loved their enemy that they and the priests adopted circumcision. Chenephres disbanded Moses' troops, and sent some to guard the frontiers and others to quarry stone for a temple at Diospolis. Nacheros, the superintendent of this work, asked Moses what other animals were particularly useful to man, and Moses said oxen; Chenephres caused a bull he named Apis to be buried in a special temple in order to conceal Moses' invention. Merris now died, and Chenephres sent Moses and a certain Chanethothes (whom he had suborned to kill Moses) to bury her body, but Moses became aware of the plot and himself buried Merris in the town he called Meroe; Merris is honored as Isis. On Aaron's advice Moses fled to Arabia; he slew Chanethothes, who had attempted to ambush him. In Arabia Moses lived with Raguel, whose daughter he married; he rejected Raguel's plea that he make war on Egypt to win kingship. Chenephres died, the first victim of elephantiasis, because he had ordered the Jews to wear linen garments to mark them out for persecution. When Moses attempted to relieve his brethren he was incarcerated but was miraculously delivered. When, at the king's request, he whispered God's name in his ear, the king swooned and Moses restored him. He wrote the Name on a tablet and sealed it, and a priest who scoffed died of convulsions. The account of the plagues follows the Biblical narrative, with slight additions; for example, "the Egyptians dedicate a rod like Moses' in every temple, and likewise to Isis, because the earth is Isis, and sent up these wonders when smitten by the rod." On the escape from Egypt alternative accounts are given: that of Heliopolis follows the Bible, that of Memphis rationalizes by saying that Moses knew the country well and waited for the ebb tide. The fragment closes with a description of Moses: "Moses, they say, was tall and ruddy, with long white hair, and dignified; and he performed these deeds when he was about eighty-nine years old."

It is obvious that this strange gallimaufry is an unskillful inter-
weaving of disparate strands, each so curtailed as to be almost
meaningless. To enucleate the several strands is a complicated task
and must involve a good deal of conjecture. But it is clear that
Moses had become the center of a mass of legend of the hellenistic
type, which, like the legends centering on Joseph or on Alexander, had doubtless been worked up into a formal romance.[25] In-
concinnities and faulty transitions in Artapanus' account would
then be due to his foreshortening material from the romance and
awkward attempts to combine it with materials from other
sources. A good analogy is offered by the *Alexander Romance*,
where "Callisthenes'" awkward fusion of materials from both
imaginative and historical sources has resulted in a baffling amalgam of sober fact and puerile fantasy.[26] And like the *Alexander
Romance*, Artapanus' influence on subsequent writers is out of all
proportion to his merit. The ascending stages of deviation from
tradition illustrated by Demetrius, Eupolemus, and Artapanus are
matched by several others cited from Alexander Polyhistor, but
the fragments are too slight for profitable analysis.

For the Greeks their mythology was a kind of ancient history
with almost Scriptural authority, and generations of poets, epic
and especially tragic, made their audiences familiar with the ancient traditions and gave them relevance to the spiritual problems
of their day. It was natural that humanistically educated Jews
should attempt to supply similar treatment for their own ancient
history, and there have survived, again in Eusebius, slight fragments of two epic poets and more considerable fragments of a
tragic poet, all elaborating Scriptural narrative. It is interesting to
observe that Alexander Polyhistor, from whom Eusebius draws
these selections also, cited them for historical data as any hellenistic scholar might cite early poets. But though a researcher might
draw upon the Jewish poets it is unlikely that they had any considerable non-Jewish audience, if only because their versification
is so inept. It is likelier that they were intended for a Jewish audi-

ence, to satisfy *amour-propre* and perhaps to communicate Bible stories to the unlearned in a more attractive form.

The first of the epic poets [27] is Philo the Elder, who is to be dated at about 200 B.C. His poem *On the Kings of the Jews* seems to have been written on a large scale; the twenty-four verses which have survived deal with the sacrifice of Isaac, with Joseph in Egypt, and with the water supply of Jerusalem. The language is so curled and enigmatic as to be virtually unintelligible; obviously this is in keeping with the hellenistic mode of purposeful obscurity of which Lycophron is the classic pattern. Aside from their form there is nothing notably hellenistic in Philo's lines. The other epic poet, probably contemporary with Philo the Elder, is Theodotus, of whom we have forty-seven verses. These deal with the narrative of Genesis 33–34—Jacob's sojourn in Shechem and the vengeance upon the violators of Dinah exacted by Simeon and Levi. The style is a good imitation of Homer—epithets, lively description, direct speeches, and all in smooth and correct versification. Eusebius names the title *On the Jews*, but because Shechem is so prominent and actually called "the sacred city" (*hieron astu*) the interesting (but unprovable) surmise has been proposed that the title was something like *On Shechem* and the author a Samaritan. Again the only deviation from tradition is in giving it a form acceptable to readers of Greek.

The most fully preserved belletristic work is the tragedy of Ezekielos on the Exodus (*Exagoge*), of which 269 lines are preserved.[28] These include a long soliloquy by Moses recounting his career down to his flight to Midian, a dialogue where Moses recounts a dream in which a royal personage enthrones him and his father-in-law offers an interpretation, a dialogue with God at the burning bush in which God gives detailed instructions concerning the wonders to be worked in Egypt and directions for the celebration of the Passover, a messenger's speech recounting the destruction of the Egyptians and the deliverance of the Hebrews, and an account of the springs of water, the palm trees, and the appearance of a remarkable bird, apparently the phoenix, at

Elim. Except for the phoenix and Moses' dream and its interpretation, which have no authority in Scripture, Ezekielos follows the Biblical narrative scrupulously. Even the additions are not deviations but the normal expansions, original descriptions, dialogue, and the like, with which dramatists regularly ornamented their material; indeed Ezekielos follows the Bible very much more closely than the Greek tragedians follow Homer. The dream sequence was doubtless required by the plot. How this was constructed we cannot say. The action was apparently divided into five episodes by regular choral interludes; unity of scene seems not to have been observed. This suggests that the play was not intended for performance. The practice of writing plays to be read as pamphlets rather than to be acted goes back at least to the fourth century, and Alexandria itself had a "pleiad" of tragedians whose works were apparently never performed.

From the literary point of view Ezekielos is squarely in the hellenistic tradition, and indeed a very creditable representative of that tradition. His language shows close familiarity with Aeschylus, Sophocles, and Euripides, but his closest affinities are, as we should suspect, with Euripides. His versification is sound, his imagery lively, his taste uniformly good. Ezekielos is much more likely than Philo or Theodotus to have had a non-Jewish audience, but the probability is that he intended his play for Jewish readers; it is in fact an effective medium for making the Biblical narrative attractive to readers whose main schooling had been in the Greek classics. Apparently Ezekielos composed a number of such dramatizations; both Eusebius and Clement speak of his tragedies in the plural. His mastery of form suggests that he was working in an established tradition, but we know of no others who dramatized Biblical episodes before or after him. For fixing Ezekielos' date there is no conclusive evidence; he is certainly anterior to Alexander Polyhistor, and probably belongs to the second century B.C. Because of his good style and his use of the Septuagint it has been assumed, probably with justice, that Ezekielos was an Alexandrian. But ignorance of geography surprising in an Alexandrian is shown by Zipporah's identification of her

country as "Libya, held by diverse tribes of dark-skinned Ethiopians"; if the error is not (as it may pardonably be) intentional
poetic license, it may point to an environment other than Egyptian,
and there is no compelling reason to deny the possibility of Palestinian authorship.

An audience like that of Ezekielos would require not only an
aesthetically satisfying presentation of the narratives upon which
Judaism was based but also an intellectually satisfying rationale
to prove its continuing validity. The philosopher of our group is
Aristobulus,[29] who is as loyal to tradition as Ezekielos and as
much at home in the humanistic environment of his age. The title
of Aristobulus' work, which appears to have comprised many
books, was *Exegesis of the Law of Moses,* or some close variant.
The general tendency of his thought is indicated by statements
in Clement (1.72, 5.97) to the effect that Aristobulus showed that
Hebrew wisdom was much older than Greek philosophy and that
the Peripatetic philosophy derived from the Law and the Prophets;
this characterization is echoed by Eusebius (*Praeparatio evangelica*
8.9, 13.11). The extant fragments do indeed proffer the claim of
Jewish priority, but show no particular connection with the
Peripatetic school. For us the most significant feature in Aristobulus
is his apparent anticipation of Philo in the mode of his allegorical
interpretation and in his use of the term *logos.*

The dating of Aristobulus is of some importance. Eusebius
(8.9) identifies him with the "Aristobulus, teacher of Ptolemy" to
whom the epistle prefixed to II Maccabees is addressed. Aristobulus
himself addresses his explanation of the anthropomorphisms in
Scripture to a Ptolemy, and Clement (1.150) and Eusebius (9.6)
identify him as Ptolemy VI Philometor (181–145 B.C.). But since
it is extremely unlikely that Aristobulus could have discussed the
problem with the king, some scholars have assumed that this dating (like the dating of Aristeas to the reign of Ptolemy Philadelphus) is a fictive retrojection, and that Aristobulus himself was
later in date. But it is altogether possible that Aristobulus had an
earlier Philometor in mind in his fictive address, and that Clement

wrongly assumed that this Philometor was Ptolemy VI. The early second-century date has also been questioned on the basis of Aristobulus' affinity with Philo; and some scholars who accept the early dating for Aristobulus explain the Philonic elements as later interpolations. The objection is valid only if we assume absolute originality for Philo, and there are not sufficient grounds for doing so.[30]

The most interesting as well as the most extensive of Aristobulus' fragments is that dealing with allegorical interpretation of Scripture (Eusebius 8.10). This purports to be an answer to Ptolemy's question as to "Why, by our Law, there are intimations given of hands, and arms, and face, and feet, and walking, in the case of the divine power (*dynamis*)." Interpreted in the "natural" sense (*physikos*, that is, not mythically) these anthropomorphic expressions all have mystical and poetic meaning. "Hand" evidently means "power," and the like. There is a long and quite eloquent exegesis of Exodus on God's descent at Sinai and the blazing of the mountain (19.18 ff.):

The descent was not local, for God is everywhere. . . . Though the places were all ablaze the fire did not actually consume . . . and the voices of trumpets were loudly heard together with the lightning-like flashing of the fire, though there were no such instruments present nor any that sounded them, but all things were done by divine arrangement. So that it is plain that the divine descent took place for these reasons, that the spectators might have a manifest comprehension of the several circumstances, that neither the fire which, as I said before, burnt nothing, nor the voices of the trumpets were produced by human action or a supply of instruments, but that God without any aid was exhibiting his own all-pervading majesty.

This is not full-blown allegorical interpretation such as Philo was later to use, or, for that matter, such as Stoic philosophers were applying to Homer in Aristobulus' own day, but it points in that direction. Intellectually and artistically Aristobulus' interpretation is a respectable effort to justify loyalty to Judaism on the part of his humanistically educated co-religionists.

Aristobulus' second fragment (Eusebius 13.12) employs the

same mode of interpretation and also claims (on the basis of previous discussion, which is not extant) that Pythagoras, Socrates, and Plato derived their doctrine of God from translations of sections of the Bible which had been made long before the Alexandrian translation of the whole. When these authors speak of the voice of God they mean his creative power. Reverent conceptions of deity are demanded by all philosophers and especially by "our faction," which the context shows means "Jews" rather than "Peripatetics." Citations from Aratus and Orpheus (the latter spurious) show that their teachings coincide with those of the Law properly interpreted.

A third fragment (also Eusebius 13.12) on the Sabbath adumbrates Philo's doctrine of the *logos*. In a manner of speaking the Sabbath is the birthday of light and also of wisdom, for wisdom produces light. The Peripatetic philosophers called wisdom a light, and Solomon taught (Proverbs 8.22) that wisdom existed before creation. God's resting on the Sabbath signifies not that he has ceased to do but that he has thus established a perpetual order. There are comments on other significances of the hebdomad, as for example that it symbolizes the *logos*. These interpretations are supported by citations, real and spurious, from Homer, Hesiod, and Linus. When, for example, "Homer" says, "On the seventh day we left the stream of Acheron," he means that through the *logos* as seventh man frees himself from forgetfulness and from wickedness of soul and attains a perception of truth.

Aside from these avowedly Jewish works there are a number of passages of manifestly Jewish authorship interpolated in the works of well-known pagan authors. The motives for such pseudepigrapha are more interesting than the content. The most extensive are a number of long passages in the *Sibylline Oracles*,[31] and 230 wretched hexameters ascribed to the sixth-century gnomic poet Phocylides. The motive for the Jewish (as for the Christian) forgeries of Sibylline Oracles is that of the apocalyptic writings, which were always anonymous. The Pseudo-Phocylides passage is harder to understand. It presents such Pentateuchal legislation as that concerning hen and chicks, for which supposititious pagan authority would hardly seem called for. Apparently the intention was to show that a respected pagan poet did not think such peculiar laws quaint.

Chapter IX

EXOTICS IN THE MAIN STREAM

THE best evidence for the efficacy of the Greek educational system in hellenized areas is the large number of writers and philosophers who are identified as "of Apamea," "of Babylon," "of Gadara," "of Samosata," or other non-Greek localities. Here we are not speaking of non-Greeks who used the language for local history or propaganda [1] but of men to whom presumably and in some cases certainly Greek was a language newly learned and whose work entered the main stream of Greek thought and letters. In almost every case, it is true, they received their higher education and pursued their careers in some genuinely Greek center, but each had received his preparatory training in his native place. In those that we shall choose to mention in the paragraphs which follow some element novel to the Greek tradition may be discerned. It may be that in every case these novelties are only natural developments out of what went before in Greece, so that no external influence need be invoked—as it need not in the case of Plato's dualism. And yet, as in the cases chosen for illustration, the novelty of doctrine or form does seem related to the origin of its promulgators. In any case these figures do show that hellenized places could prepare their students for a career in letters or philosophy, and in any case their contributions do illustrate a change of attitude in the hellenistic age.

The number of persons of non-Greek origin whose names have been recorded is very large.[2] Sometimes, as with Stoicism, a whole

philosophic trend seems to be promoted by men from a certain area, sometimes a remote area is the seat of a more or less
influential school, as Antioch was for rhetoric or even Susa for
philosophy, sometimes a single otherwise undistinguished city, like
Gadara, will produce a succession of men who introduce significant innovations, and sometimes a single towering figure, like
Posidonius of Apamea, will alter current concepts of the meaning
of history. For the process as a whole the actual dates are unim-
portant. Any list of the dozen Greek classics which have markedly
influenced subsequent European literature must include the name
of Lucian of Samosata; and though Lucian belongs to the second
century A.D. he spoke the Syrian language as a boy and had to
learn Greek.

It may well be, as many thoughtful students have maintained,
that Stoicism is the most important single creation of the hellenistic
age.[3] Whether or not its founder Zeno was a Semite cannot be
positively determined. He came from Citium, on Cyprus, which
was a meeting place of Greek and Phoenician, and his father's name
was Mnaseas, which may be either Greek or cognate with the
Biblical Manasseh. In any case, his contemporaries thought of
him as a Phoenician, and attributed such traits as his niggardli-
ness to his "barbarism" (Diogenes Laertius 7.16). His education, from the age of twenty-two when he came to Athens, was
Greek. He attended the lectures of Polemon, head of the Academy,
but was most deeply influenced by the Cynic Crates. But Zeno's
teachings are not related to the classical succession in the same
way that other hellenistic doctrines are. The Academy and the
Peripatetics carried on the tradition of their founders, and the
Epicureans, who were the Stoics' principal rivals, derived in a
straight line from Democritus and Leucippus and the sophists.
Stoicism is a new thing. Its salient characteristic is a passion for
righteousness, and it has more than a touch of mysticism. If a
novelty implies an impulse from without it is natural to think
that Zeno's early background may have included traditions cog-

nate with or deriving from the passion for righteousness which motivated the prophets of the Old Testament.

Whether or not the founder was a Semite, it is remarkable that so large a number of his successors did derive from the east. Chrysippus, the "second founder" of the school, was probably from Tarsus, and Chrysippus' successors were Zeno of Tarsus and Diogenes of Babylon. Diogenes' reputation drew many students from Asia. Diogenes' successors in turn were Antipater of Tarsus, Archedemus of Tarsus, and Boethus of Sidon. The remains of these teachers are too fragmentary or indirect to permit of any meaningful judgment on their form, but an occasional oddness of phraseology does catch the eye. This, for example, is how the Stoics described the relationship between the parts of philosophy (Diogenes Laertius 7.40):

They likened philosophy to an animal: logic corresponds to the bones and sinews, ethics to the fleshy parts, physics to the soul. Or to an egg: logic is the shell, the part beneath it ethics, and the innermost part physics. Or to a fertile field: logic is the hedge enclosing it, ethics the crop, physics the soil or the trees. Or to a city well fortified and governed by reason.

The similes and the cumulation of alternatives connected by "or" with the simplest and ethically most valid at the end is wholly characteristic of the style of the *midrash*. Stylistic modes are often more impressive than similarities in doctrine. Of these there are many, and in their case the direction is surely from the Stoics to the rabbis. In explaining apparent violations of theoretical equality, for example, Chrysippus said that some seats in the theater must inevitably be better than others, and the rabbis that one day in the week must inevitably be more honored than others.

For range, for originality, and for influence the ancient thinker who ranks next to Aristotle is Posidonius of Apamea, on the Orontes (135–50 B.C.).[4] Not only did all serious historians and philosophers who came after him use his histories, and more important, his philosophy of history, but his teachings were borrowed by Lucretius and Vergil, Seneca and Pliny. Again, Posidonius studied in Athens and made his permanent home in Rhodes, so that Syrian Apamea was responsible only for his preparatory education. But the elements in his teaching which were both new and seminal do make him seem the channel of eastern ideas which demonstrably shaped western development. For the sake of objectivity as well as brevity I transcribe the description of Posidonius' philosophy of history from Piero Treves' entry in the *Oxford Classical Dictionary:*

According to Posidonius the end and destiny of the human race is exactly reflected in the vicissitudes of history. Political virtue, therefore, consists in turning humanity back to its state of prehistoric innocence, in which philosophers were the lawgivers and instructors of their fellow men and acted as intermediaries between the world of matter, in which men are compelled to live, and the world of God, from which alone law-abiding morality can spring. Thus politics and ethics are one, and any form of moral or political activity becomes a religious duty, by fulfilling which man frees himself and acquires knowledge of the gifts of the spirit, which enable him to enjoy a superior form of existence after death. Since the God of Posidonius is the creator neither of matter nor of soul, the latter cannot be considered immortal in itself. But since it is composed of the same substance as the heavenly bodies, it escapes from the human prison and returns to the sublime abode whence it originally came.

This might well serve as an account of the theory of history premised in the Bible. We sense in Posidonius not merely detached scholarship but something like missionary zeal. His theories were not the by-products of his historical studies, but rather his historical studies, like his work in other disciplines, notably astronomy, were calculated to prove and propagate his theory. The basis of his thought is religious.[5] Chrysippus had begun his treatise on law with the statement "Law is king of all, of things both divine and human," and Posidonius declared that there is no other source and origin of law than the will of Zeus and Nature, or, in Stoic language, God. He criticized current beliefs freely, both the Olympian and the popular varieties. There is a strong likelihood that Posidonius was the principal source not only for the philosophical elements in the Jewish-Greek writers, notably Philo, but also for Wisdom of Solomon and IV Maccabees.[6] Because Posidonius made the will of God the sole authority it was easy for Thomas Aquinas to take his doctrine over literally, of course giving "will of God" a different meaning.[7] Posidonius' doctrine permeated Europe because it was the basis upon which Augustus' principate was founded and so the basis for the central stream of political theory which Rome transmitted to Europe.

But it is not a doctrine which would normally have grown out of antecedent Greek speculation, which, for one thing, was centered on the conditions of the city-state. Posidonius' chief debt was to the Stoic tradition which, indeed, he endeavored to restore to its pristine purity, but it is likely that he himself had some knowledge of Jewish thought. Even as a deracinated Syrian he must have been interested in events in Judaea whose newly won independence was a subject of current discussion, and we know that he was familiar with the name and work of Moses: he thought that Moses had led his followers to the conquest of Jerusalem because he was displeased with Egyptians and Greeks for representing gods in the shape of animals or humans.[8] To be sure this smattering of knowledge and the trend of his teaching do not necessarily imply that Posidonius derived his theory from the Biblical narrative, but given his origin and interests and the numbers and influence of the Jewish community in the eastern Mediterranean in his day it is altogether possible that he was indeed influenced, as we shall see that Vergil probably was,[9] by Biblical materials. In any case, whatever the explanation of the coincidences may be, they are evidence of a fusion of ideas in an extremely important area.

We turn from philosophy to belles-lettres, where a series of writers from the single town of Gadara will provide sufficient illustration. Gadara was a city of the decapolis, a little east of the Jordan, near the southern shore of Lake Tiberias.[10] It is commonly identified with Ramoth Gilead of the Bible; its modern name is Umm Keis. The site has impressive hellenistic and Roman remains—two theaters, temple, basilica, colonnades. Clearly it was not a Greek enclave, but a native city in which the Greek way of life had become normal—as its history shows. Gadara was important enough to be a fortified city when Antiochus the Great took it in 218 B.C. About 100 B.C. the Jewish king Alexander Jannaeus took it after a ten-month siege. It was "freed" by Pompey in 63, and counted its era from that date, as the numerous coins show. In 30 B.C. Octavian gave the city to Herod the Great. The Gadarenes complained of Herod's rule before Agrippa at Mitylene in 22 B.C. and before Augustus himself in Syria in 20 B.C. After the death of Herod (4 B.C.) Gadara was an independent city under Rome.

Strabo, writing in the first decade of the common era, names the famous Gadarenes (16.2.29) as "Philodemus the Epicurean, and Meleager, and Menippus the serious comic (*spoudogeloios*), and the contemporary orator Theodore." The earliest of these is Menippus, who lived in the first half of the third century B.C.[11] Of his work nothing has survived, but the original and incisive character of his satire is attested by authors down to Marcus Aurelius, who spoke of him (6.47) as "a mocker of man's perishable and transitory life," and his name was permanently attached to the form he was presumed to have invented. On the basis of ancient opinions we may deduce that Menippus' characteristics were keen humor, freedom from tradition in form and matter, scornful mockery of the follies of humankind, especially when those follies were sanctioned by traditions of religion or philosophy, and above all an impulse to preach. It has been suggested that his homilies, classed as Cynic diatribes,[12] influenced a number of Christian preachers; we can be sure that they influenced the Roman Varro, for he named his satires "Menippean."[13]

Varro's Menippean Satires, again, are lost, but we know that they exerted great influence on later Roman writers. It is presumed, for example, that Horace's second book of Satires was inspired by Varro.[14] The subject of Horace 2.3, which is twice as long as his next longest satire, is "that every silly man is mad"; Varro's most popular Menippean satire, as shown by the frequency of the fragments, was his *Eumenides*, of which the subject was "that every silly man is mad." Other influences have been detected in Horace, in Seneca, in Juvenal, and in Petronius. Our fullest notion of the contents of Menippus' work is provided by his fellow Syrian Lucian, of whom it has been cogently argued that many of his pieces are virtually lifted from Menippus.[15]

Menippean satire denoted serious criticism with a light touch —*ridendo dicere verum*—but its most salient characteristic was its intermingling of prose and verse. Not only, then, are Seneca's *Apocolocyntosis* or "Satire on the Deification of Claudius" and Petronius' *Satyrica* Menippean satires, but so is Boethius' *Consolation of Philosophy* also. Now the intermingling of prose and poetry in a literary form is unexampled in antecedent classical literature, but it is a well-established Semitic form. Its Arabic name is *maqama*, or "session"; it is a harangue in artistic prose, interspersed at appropriate points with bits of verse in strict meter. The outstanding Arabian exponent of the form was Ibn Hariri,[16] but there are many other examples and traces even in the *Arabian Nights*. The example of a Menippean satire most familiar to European readers is *Aucassin and Nicolette*, which is amusing, critical of tradition, and interspersed with verse; *Aucassin and Nicolette* was written in the Provence when Arab influence was a considerable factor. We cannot, of course, trace the literary form of the *maqamat* back of the classical period of Arabic literature, but Ibn Hariri was obviously following an old tradition. If it was as old as Menippus we should have an example of a hellenized easterner contributing a native property to the general literary tradition.

Meleager,[17] the second of our Gadarenes (c. 140–70 B.C.), also wrote Menippean satires, which are unfortunately lost, but he is best known as the first compiler of a critical anthology. His *Garland*, enlarged by later hands, is the basis of the *Palatine Anthology*. Meleager's own poems, of which some one hundred thirty are included in the *Anthology*, pioneer a new mood in Greek poetry. Meleager's father was a Syrian Greek, his mother in all likelihood a native. He refers to himself as a Syrian (7.417.5–6) —"If I am a Syrian, what wonder? Stranger, we dwell in one country, the world; one Chaos gave birth to all mortals"—and exhibits his knowledge of eastern languages (7.419.7–8)—"If you are a Syrian, *Salam!* If you are a Phoenician, *Naidius!* If you are a Greek, *Chaire!* And say the same yourself." Gilbert Murray sensed that Meleager's Greek betrays the foreign late learner: "One suspects that, at home in Gadara, Greek was only his second language, and that he had talked Aramaic out of school." [18]

What is new in Meleager is sensuousness, passion, mysticism, capacity for heights and depths of feeling, a delight in flowers and smells. His most perceptive critic writes of him as follows: [19]

We possess about a hundred amatory epigrams by this poet . . . unequalled in the width of range, the profusion of imagination, the subtlety of emotion with which they sound the whole lyre of passion. . . . Greek becomes in his hands almost a new language, full of dreams, at once more languid and more passionate. . . . In Meleager the touch of Asiatic blood creates a new type, delicate, exotic, fantastic. . . . The atmosphere is loaded with a steam of perfumes. With still unimpaired ease and perfection of hand there has come in a strain of that mysticism which represents a relapse or reaction from the Greek spirit. Some of Meleager's epigrams are direct and simple, even to coarseness; but in all the best and most characteristic there is this difference from purely Greek work, that love has become a religion; the spirit of the east has touched them. . . . Love appears in a hundred shapes amidst a shower of fantastic titles and attributes. . . . The air all round him is heavy with the scent of flowers and ointments. . . . For a moment Meleager can be piercingly simple; and then the fantastic mood comes over him again, and emotion dissolves in a mist of metaphors. But even when he is most fantastic the beauty of his rhythms and grace of his language never fail.

Perhaps one point may be added. It may be that Meleager's exquisite and ecstatic perception of love, the concept of love which is truly romantic, comes only as the reaction of a Greek attitude of enjoyment upon the oriental reverence for chastity.

It is not too much to say that in respect to sexual emotion Meleager marks the principal turning point in the history of poetry from Homer to modern times. The direction he pioneered was followed. The Romans, particularly Ovid and Propertius, learned from him, and as F. A. Wright has written,[20] "from him more than from any other the singers of the early renaissance in France and

Italy derive." Here, then, is another considerable contribution from the east.

Of Philodemus, our third Gadarene, much more is known than of his older fellow townsmen.[21] He was the domestic philosopher and dependent of L. Calpurnius Piso, the consul of 58 B.C. and subsequently the father-in-law of Julius Caesar. His library, comprised mainly of his own philosophical treatises, was recovered from the ruins of Herculaneum. In his invective against Piso, delivered in 55, Cicero has some caustic things to say of Philodemus as a demoralizing influence upon his pupils, but he is very appreciative of Philodemus' learning and breeding in his philosophical writings. Indeed it is assumed that Philodemus was Cicero's source for the presentation of Epicurean doctrine in *De natura deorum* and *De finibus*. Similarly, there is a strong possibility that the *Ars Poetica* of Horace was largely based on a work of Philodemus.[22]

But Philodemus has, and probably had, a greater vogue as a poet than as a philosopher. There are some twenty-five of his epigrams in the *Anthology*, which show a passion and sometimes a coarseness hard to reconcile with even an Epicurean philosopher. There are definite echoes of his extant poems in Catullus and Horace, Ovid and Martial.[23] More impressive still, a fragment of Philodemus' treatise *On Flattery* shows the names of Quintilius and Varius certainly and Vergil and Horace probably, all in the vocative case. Competent scholars have taken this fragment to indicate that Philodemus was actually the teacher of the great Augustans. In a very real sense, therefore, Philodemus would be what Professor Körte has called him, "the bridge from the hellenistic world to the Roman." [24] It was Rome, of course, which absorbed hellenistic culture for transmission to Europe, and it is of interest to note that a hellenized easterner was an important agent in the process.

The Gadarene group may have been exceptional but it was not unique. If they and other hellenized easterners contributed new ingredients to the fusion which became European culture, their ingredients had already been touched by the earlier current whose direction was west to east. This might be expected in such areas as satire and romantic love, but it is no less true in the area of religion, where the eastern contribution is generally thought to have maintained a character untouched by and even hostile to western influences. One of the ways in which a literary form affected the course of history is implicit in the new concept of history which religion promoted; we shall next look at the character of historiography in the hellenistic age to see how this might be so.

Chapter X

HISTORIOGRAPHY

THE revolutionary distinction of classical Greek historiography is that it is anthropocentric. In the ancient Near East, as we shall presently notice, annals of the past were preserved and interpreted in the interest of religion; Greek history is rational and humanist. Herodotus merely declares that his purpose is to preserve the great deeds of the past from oblivion, and Thucydides uses history as a laboratory specimen to study political behavior; their real concern is with the present and the future. In the hellenistic age history assumes new functions, of which the principal is that of reassuring the individual concerning his place in the larger scheme of things. "Not to know what happened before you were born," says Cicero (*Orator* 20), "is to be forever a child, for what is the span of the life of man unless it is tied to that of his ancestors by the memory of earlier events?" Each of the Roman historians, and in particular Livy, who is their best spokesman, makes the chief use of history moral edification. The tendency appears early in the hellenistic age. When men feel that they have fallen from a high estate which they once enjoyed and begin to look back wistfully on a more glorious past and when they come to regard the achievements of the past as classical paradigms, knowledge of the past acquires a special value and entitles its possessor to a privileged status as scribe and eventually as saint.[1] History now supplies not only knowledge but wisdom, as we can see from a passage in Plutarch (*On Tranquillity* 14):

The foolish overlook and neglect the good things that are there because their imagination is always straining towards the future. . . . The logic of the schoolmen who deny the principle of growth on the ground that being is in constant flux would continually transform each of us into a different man; so those who do not retain and cherish the past in memory but allow it to flow away, actually make themselves empty and impoverished day by day and dependent upon the morrow, as though all that had occurred yesterday and the day before had not happened at all and had no relevance to them.[2]

With the new view of the function of historiography new practices are introduced. In general these are analogous to the innovations to be noticed in other literary and artistic expressions of the contemporary mood. As in art or philosophy we find that the enlarged geographical horizons create interest in the total history of large complexes of people and eventually in universal history, and we find too the obverse of the coin in the enhancement of the individual, whether in preoccupation with local history or in greater attention paid to personages in general history. There is the same freedom given to fancy as we find in plastic art, and an even greater striving for sensationalism at the expense of literal fact. Perhaps most significant of all, the remote past is idealized and history becomes an instrument of propaganda, whether for an individual or a policy, or for the manifest destiny of a nation, or for inculcating some specific philosophical or theological ideal.

For all these tendencies there were of course germs in what had gone before. Men have always had a special interest in their particular locality and local records had always been kept. Remote places had always engaged at least a romantic interest and Herodotus did indeed deal with them, though his book, like his predecessor Hecataeus', is rather travel book than history. Thucydides' history is indeed philosophical, yet he reveals his own convictions, as any thoughtful writer must; to that degree his work is propagandist, though his propaganda has no such limited and specific objectives as we shall find in later writers, and he is skillful enough to appear totally objective. Xenophon had made individual character responsible for great actions in the *Anabasis* and especially in the *Cyropedia*, which certainly takes liberties with facts for the sake of promulgating an ideal. The most outspoken propaganda of all is the treatise called *On the Constitution of the Athenians*, of about 424 B.C., included in the works of Xenophon but ascribed to a figure we call the "Old Oligarch." But in the hellenistic age these various tendencies became the central preoccupation of historians, and the new approach affected not only historiography but also history. The past came to be considered a guide to the future more literally than it had ever been before,[3] and hence a particular view of the past had a greater role in shaping aspirations for the future.

The new approach was initiated by Isocrates, who himself, indeed, wrote no history, but rather orations or more properly essays, but who propagated his views through the fourth-century historians, virtually all of whom were his pupils. In the first place Isocrates made of history an art, not a science as Aristotle would have had it. This implied not only a high concern for rhetorical style but also heightening the reader's interest by all the devices appropriate to melodrama and arousing his pity and fear.[4] How this sensationalism affected hellenistic historiography we shall see in the sequel. But Isocrates also wished to make history edifying, and to this end he took a new attitude towards tradition. In his own writings we can see a new tendency to idealize the past and make of it an armory of examples for guiding political attitudes and actions in the present.[5] Political leaders had always exploited ancient myths and oracles to justify and promote policy,[6] but their materials had or were given the halo of religion; examples of actual history would not serve. Isocrates raised history itself into a kind of hagiographa. It was Isocrates, furthermore, who promoted the universal rather than the parochial view. Thucydides had limited his scope to Athens and Sparta, and Herodotus and Xenophon brought barbarians in only because they impinged on Athens and Sparta; the fourth-century historians, who were pupils of Isocrates, took a wider view. And finally it was Isocrates who promoted the practice of glorifying individual figures as catalysts of history. This is not merely another aspect of his idealization of the past, but a concept of how history is made. His *Address to Philip* and his *Evagoras* illustrate the point.

The outstanding historians of the fourth century were Theopompus and Ephorus, both pupils of Isocrates.[7] Theopompus wrote a *general* history of Greece, called the *Philippica*, in fifty-eight books, from 362 (where Xenophon's *Hellenica* ends) to the death of Philip in 336 B.C. We know little of his work except that he realized that the history of all Greece was now, if never before, a single piece. Ephorus' distinction was that he was the first to write universal history. He began with the return of the Heracleidae, which he considered the earliest verifiable fact in history, and went down to 341 B.C. There are extensive excerpts of Ephorus in Diodorus Siculus, particularly of passages dealing with barbarian countries. Assyrian and Persian history was treated in the fourteen books of Ctesias, who was physician to Artaxerxes; we have the epitome of Photius, made from an epitome of the age of Nero. Towards the end of the fourth century Pytheas of Marseilles sailed out from the Pillars of Hercules and to the British Isles, and brought back reports which can only be excavated from Strabo, who disbelieved them. Antiphanes of Berge wrote an apparently fantastic account of the same regions, perhaps in parody of Pytheas; his name became the ancient equivalent for Baron Munchausen. The man probably responsible, but only through others who used him, for our knowledge of hellenistic history after Alexander is Hieronymus of Cardia, whom Tarn called [8] "probably one of the greatest historians Greece produced"; but his work is lost.

After Alexander the writing of history was quickened, with Alexander himself, significantly, the favorite subject. A number of men in his inner circle published works based on official records and their own memories: Ptolemy, who became king of Egypt; Nearchus the admiral, and another naval officer named Androsthenes; Callisthenes, the nephew of Aristotle, who wrote a fulsome history of Alexander as well as ten books of *Hellenica* on the period 387–357 B.C. but whom Alexander subsequently put to death for plain speaking; and Aristobulus of Cassandrea. Arrian (second century A.D.) says in the preface to his seven-book *Anabasis of Alexander* that Aristobulus' account, as well as Ptolemy's, is "strictly authentic"; but Lucian (*How to Write History* 12) says that Alexander himself was so disgusted with Aristobulus' gross flattery that he threw a book of his overboard and said that its author should be thrown after it. Others in the outer circle, like Onesicritus, Chares, and Ephippus, wrote books filled with trivialities or inventions. On the basis of these earlier works Clitarchus of Alexandria subsequently produced a rhetorical history which was widely used and became the authorized version of the career of Alexander. Much later a writer using the name of Callisthenes produced an early version of the *Alexander Romance* which was then enlarged with spurious correspondence [9] and became one of the world's most widely read books.[10]

As in the case of hellenistic philosophy and art, expansion to the universal had as its obverse contraction to the particular. In historiography the particular took the form of local histories; we are best informed about those of Athens, called *Atthides*.[11] The best-known writer of an *Atthis* is Philochorus, who was put to death by Antigonus Gonatas about 261 B.C.; a considerable continuous passage is preserved in Dionysius of Halicarnassus, and new fragments have been discovered in the present century. Probably derived from *Atthides* is the invaluable *Marmor Parium*, a chronicle of Athens inscribed on stone at Paros in 263 B.C. and discovered in Smyrna. The Parian Marble supplies scattered data from the time of Cecrops down to the date of its engraving, and is particularly interested in religious festivals; hence it is our principal source of information for tragic contests, sometimes supplying the names of competitors and winners as well as dates. When the present has no room for glory men find solace in the glories of the past.

The glorification of important personages was part of the Isocratean tradition, but the study of character for its own sake and the writing of biography was a special contribution of the Peripatetic School; it is the Peripatetic tradition which the hellenistic biographers, culminating in Plutarch, follow.[12] Theophrastus, Aristotle's successor as head of the school, wrote a book of *Characters*, describing such common types as the Flatterer, the Newsmonger, and the like. The delineation of the individual, especially under strong emotional stress, is as characteristic of hellenistic literature as it is of art. Historiography was not immune, and indeed it is its emotionalism which is the quality (or defect) that particularly characterizes the hellenistic historians.[13] Not only were they rhetorical and sensational but they deliberately aimed to work on the emotions of their readers.

The outstanding historian of the "pathetic" school was Duris (340–260 B.C.), pupil of Theophrastus and tyrant of Samos. Another writer of the same class, better known because more freely used by Plutarch, is Phylarchus. An impatient criticism of him by Polybius (2.56.7) will show us Phylarchus' approach as well as Polybius' own:

In his eagerness to arouse the pity and attention of his readers he treats us to a picture of clinging women with their hair disheveled and their breasts bare, or again of crowds of both sexes together with their children and aged parents weeping and lamenting as they are led away into slavery. This sort of thing keeps up throughout his history, always trying to bring horrors vividly before our eyes. Leaving aside the ignoble and womanish character of such a treatment of his subject, let us consider how far it is proper or serviceable to history. A historical author should not try to thrill his readers by such exaggerated pictures, nor should he, like a tragic poet, try to imagine the probable utterances of his characters or reckon up all the consequences probably incidental to the occurrences with which he deals, but simply record what really happened and what really was said, however commonplace. . . . Apart from this, Phylarchus simply narrates most of such catastrophes and does not even suggest their causes or the nature of these causes, without which it is impossible in any case to feel either legitimate pity or proper anger.[14]

But there is something to be said for Phylarchus. The *Lives of Agis and Cleomenes*, mainly based on Phylarchus, are surely the most gripping in Plutarch. Moreover, they are propaganda for a program, and very effective propaganda.

Effectiveness as edifying propaganda is indeed the object of such history, and was the basis of the rules for narrative composition followed by the self-conscious litterateurs of the hellenistic age.

In the formulation of Asclepiades of Myrlea,[15] echoed in other theorists,[16] narrative prose falls into three categories: true history (*alethes historia*), false history (*pseudes historia*), and history as it may likely have happened (*plasma* or *hos genomena*). The first category includes unadorned chronicles; the second such fantasies as Lucian's *True History*, of which the author himself says that it contains no truth; and the third must be based on truth but admits of elaborations provided they have verisimilitude and are edifying. By our standard such an approach blurs any line of demarcation between history and fiction, and it appears indeed that the earliest romances did contain a nucleus of history which was elaborated for an edifying effect. Eventually the historical element was reduced to a mere background for the love story which preempted the foreground, but the extant romances preserve the form of history.[17]

The merging of categories which are distinct in his own mind creates difficulties for the modern reader, especially in works involving religion. Either he accepts as literal truth things the author never intended he should, or in his impatience with manifest untruths he rejects the truth which the author meant him to accept. *Aristeas* is a case in point.[18] In the preface to that book Humphrey Hody, the great seventeenth-century English editor, says that he is aware that better manuscripts are available on the continent but that he would not trouble his friends to report these readings because the book was manifestly false: it represented Demetrius of Phalerum as being on good terms with the second Ptolemy whereas history showed that he was on good terms only with the first Ptolemy. By hellenistic standards the author of *Aristeas* was a conscientious workman, trying to make his kernel of truth as edifying as possible, and one of the recognized ways of making a story effective was to associate it with some great name. A nineteenth-century student of III Maccabees was disturbed because, as he had taken pains to learn from a colleague in zoology, the seventy elephants which Ptolemy IV had at Raphia could not in a single generation multiply to the five hundred he is represented as having in that book. All the author intended, of course, was an impression of a huge number of elephants; he never expected his readers to count them. All of III Maccabees may be a fiction, but the author believed its essentials; the fact that Josephus (*Against Apion* 2.5) has an independent version shows that it was accepted as history.

Other Apocryphal books as well can be more fairly appreciated in the light of hellenistic historiography. This is notably true of Judith, which we shall consider in the chapter on love stories,[19] and of II Maccabees, which we shall glance at in the present chapter. The finest flowering of all is surely Livy's history of Rome, where all the hellenistic canons are applied, but with good sense and high art.[20] Livy's merits shine the brighter when his early books are compared with the parallel account in Dionysius of Halicarnassus. Dionysius wrote his twenty books of *Roman Antiquities* in the interest of interracial comity, to show that Romans were much like Greeks. In obvious imitation Josephus later wrote twenty books of *Jewish Antiquities*, to show that Jews were much like Greeks.

Josephus was addressing a Greek-reading audience and he (or his "ghosts") observed all the canons of hellenistic historiography: [21] he is rhetorical, he is pathetic, he glorifies the past and its great figures, and he woos his readers. This is easy to see in the *Antiquities*, where we can read his own sources and perceive how he dealt with them. All his deviations from Scripture, by way of expansion or omission or redistribution of emphasis, are obviously in the interest of attracting readers nurtured in hellenistic history.[22] But there is a possibility that the two skeins represented in the *Antiquities* had interacted upon one another before Josephus' time, and in order to assess this possibility we must glance at antecedent historical writing in languages other than Greek.[23]

Until the rise of Greece, R. G. Collingwood has said,[24] the whole of the Near East was dominated by two forms of quasi-history, theocratic history and myth. Justifiable as such a statement may be from a rationalist Greek point of view, it is far too sweeping, for all the peoples of the ancient Near East preserved memories of their past, and among the Israelites, at least, these records were made the basis of what can fairly be called history by any definition of the word. At the farthest remove from what we should call history were the Egyptians, of whom Ludlow Bull says: [25]

In the writer's view it seems fair to say that the ancient Egyptians cannot have had an "idea of history" in any sense resembling what the phrase means to thinkers of the present age or perhaps of the last 2400 years. They do not seem to have developed a philosophy of history so far as can be observed in the surviving fragments of their literature. They do not seem to have thought in terms of cause and effect or of trends that were observable in their own story or in those of neighboring peoples in the ancient world. There was a definitely static quality about the Egyptians' view of life and of their past.

This is far less true of ancient Mesopotamia,[26] though we have no "books" which can be read as history. The only writings which have sufficient size and scope and finish to make them useful for our purpose are the Assyrian royal inscriptions [27] and the documents embedded in the text of the Old Testament. The Babylonian building inscriptions, upon which the Assyrian were based, followed a stereotyped form: [28] dedication to the god, titles of the king, the nature and circumstances of the dedication, curses upon any who injure the dedication and prayers for any who restore it. Gradually the titles of the king and the circumstances of the dedication were elaborated to include a good deal of history. By the Sargonid period (eighth century B.C.) the dedication was suppressed and room was made for a complete history of a reign, recounted by years or campaigns but with conscious literary art. It is clear that very careful records of the past were kept and that they were presented in high style; but the history is of the prowess of a dynasty, not of a people. Like other ancient historical records it is essentially hieratic in character, not a book one might read and assimilate. Dr. Campbell Thompson speaks for all readers when he says, "The vainglorious story of conquest which every Assyrian monarch bequeaths of himself to posterity is a bloody record of cruelty and terror, and the disgusted reader loses sight of whatever literary excellence there may be in it in his loathing for the complacent story of slaughter." [29]

The Israelites too kept careful record of their kings, but the documents we call J and E are a great deal more than royal chronicles: they are true history, mature, artistic, and complete, and they deal with a people, not a dynasty.[30] It is clear that these documents circulated as separate books as late as 400 B.C., for it can be shown that J and E survived after they were amalgamated into JE, and JE after it was worked over by D, and JED after P was mortised into it. It was only after they were made into a Bible that the components lost their individual existence. Separately, before they were welded into a whole with other documents, they were doubtless the chief factor in giving the Hebrews a sense of individuality and unity. The merits of J and E have been unstintingly and deservedly praised. Eduard Meyer, who was the greatest ancient historian of our century and completely objective with reference to the Bible, wrote: "No other oriental nation was able to create such an historical literature. Even the Greeks succeeded in producing one only at a much later stage of their development, in the fifth century." [31] What distinguishes their history is that they made it their people's charter. Their theme is the relations of God to mankind as exemplified in the career of his elect; the career is of moment because it epitomizes that relationship. The past constitutes the people's distinction and is the constitution which must control the people's future. Not the country or its politics are the main concern, but the people; it is significant that neither document speaks of the division of the kingdom. What gives the history its power is the unquestioned conviction that has gone into it; it can no more be doubted than the gathering of water on the face of the earth or the firmament above it.

Even when it is interlarded with later documents and canted to less grandiose ends the history of J and E retains this power. The power is dissipated when, as in books of Chronicles,[32] the history is obviously manipulated and unconscionably exaggerated by a lesser hand in the interests of particular propaganda. The past is exploited rather than revered. Levites and temple musicians are glorified in the interest of a class, a mechanical kind of divine retribution is emphasized in the interests of discipline, and David is made a wooden saint in the interest of a dynasty. Where, for example, I Samuel 24.1 has, "And again the anger of the Lord was kindled against Israel, and he moved David against them to say, Go, number Israel and Judah," I Chronicles 21.1 has, "And Satan stood up against Israel, and provoked David to number Israel." Under the heading of "The First Apology of Judaism," Professor Pfeiffer writes:

It is an error to consider the Chronicler as a writer of history. It is futile to inquire seriously into the reality of any story or incident not taken bodily from Samuel or Kings. His own contributions should be classed, with the Books of Jonah, Esther, Tobit, Judith, and the like, as historical fiction. . . . Anachronisms may be detected on every page of his book; imaginary characters appear on the scene and historical ones are unrecognizable in their new roles, miracles abound, and, were it not for the devout, earnest purpose of the author and for his ecclesiastical pedantry, the fantasy and picturesque detail of his tales would make him an eligible contributor to the Arabian Nights.[33]

This description would fit Demetrius and Artapanus, who are only a century removed from Chronicles, it would fit the Greek romances, which followed the canons of hellenistic historiography, and in a peculiar sense the history of Livy, though Livy was a much more sophisticated man and a much subtler artist. Though the date of Chronicles may be put as low as 200 B.C.[34] it is not here suggested that their author learned his techniques from the Greeks, though it is not impossible that he did. What might be said is that both Chronicles and hellenistic historiography are symptoms of a new nationalist climate. If there was influence it probably moved in the other direction, when Livy and his congeners provided a religious sanction for Romans in the history of Rome.

Later books included in the Septuagint and classified as history all exhibit the effects of hellenistic historiography in greater or

less degree. The most independent, and the best as history and
literature, is I Maccabees,[35] which describes events from the uprising at Modin in 167 B.C. to the murder of Simon the Maccabee
in 134. The book was written shortly after that date and rests on
autopsy or official sources. Its data are reliable though it naturally
shows a strong bias in favor of the Hasmoneans, who, the author
implies, were divinely appointed to save Israel (5.61–62): "This
great event befell the army because they did not obey Judah and
his brothers, imagining that they could perform some heroic deed.
They were not of the family of those men into whose keeping
was entrusted the power of saving Israel." Successes are regularly
ascribed to divine help (e.g., 4.55, 12–15). The day of prophets
and miracles is past (9.27) but heaven will still hear and answer
prayer (e.g., 3.18 f., 3.44, 4.30 ff.). But though the book was
written in Hebrew (which is lost), its sensationalism, its miracles,
and in particular its use of letters and documents to make important junctures in the story are evidences of the effects of hellenistic practices.

Hellenistic practices are most palpable in II Maccabees.[36] Its
author declares that his work is an abridgment and popularization
of a five-book history by Jason of Cyrene, of whom nothing is
known. It covers a shorter span than I Maccabees, only the fifteen
years from 175 B.C. to 160, and is far less trustworthy. The style
is turgid and overloaded, there are long rhetorical descriptions,
details are exaggerated, the enemy is spoken of with abusive
epithets, and the author obtrudes his own reflections at unnecessary length. Two of the fifteen chapters are prologue; one an account of Heliodorus' miraculously thwarted attempt to plunder
the temple; and two an account of the martyrdoms of Eleazar and
of Hannah and her seven sons, which is the subject of IV Maccabees. The epitomist explains (2.23 f.) that Jason's "dense mass
of material [is] intended primarily only for those who wish to
plunge into historical narratives. We have rather taken thought
of those who like to read for pleasure (*psychagogia*), for those
who prefer ease (*eukopia*) in the things they are to remember, in
order to supply edification (*ōpheleia*) to all who encounter our

work." The program of hellenistic historiography could not be more succinctly expressed than by the words *psychagogia, eukopia*, and *ōpheleia*—with the inevitable concomitant of indifference to historical fact.

III Maccabees [37] can hardly be admitted into the category of history even on the most generous construction. The story it tells is as follows: Ptolemy IV is miraculously prevented from entering the temple at Jerusalem after his victory at Raphia in 207 B.C., and in his annoyance determines to annihilate the Jews of Egypt. He collects them in the hippodrome, to be trampled down by five hundred elephants which have been infuriated by drink. A series of odd miracles saves the Jews: one day the paper and pens of the registrars give out, another day the king oversleeps, on another he has a fit of amnesia: finally two angels cause the elephants to trample the enemies of the Jews instead. The Jews are then feasted and receive permission to kill three hundred renegades of their own people. It is virtually certain that III Maccabees was written about 25 B.C. and expresses a violent reaction to a new census instituted by the Romans, which would affect the Jews adversely; yet the elephant story was not invented by the author but belonged to the body of what he considered history. Josephus (*Against Apion* 2.5) tells the story in a form which shows that he did not derive it from III Maccabees, and places it in the reign of Ptolemy Physcon. Though we may regard III Maccabees as fiction, then, its author regarded it as a historical narrative, suitable for presentation in the hellenistic manner.

This confounding of what to us are disparate genres affords an insight not only into the character of hellenistic historiography but also into that of the romance, which, as has been observed, started its career as a species of history calculated to promote cultural survival among the defeated peoples of the eastern Mediterranean. III Maccabees belongs to that category as clearly as does the *Ninus Romance*, which is roughly contemporary with it, and it is interesting to observe how many motifs it shares with even the fully developed romances which are extant.[38] To begin with there is (a) the introduction of a well-known character from a familiar period of history; Ptolemy Philopator here corresponds to the historical personages in Chariton or Heliodorus. (b) It is virtually a fixed element in the romances that the denouement is presented in a quasi-judicial or judicial process before a large assembly, frequently in a theater or hippodrome, where the hero or heroine is brought to the very brink of horrible destruction and then by a reversal through an agency which seems providential is not only delivered but gains the upper hand, to the applause of a multitude. This is fully exemplified in III Maccabees. (c) The judicial crisis gives rise to pathetic scenes and rhetorical forensic speeches involving extravagant exaggerations. (d) Another characteristic of the style of the romance is their very generous use of literary allusions and echoes. III Maccabees follows the same practice, except that its allusions are, as we should expect, to Hebrew literature. The long supplications offered by the priests Simon (2.1–20) and Eleazar (6.1–15) correspond closely to the form and spirit of extant Hebrew prayers, and they are spectacularly answered. (e) That the religious interest should be dominant in III Maccabees is to be expected; but it must be observed that the religious interest is also prominent in the romances, and may well be, as has been maintained, the chief motive for writing them. (f) A literary device common to the romances is the use of quoted letters, especially to set forth vital and unexpected changes in circumstances. In III Maccabees Philopator's two great decisions, to annihilate the Jews and to atone to them, are set forth in letters (3.12–30 and 6.41–7, 9). Where III Maccabees obviously diverges from the romances is in the absence of a personal hero and a love story. The absence of the personal hero may be explained by the circumstance that only Moses could serve as a national hero, after the fashion of Ninus and the others; and Moses is in fact the sole hero in Artapanus and Ezekielos and the others. The actual hero of III Maccabees is patently the whole Jewish community, as in Deutero-Isaiah's concept of the Suffering Servant. As for a love interest, so pious a work could hardly make room for one, but it may not be too fanciful to see the emphasis on quite irrelevant brides being torn from their nuptial chambers as a strained effort to supply a surrogate for an element the author knew a work like his should contain.

From Isocrates onwards history had been patriotic; the books of the Maccabees show how the motive of patriotism was enhanced by a religious motivation, and we shall see how the new conception of patriotism was celebrated by Livy and Vergil to become the rationale of Roman citizenship. But now we turn to other forms of literature in which a Greek basis was adapted and transformed in the east, and first to drama.

Chapter XI

DRAMA AND DIATRIBE

MODERNS are apt to be more immediately and deeply impressed with tragedy than with other achievements in the Greek repertory, and it is not unlikely that sensitive ancients who encountered Greek genius as a fresh experience reacted similarly. We have seen that classical drama was studied in the schools which were to be found in every hellenized community, and that many of these communities possessed theaters; [1] it would be strange if a novelty of such grandeur, artistically and intellectually, would fail to touch thoughtful minds in the east.

For those who wrote in Greek there can be no question; it may be stated categorically that every bit of Greek writing we have (aside from such things as tax receipts and bills of sale), whatever the origins of the writer, shows knowledge of Greek tragedy. Every work in the Apocrypha and Pseudepigrapha of the Old Testament has expressions from or allusions to tragedy which the reader was obviously expected to recognize. Sometimes, as notably in IV Maccabees, the whole conception of a work seems to be influenced by tragedy.[2] Here the author sets a scene typical of tragedy, and carries his action forward by dialogue between the tyrant and his victims. The seven brothers are actually called a chorus at several points, and like a chorus the author has them speak with a single voice, and at a point of stress break into separate ejaculations and then join again in a triumphant finale (13.11 ff.). When he wishes to speak of a retributive curse pursuing a wrongdoer he uses *alastor* (9.24, 11.23, 18.22), which must evoke the atmosphere of tragedy. When he wishes to underscore the innocence of the martyrs and the injustice of the persecutor he copies the device which Euripides uses in the *Trojan Women* and constructs a damning epitaph. Like good Greek tragedy, and unlike melodrama, IV Maccabees avoids making its tyrant a capricious monster, brought to his knees crushed and groveling in the last act. The tyrant is a reasonably good man, and all the cast —and vicariously the audience—learn by suffering.

Not only was something of the spirit and technique of tragedy adapted for philosophic discourses, but the form itself was imitated. The *Exodus* of Ezekielos, which has been described above,[3] is a very respectable piece, and though the next extant production of the kind is the *Christus Patiens*, ascribed to Gregory of Nazianz (fourth century) but probably of much later date, there must have been other dramatizations of scriptural themes more nearly contemporary with Ezekielos. Indeed, the practice of elaborating episodes briefly told in the Bible into a rounded and edifying story which is found in nondramatic writers may owe something to the example of the classical tragic poets.[4]

But were writers who wrote in their native languages and in their own countries affected by Greek tragedy? Aside from Latin, which adapted Greek drama wholesale, the question must reduce itself to a consideration of Hebrew, for the reason that it is the only language in which belles-lettres survive from the period with which we are concerned. It has been maintained (but certainty seems impossible) that Sanskrit plays of the Gupta period, like Kalidasa's *Shakuntala* or Harsha's *Priyadarsika* show knowledge of what the Greeks had done, but their date is too low to be meaningful to us. Similarly the so-called Edfu drama of Egypt[5] is too high as well as too amorphous to be meaningful for our purposes.

Certain things in Hebrew do seem to bear striking resemblances to things in Greek tragedy. We shall notice the dependence of the Testament of Joseph on the Phaedra legend, but its author may have learned the story from an intermediate treatment of it.[6] In the ancient Hebrew prayer called Eighteen Benedictions (of which the framework is almost surely pre-Christian)[7] there is a curious parallel in the order of the blessings to the order of blessings pronounced by the chorus of Danaids in Aeschylus' *Suppliant Women* (630 ff.) [8] Striking as the similarity is, it is only the order we can argue from, for the blessings fit admirably into either context.

So it is with doctrine, especially in the case of Aeschylus. His exaltation and spiritualization of his supreme deity, in all his extant plays except the questionable *Prometheus*, could hardly offend anyone nurtured on the Old Testament. Passages like the following, again from the *Suppliant Women*, might well have come from the pen of an Old Testament prophet: [9]

Whereon Zeus hath set his desire, that is hard to trace: verily it flareth everywhere, even in the gloom, howbeit attended by events obscure to mortal man.

Secure it falleth, and not upon its back, whatsoever is decreed unto fulfilment by the nod of Zeus; for the pathways of his understanding stretch dark and tangled, beyond ken to scan.

From their high-towering hopes he hurleth mankind to utter destruction; yet he arrayeth no armed violence—all that is wrought by the powers divine is free from toil. Seated on his holy throne, whence he removeth not, nevertheless in mysterious wise he maketh his thought to deed. (87–103.)

He doth not sit upon his throne by authority of another and hold his dominion beneath a mightier. None there is who sitteth above him whose power he holdeth in awe. He speaketh and it is done—he hasteneth to execute whatsoever his counselling mind conceiveth. (595–599.)

The same is true of Aeschylus' new insistence on individual rather than inherited responsibility for wrongdoing, which is the main substance of the *Oresteia*. The prophets made the same point, and with the same air of novelty. In Jeremiah 32.29 we read: "In those days they shall say no more, The fathers have eaten a sour grape, and the children's teeth are set on edge. But every one shall die for his own iniquity: every man that eateth the sour grape, his teeth shall be set on edge." And in Ezekiel 18.2–4 we read: "What mean ye . . . saying, The fathers have eaten sour grapes and the children's teeth are set on edge? . . . The soul that sinneth, it shall die."

Nor are rudiments at least of dramatic form unexampled in the ancient Near East, at least during the centuries when other parallels with high Greek antiquity have been noticed. The pioneering work of Jane Harrison, Gilbert Murray, Francis Cornford, and latterly George Thomson has persuaded most students of classical drama that both tragedy and comedy originated in a seasonal ritual; when the ritual is interpenetrated with interpretive myth drama is born. On the basis of various ancient Near Eastern texts Theodor H. Gaster has shown that a primitive kind of drama, analogous, in all probability, to the antecedents of perfected Greek tragedy, did in fact exist in the literatures which affected the Old Testament.[10] Gaster points to vestiges of this drama in various passages in the Old Testament, but he cannot of course claim that these were felt as drama by the audiences for which they were intended—any more than audiences of New Comedy were aware that the infants who were exposed and subsequently recognized were descendants of the year baby in the annual vegetation cycle.

For any meaningful comparison we must look at Greek tragedy only in its developed form, as the hellenistic age looked at it; and as in the case of the *Suppliants*–Eighteen Benedictions parallel, influences can be recognized only if externals suggest that influences are arguable. The only non-Greek work which bears a recognizable resemblance to the form of Greek tragedy (whether or not the resemblance is accidental or sufficiently close) is the book of Job.[11] Job is the only book in the Bible, not historical or lyrical in form, in which what is said is not said in the author's own person but is distributed among a cast of speakers who use highly poetic language and build up to a climax, and in which, therefore, artistic structure is of paramount importance. It is the only book in the Bible which begins with what amounts to "Once upon a time."

Over the centuries this has disturbed the devout, who have found it unthinkable that Scripture should represent as having happened things which were only imagined. Theodore of Mopsuestia (d. 428), the most critical mind among the teachers of the

ancient church, denounced Job as an imitation of a Greek tragedy. Its author, he declared, being familiar with Greek literature
and a friend of the Greeks, was prompted by an unholy ambition
to make of the ancient true story of the Edomite Job a drama
after the pattern of the Greek poets. He invented the speeches he
put into the mouths of the characters—some of which are injurious and almost blasphemous—as well as the prologue in heaven
with its scandalous wager between God and Satan, and the myth-
ical monsters in Chapters 40–41. Theodore therefore excluded Job
from his Bible as a work of fiction. Theodore's opinion was condemned at the Council of Constantinople in 553.

The alternative of accepting Job as edifying allegory, which
seems natural to the modern reader, was slow in establishing itself.
Maimonides (1135–1204), the greatest of the medieval Jewish
philosophers, declared in his *Guide to the Perplexed* (3.22) that
Job never actually existed and that his story was intended only to
point a moral.[12] In 1587 Theodore Beza began a course of lectures
on Job in Geneva by dividing the book into acts and scenes, and
in the eighteenth century Bishop Lowth tells us that virtually all
scholars regarded Job as a drama and discussed it, as they would a
Greek tragedy, with reference to its division into acts, its catas-
trophe, its *deus ex machina*. Lowth himself devotes an entire lec-
ture to the problem in his volume on Hebrew poetry (1753); he
finds that Job conforms to the prescriptions of Aristotle's *Poetics*
in every respect except "action." Lowth concludes that Job may
be called a dramatic poem but not properly a drama,[13] and his has
been the dominant critical view. This view, it may be remarked,
does nothing to weaken Theodore of Mopsuestia's opinion that
Job was a deliberate imitation of Greek tragedy; the Greeks themselves wrote plays which were not intended to be acted, and, as
we shall presently notice, there are grounds for thinking that the
Prometheus itself, which is the closest Greek analogue to Job,
belongs to this category. But before we pursue the possible relationships of Job to Greek tragedy further we must consider some
of the critical problems involved in the text of Job.

These are numerous and vexatious and have been debated end-
lessly, because the inner meaning of the book depends upon them.
First the question of date. Most handbooks agree in placing it at
about 400 B.C., but rather on intuition than on anything like definite evidence. The tendency of all critics to push the date as far
back as possible seems to be based on an unconscious analogy to
Greek or Elizabethan drama. The language of Job is the loftiest
and most ornate in the Old Testament, and everyone knows that
poetic language descends from the grandeur of Aeschylus to the
almost colloquial simplicity of Euripides, from the rhetorical and
poetic utterance of the Elizabethans to the vernacular of G. B.
Shaw. But then, it must be remembered, language moved in the
other direction also, from the simplicity of Euripides to the tur-
gidity of Seneca, from Shaw to Eliot and Pound. When it ob-
serves a canon of form a literary work becomes difficult to date.
Quintus of Smyrna's *Posthomerica* or Musaeus' *Hero and Leander*
may be recognized as late productions by their un-Homeric sentimentality, but their form and language is deceptive, and through
the Humanist period Musaeus was actually thought to be older
than Homer. Actually there is no valid philological reason to
prevent our dating Job a century or two after 400.

The more serious problem involves the question of possible interpolations. The crucial sections are the prose prologue and
epilogue (1.1–2.10 and 42.10–17), the poem on divine wisdom
(28), and the speeches of Elihu (32–37). The objection to the
prologue is its crude anthropomorphism which is out of keeping
with the main body of the book. The objection to the epilogue is
that it seems to negate the main teaching of the book: after so
much effort has been expended to persuade us that there is no
connection visible to human eyes between a man's merit and his
lot in life, we are shown that Job does in fact receive a reward
for his righteousness. The objection to Chapter 28 is that it seems
unrelated to its context. The objection to the Elihu speeches is
that in part they repeat, less effectively, what had been said before, and in part anticipate the speech of God out of the whirl-

wind. This section has been almost universally condemned as an interpolation, on the analogy of similarly pious interpolations to correct heterodoxy in a book like Ecclesiastes.

On the other hand, without the prologue the whole book would be unintelligible. In logic the epilogue is not so indispensable, but it is asking too much even of a spectator who has been intellectually persuaded to leave Job hopelessly suffering on his ash heap. There is evidence for the existence of a far simpler folk story of Job, reflected in our prologue and epilogue; this our author has filled out with profound and noble poetry, leaving the folk story unchanged at beginning and end. There remain Chapter 28 and Elihu's speeches to consider.

An ingenious defense of the integrity of these passages was offered by Horace M. Kallen a generation ago in his *The Book of Job as a Greek Tragedy*.[14] Kallen's thesis is that the author of Job was directly inspired by witnessing a production of Euripides, possibly of the *Bellerophontes*, probably in Egypt. The prologue and epilogue follow Euripidean practice, and the apparently unrelated poem and the remarks of Elihu, as well as other pieces which Kallen mentions, are appropriate where they are as choral interludes and would perhaps have been more easily recognizable as such before the text was regularized to approximate the form of other Old Testament books. In Euripides more than in his predecessors, it will be remembered, the choral odes tend to be detached from the dialogue. And finally, there is the characteristically Euripidean *deus ex machina*.

Whatever we think of arguments based on prologue, epilogue, and chorus, the *deus ex machina* argument does have a certain cogency, greater than Kallen realized. In Euripides this device is used to leave the play intentionally open-ended, to satisfy the spectator who wishes an orthodox or a happy ending, and simultaneously to nurture ·doubts in the minds of the less conventional.[15] Indeed in such plays as *Alcestis, Medea, Ion, Iphigenia in Tauris*, Euripides makes the epiphanies so hard to credit that he seems more interested in instilling doubt than in satisfying the conventional; "Take this ending if you like," he seems to say, "but I hope you won't." The voice out of the whirlwind in Job has a similar effect. That God has greater power, which is its main burden, had been pointed out by other speakers and freely acknowledged by Job. What Job had desiderated was a rationale, and to this the response is that God's ways are unsearchable. Job yields (42.1–6), but out of faith rather than logical conviction. Those who persist in demanding logic need not follow Job, and it does not appear that the author intended to declare that they must. As with Euripides' gods out of the machine, the spectator is left to accept or reject.

Even if this interpretation is only fanciful it remains true that Job's attitude of *demanding* a self-justification of God is unexampled in Old Testament literature. In support of his thesis of a Euripidean model Kallen points out that Euripides and Job have the same questioning attitude to their respective orthodoxies. Nathaniel Schmidt, among others, declared that such an attitude was inconceivable in an Old Testament context without direct inspiration from the Greeks, and specifically, Schmidt suggested, Aeschylus.[16] Robert Pfeiffer, whose learning and taste are unexceptionable, sees no reason to think that the author of Job was a Jew and maintains that he was not.[17] For our purposes it is not essential to identify the author of Job otherwise than by saying that he was certainly not a Greek; Greek elements in his book, if they are present, are in any case an importation.

Where hard evidence is nonexistent or equivocal the opinions of perceptive ordinary readers are as valid as those of the philologians. It proved so in the case of Homeric studies; while philologians were fragmenting *Iliad* and *Odyssey* into bits and pieces poets came to insist more and more on their unity, and were justified by new discoveries regarding the nature of oral poetry. In the case of Job numberless readers have noted its general resemblance to the *Prometheus*, on the obvious grounds that both demand justification of a supreme deity, each sets up an adversary to the deity, each employs extraordinarily lofty and artful language, each is essentially undramatic, except in an intellectual sense, though each preserves a dramatic form, and finally that each does offer a kind of justification. There are subtler and more compelling parallels, but before we consider them a word must be said concerning a critical problem involved in the *Prometheus*.

Except for the fact that Aeschylus is known to have composed a Prometheus trilogy and that the *Prometheus* is included with plays known to be Aeschylean in our manuscript tradition, there can be no complete certainty that the play we have is the play Aeschylus wrote, and a number of respectable scholars have maintained (though preponderant opinion is decidedly against them) that our *Prometheus* is not Aeschylus' but a sophistic production of the fourth century intended not for stage presentation but for reading.[18] We know that plays were written by philosophers of various schools to embody their teachings but not to be acted,[19] and divergences from normal Aeschylean techniques of language and construction are very marked. Technically there is so little to relate the *Prometheus* to Aeschylus' acknowledged plays that scholars have significantly oscillated between assigning it to the beginning of his career and its end. (For the others, except the Danaid trilogy, a firm dating has come down from antiquity.) But the sharpest inconcinnity between the *Prometheus* and the rest of Aeschylus is in theology. The six other plays are quite consistent in their exaltation of Zeus, quite in the temper of the passages from the *Suppliant Women* cited above. The second of those passages (599 f.) declares that Zeus' sovereignty is absolute. In *Prometheus* (516 f.) we have the following exchange: "Can it be that Zeus has lesser power than they [sc. Fates and Furies]?" "Yes, he cannot escape what is ordained." It is hard to believe that so critical a picture of Zeus as the *Prometheus* presents can have come from the hand that glorified Zeus in the other plays.

Even without the theory of fourth-century authorship Aeschylus would still have been available in book form (though we know from statistics of papyri and quotations that he was little read), but it is easier to imagine that a hellenized non-Greek would be more likely to be attracted by a fresh pamphlet reflecting contemporary discussions and to make it the point of departure for his own treatment of the same subject. It is easier too if we under-

stand that the Promethean view of deity was not too remote from
his own, as in fact it was not. The conception of the Promethean
Zeus as unjust as well as ruthless, illustrated and propagated by
Shelley's treatment, stems from the revolutionary temper of the
romantic era and does not fairly reflect the ancient play. There
Zeus upon coming into power found mankind a miserable lot. He
despised them and (234 ff.) "desired to bring the whole race to
nothingness and to create another, a new one, in its stead." Prometheus, who was a Titan and so in a sense man's elder brother,
made it possible for wretched man to survive by propping him up
with clothes and medicine and fire and means of livelihood and
finally deceptive hope. In other words, out of sentimentality,
grateful to man indeed but misguided and based on a presumption
of knowledge he could not have, Prometheus dared question the
wisdom of Zeus. But in the *Prometheus*, if nowhere else, Zeus is
merely a convenient poetical personification of the supreme power
which controls the world. Unlike Jehovah, who himself made the
world, Zeus is, to be sure, new to his power; but the concern of
the Promethean Zeus for the management of the world is much
greater than the older Zeus', and there is a much greater interval
between him and lesser deities. In other words, there is here a
conscious approach to monotheism, and the sole god is not so
much a personage as a personification of the master force in the
cosmos. Men are by no means his principal concern; mankind is
only a single element in the world and can be dispensed with for
the better functioning of the world's economy.

If we look at Job from the theological point of view we shall
find it as near this conception as it is remote from the traditional
beliefs, as maintained by Job's friends. For them (as for the unconsciously arrogant devout generally) God's main business is
with rewarding and punishing mankind. The friends insist on
God's omnipotence and the universality of sinfulness, and Job
agrees with them; but they insist too that sin and pain must be
related as cause and effect, and here Job disagrees. However
wisely and beautifully the world may be ordered, pain is inherent
in the human condition; it is not a requital for human conduct.
We may note, incidentally, that this is the regular view of Greek

tragedy; its sufferers are not sinners but men caught by (to them)
unintelligible ordinances of heaven, and they achieve their tragic
stature in despite of those ordinances. Only when we come to
Seneca do we encounter conscious villains, whose wrongdoing is
therefore in the nature of sin. If we speak of Job as a theodicy, as
it is customary to do, the justification of God lies not in a demonstration that there is after all a causal nexus between a man's behavior and his lot, but in the suggestion that God's laws are not
susceptible to measurement by human standards: his geometry is,
as it were, non-Euclidean.

Now to view evil as inherent in man's lot and not as a punishment for the wicked is to deal with it from a philosophical point
of view unknown elsewhere in the Old Testament, as Professor
Pfeiffer points out.

Job's theology [he writes] is more akin to the Greek than to the
Israelitic notion of the deity. . . . The functions and attributes of
the deity in Job indicate that the author conceived of his God primarily as a cosmic force, not as the patron God of a nation, primarily
concerned with human affairs. This anonymous deity is not connected
with any nation, nor is it the object of worship. Although God appears
as a person in addressing Job out of the whirlwind, the personality of
this God is a postulate of religion and a poetic device required by the
drama, rather than a philosophic conclusion. In essence God is a universal force, and as such can hardly have the characteristic of human
personality.[20]

Such parallels in essence are much more cogent than external
similarities like prologues or descriptions of strange creatures. The
flaw in the criticism of Lowth and his successors is that they were
concerned with form exclusively, making Aristotle's *Poetics* their
guide. The author of Job was not an Alexandrian litterateur nor a
Roman schoolboy but an original and profound poet. If he learned
from the *Prometheus* at all it would be a view of the nature of the
divine. The likeness in substance may reinforce a belief in the influence of form, not the other way round.

It is the standard of the schools, again, which has led scholars to
question the hellenistic character of what surely is the most characteristically hellenistic book in the Old Testament canon—Ec-

clesiastes.[21] The denial of divine concern for human conduct and particularly of rewards and punishments in a future existence, and the admonition, consistent with this lack of belief, to seek pleasure is thoroughly Epicurean. But though Epicureanism is the dominant note Ecclesiastes shows touches of Stoicism also: admonitions to do one's duty, to be content with one's lot, to welcome death. Such a statement as "Then shall the dust return to the earth as it was, but the spirit shall return to God who made it" (12.7) is Stoic; it was the Stoics who taught that the souls of men are splinters of the divine world-soul and are reunited with it after death. There is a suggestion of Stoicism also in the doctrine of the cyclic recurrence of natural phenomena (1.5 ff.). But, it has been argued, adherents of one school avoided the doctrines of the other, and hence Ecclesiastes could have learned from neither. For teachings of duty and discipline, furthermore, there is no need to seek western sources; and for the apparently Epicurean passages there are sufficient antecedents in the ancient literature of the Near East, sometimes strikingly close. In the Gilgamesh epic, for example, the barmaid Siduri admonishes the weary hero as follows (Babylonian version, iii):

> Thou, Gilgamesh, let full be thy belly,
> Make thou merry by day and by night.
> Of each day make thou a feast of rejoicing,
> Day and night dance thou and play!
> Let thy garments be sparkling fresh,
> Thy head be washed; bathe thou in water.
> Pay heed to the little one that holds on to thy hand,
> Let thy spouse delight in thy bosom!
> For this is the task of mankind! [22]

And in the Egyptian Song of the Harper we have:

> What are their [sc. the dead] places now?
> Their walls are broken apart, and their places are not—
> As though they had never been!
>
>   .   .   .   .   .   .
>
> Let thy desire flourish,
> In order to let thy heart forget the beatifications for thee.
> Follow thy desire as long as thou shalt live.

> Put myrrh upon thy head and clothing of fine linen upon
> thee,
> Being anointed with genuine marvels of the god's prop-
> erty.
> Set an increase to thy good things;
> Let not thy heart flag.
> Follow thy desire and thy good.
> Fulfill thy needs upon earth, after the command of thy
> heart,
> Until there come for thee that day of mourning.[23]

But there is as great a difference between Ecclesiastes and the shrugging despair of these prescriptions as there is between Epicureanism and the travesty of it suggested by "Eat, drink, and be merry." In Ecclesiastes we have not merely resignation but an effort to understand. "Only a Jew having some slight acquaintance with hellenism," Professor Pfeiffer notes, "would have been inclined to glance behind the scenes, behind the comfortable accepted views of the community, in order to test the validity of his people's faith, thereby reaching philosophical conclusions that were both novel and revolutionary. . . . If, then Ecclesiastes heard echoes of Greek thought and was deeply stirred thereby, as seems certain, we may say that in a sense his book is the first attempt to make a synthesis of Judaism and hellenism." [24]

Ecclesiastes heard more than echoes. If the author of Job learned from the Greeks he shaped what he learned into a new creation; Ecclesiastes is a closer imitation of a Greek genre, in form and spirit. That genre is the diatribe, which was invented by the Cynic-Stoic preachers and enjoyed an enormous vogue in the hellenistic age; we have seen that both Menippus and Meleager wrote diatribes. Even in syntax Ecclesiastes seems to be striving for Greek form; consider the one sentence which occupies the first seven verses of Chapter 12:

Remember now thy Creator in the days of thy youth, while the evil days come not, nor the years draw nigh when thou shalt say, I have no pleasure in them; while the sun or the light or the moon or the stars be not darkened, nor the clouds return after the rain; in the day when the keepers of the house shall tremble, and the strong men shall bow themselves, and the grinders cease because they are few, and those that look out of the windows be darkened, and the doors shall be shut in the streets, when the sound of the grinding is low, and he shall rise up at the voice of the bird, and all the daughters of music shall be brought low; also when they shall be afraid of that which is high, and fears shall be in the way, and the almond tree shall flourish, and the grasshopper shall be a burden, and desire shall fail; because man goeth to his long home, and the mourners go about the streets; or ever the silver cord be loosed, or the golden bowl be broken, or the pitcher be broken at the fountain, or the wheel broken at the cistern; then shall dust return to the earth as it was; and the spirit shall return unto God who gave it.

Because of the "atomistic" character of Hebrew this sentence is more monstrous in that language than it is in English, and it is hard to see why a practiced writer would compose so awkward, and needless, a construction unless he were imitating some alien form.

One of the indications that Ecclesiastes is of the character of a diatribe is the very inconsistency which has led some scholars to deny Greek influence. The inconsistencies which seem to mar the unity of the text and which have led some critics to posit as many as five separate strands in the little book [25] are perfectly consistent with the traditional form of the diatribe. In calling attention to the affinities to the diatribe shown by the Pauline Epistles Paul Wendland writes: "The diatribes with their lively interruptions of the discourse by means of interjections and questions or by the utterances of an opponent, with their propensity to short paratactic cola which causes relationships to be expressed by coordination rather than subordination, supply striking parallels to the paraenetic portions of Paul's Epistles." [26] Such, indeed, is the essential style of the diatribe, and it is this style which sets Ecclesiastes apart from other books in the Old Testament. Arthur Allgeier in his commentary on that book [27] has recognized that Ecclesiastes is in the nature of a diatribe and welcomed the fact as a rehabilitation of the integrity of the text. Virtually every writer of ethical essays in the Greco-Roman period, both Greek and Latin, more or less adapted the diatribe form.[28] In Epictetus and in Dio Chrysostom and particularly in Seneca (who though nominally a Stoic uses Epicurean texts in many of his *Letters to Lucilius*) we see that the diatribe makes free use of any striking ethical statements that might be in the air, whatever school they may derive from. It is the same with Ecclesiastes; the air he breathed seems to have been not only touched but saturated with dicta of the hellenistic teachers. The book closes on a devout note which is tantamount to a rejection of all that has gone before (12.13–14): "Let us hear the conclusion of the whole matter: Fear God and keep his commandments, for this is the whole duty of man. For God shall bring every work into judgment, with every secret thing, whether it be good or whether it be evil." This note has been explained by almost every modern critic as the addition of a devout editor who was disturbed by the heterodoxy of the book. Even such a note might have been uttered by the writer of a diatribe.

From the point of view of its influence upon Ecclesiastes the diatribe must certainly be considered a Greek form, and yet its very introduction into Greek was, as we have noted, the work of a man from Gadara, and it was carried forward by another man from the same place. The strands become difficult to untwine, but the influence of the mingled skein upon Christian sermons, upon wandering missionaries, and even upon the monastic ideal and practice was incalculable.[29] The influence is palpable in, and was most widely and effectively propagated by, the most famous missionary sermon of all, St. Paul in his address to the Athenians on the Areopagus (Acts 17.22–31). Here, for convenience, is the text, in the Standard Revised Version:

[22]So Paul, standing in the middle of the Areopagus, said: "Men of Athens, I perceive that in every way you are very religious.[23] For as I passed along, and observed the objects of your worship, I found also an altar with this inscription, 'To an unknown god.' What therefore you worship as unknown, this I proclaim to you.[24] The God who made the world and everything in it, being Lord of heaven and earth, does not live in shrines made by man,[25] nor is he served by human hands, as though he needed anything, since he himself gives to all men life and

breath and everything.[26] And he made from one every nation of men to live on all the face of the earth, having determined allotted periods and the boundaries of their habitation,[27] that they should seek God, in the hope that they might feel after him and find him. Yet he is not far from each one of us,[28] for 'In him we live and move and have our being'; as even some of your poets have said, 'For we are indeed his offspring.' [29]Being then God's offspring, we ought not to think that the Deity is like gold, or silver, or stone, a representation by the art and imagination of man.[30] The times of ignorance God overlooked, but now he commands all men everywhere to repent,[31] because he has fixed a day on which he will judge the world in righteousness by a man whom he had appointed, and of this he has given assurance to all men by raising him from the dead.

This speech Eduard Norden has analyzed in detail in his *Agnostos Theos*, which is a model of philological acumen and precision, and has demonstrated that it belongs to a standard type in its occasion, "text," and individual motifs and expressions.[30] One or another of several religious teachers Norden cites, who cannot have been influenced by St. Paul, is represented as visiting Athens in the course of a missionary journey, choosing as a text some local monument he has noticed on a walk, and reproving the audience for falsely associating the Deity with material objects and tendance. Each of the four motifs of correcting ignorance (23), worshiping God not through material representation but in spirit (24 ff.), calling for repentance (30), and referring to resurrection (31) appears in Poimandres (1.27 f.),[31] Odes of Solomon (33), and the Sermon of Peter.[32] The Stoic texts, down to verse 29, including the quotation from Aratus, are commonplaces in the diatribes and have numerous parallels. An altar of doubtful identity is made a text for diatribe by Maximus of Tyre in the piece entitled "Should a man set altars up to the gods" (No. 8), and notably in a first-century letter falsely ascribed to Heraclitus (No. 4).[33] This piece shows several interesting parallels to our text, as an excerpt will show:

But you, ignorant men, first teach us what God is in order that you may be believed when you speak of impiety. Where then is God? Is he shut up in the temples? You, I suppose, are pious when you set God in darkness? A man would consider himself slandered if he were called "stone," and is it a true description of God to say that he is formed of rock? You uneducated men, don't you know that God is not something made by hand, and has no base large enough, and has not merely a single precinct, but that the whole universe is his temple?

The strongest evidence for the "literary" character of the discourse on the Areopagus emerges from a comparison with an episode in the career of Apollonius of Tyana (whom we shall consider more fully in a subsequent chapter). The summaries of the accounts of the two men which Norden exhibits in parallel columns [34] make some connection between them almost certain. Here is the part on Apollonius:

A religious teacher from Asia Minor travels through the world to preach religion to men ignorant of true divinity. About the middle of the first century he reaches Athens, and finds evidence of the people's religiosity in their numerous sacred monuments. He uses an inscription on an altar to teach that the proper worship of god is spiritual.

It is extremely unlikely that such an inscription as "To the unknown god" (more accurately "To an indeterminate god") could have occurred, though there are sufficient parallels for the phrase in the plural. The use of the singular is then a deft device to give the discourse the turn desired. To say that the author of the discourse adapted standard forms is by no means to impugn his earnestness and his sincerity; it would be much more remarkable if a literate man addressing a literate audience did not use the forms associated with his subject. In this case the origin of the form may have been eastern, but it had become fully naturalized in the west; now the east endowed it with new meaning and returned it to the west for eventual penetration into the whole of European civilization.

Chapter XII

LOVE, TRIANGULAR
AND PURE

"FEW people would fall in love," La Rochefoucauld has said, "if they had never heard of love." The relationship between men and women is, to be sure, a condition of human survival, but the civilized conceptions of love and its treatment in literature exhibit various and marked differences from the elemental basis. What may seem to be natural responses may really be conventions grown so pervasive that they are no longer recognized as such, as Denis de Rougemont has shown in his *Love in the Western World*. Refinements of the elemental basis do tend to take similar directions, and it is therefore easy for a reader bred to the western tradition to adjust his understanding to the different conventions in the *Ramayana* or *Kalevala*, *Genji* or the *Arabian Nights*, or for that matter in Greek tragedy, but adjustment is required nevertheless. Our problem in the present chapter is to see how certain of the western conventions of the literary treatment of love took shape.

Expression of the lover's ecstasy is a matter for lyric; we have seen how Meleager may have contributed to the tradition of the love lyric, and we shall presently try to place the Song of Solomon in the tradition of erotic lyric. But for the storyteller there is nothing to say when the course of love runs smooth except, "And so they lived happy ever after." Difficulties to be overcome offer the storyteller scope, and the possibilities are enriched when there is a rival. The love triangle plot is indeed old and prolific.

In its earliest form the plot seems regularly to involve a woman of position, her husband, and a younger man who is a rival rather for the husband's status than for his wife's sexual favors. In origin this pattern probably derives from matriarchal societies,[1] where the position of queen's consort has political meaning; but even in societies where matriarchy did not, or did not longer, prevail, admission to the queen's bed symbolized accession to the throne. In the Old Kingdom in Egypt, for example, the founder of a new dynasty legitimized his position by marriage with a queen of the preceding dynasty,[2] and in ancient Israel Ahithophel advises Absalom to take possession of his father David's harem in order to secure his succession.[3] Two elements inherent in the origin of the pattern are that (a) the woman takes the initiative, though her motive may not be erotic, and (b) the rival has some quasi-legitimate claim, usually based on kinship. Where these elements would not seem extraordinary in a matriarchy, they would be startling in a society where the woman was never allowed the initiative and where incest was anathema. Hence stories which may reflect an ordinary process of succession in their origin become the subject of stark tragedy when transposed to a later age.

In our earliest example, which is the plot of the *Odyssey*, the pattern seems already to have been modified to suit later conditions and tastes; yet some of the essentials are present. Penelope is handsome, but the suitors are motivated by political rather than erotic reasons, and though she does not take the initiative it is clear that the choice must be hers. Telemachus, whom the suitors plan to kill, is a surrogate for his father. Whether and to what degree traces of an earlier matriarchy survive in Homer is a disputed question.[4] The description of the royal ménage in Phaeacia does suggest that some matriarchal traits have been consciously suppressed. Athena (in the guise of a young girl) praises Arete's intelligence and her skill in resolving quarrels (7.73–75), and it is Arete who speaks of Odysseus as *her* guest and bids the Phaeacians to give him presents. But at once an elderly Phaeacian remarks that the queen's bidding is just and should be heeded, yet the decision must rest with Alcinous the king (11.338–46).[5] Perhaps in the case of Penelope as in that of Arete the harsh or antiquated aspects of the story have consciously been toned down. The tragic poets often present the old tales in unmodified form. The *Odyssey's* version of the Clytemnestra-Agamemnon-Aegisthus triangle, for example, is more "modern" than Aeschylus'. In Zeus' own exculpation at the opening of the poem (1.32 ff.) the blame is placed solely on Aegisthus, and in the recital of Agamemnon's ghost (11.409 ff.) it was Aegisthus who invited him to his house, feasted him, and then killed him like an ox at his crib, though the wicked wife is spoken of as an accomplice.

In one Homeric triangle—that involving Antea (*alias* Stheneboea), her husband Proetus, and the handsome Bellerophon (*Iliad* 6.160 ff.)—the motive of the woman, who does take the initiative, is declared to be sexual; and it was this factor, naturally, that Euripides and later writers seized upon. But the alternative which Antea offers her husband, "Kill Bellerophon or you must die," suggests that more than a point of honor is involved; surely if Antea had had her will Bellerophon would have succeeded to Proetus' position as well as his queen. In the story of Phoenix (*Iliad* 9.447 ff.) our text furnishes no clear ground for surmising a dynastic issue, and yet Phoenix' sole motive for corrupting his royal father's concubine, as he tells the story, was to confirm his own mother's status. A similar motivation may lie behind Reuben's corruption of Bilhah (Genesis 49.4); Reuben was Jacob's first-born, the son of his senior wife, Leah, and his tribe must have been more powerful than its later position would suggest.

Poets must be expected to adapt the ancient stories they use to their own conceptions, and it is in fact in a historian that we find the triangle which corresponds most closely to the ancient pattern. In the story of Gyges and Candaules' wife (Herodotus 1.8–12) it is the woman who takes the initiative and the issue involves kingship.[6] The lady says, "Receive the kingship of the Lydians which is yours if you take me." We know that Candaules' wife was very beautiful, but her beauty was of no weight in swaying the reluctant Gyges, nor was the lady motivated, so far as we are told, by any consideration other than avenging Candaules' insult. Indeed the phrase which opens the story, "It happened that Candaules was in love with his own wife," seems to indicate surprise if not disapproval of love entering in as a factor in a serious matter.

That the kingship is annexed to the lady appears from the Oedipus story. Oedipus married Jocasta when he had discomfited the Sphinx not because he was ravished by the charms of a woman old enough to be his mother but because marrying her was part and parcel of succeeding to her late husband's position. As Sophocles' play proceeds we see evidence of mutual affection and dependence between the king and queen, but these personal relationships are only incidental means of giving depth to the central story, as is the relationship between Antigone and Haemon in the *Antigone*. No one thinks of the love interest in these plays as central, nor is it central in the *Trachiniae*, where there is rivalry of a sort between two women.

In tragedy the clearest reflection of the ancient triangle pattern is the *Agamemnon* of Aeschylus. Here possession of the lady symbolizes if it does not actually confer kingship, and the junior rival has a quasi-legitimate claim, based on kinship, upon the status he covets. To give the history moral relevance for a fifth-century audience it was obviously necessary to indicate the personal as well as the political relationships between the principal personages. What gives the *Agamemnon* its special interest, from the present point of view, is that in itself it illustrates the transition from political to erotic motivation. In forming their illicit liaison Clytemnestra was motivated by vengeance and Aegisthus by ambition, and these motives are emphasized in the play. But as the play proceeds we see that Clytemnestra trusts Aegisthus and loves him. At lines 1435 and following she speaks of Aegisthus as kindling the fire on her hearth; that only the master of the house had the right to do, and by assigning the function to Aegisthus, Clytemnestra formally bestows lordship upon him. And at line 1654 she addresses him as "best beloved." In the *Choephorae* Electra and her partisans quite understandably emphasize the erotic

ROMANCE
BOURGEOIS —

motivation for Clytemnestra's crime, as at lines 132 and following.
But the definitive assessment of the relative importance of the factors involved is indicated by the intervention of Apollo in the
Eumenides. Regicide is the culmination of political subversiveness,
and it is sound political order which most concerns Apollo. It is
the personal relationships and the individual psychologies of the
persons involved which give the *Agamemnon* its immediacy and
poignancy, but no one in his senses would sum it up as a triangle
play.

It is only when the pitch of tragedy starts its descent from the C. OLD
heroic to the bourgeois, when domestic problems supplant theol- HISTORY
ogy, that we can expect love to displace politics as the dominant
motivation. It was Euripides who began to represent men as they
are instead of as they should be, who clothed the traditional
triangle with individual passions and so made it universally accessible and moving. His *Hippolytus* marks the major turn in the
history of the triangle motif from its origins in pre-history to
modern times. The play is his own invention.[7] The myths the
tragedians quarried from showed no such connection between
Phaedra and Hippolytus as between Clytemnestra and Aegisthus.
For the disparate motifs which Euripides tied together,[8] the body
of legend did, of course, supply suggestions. The Potiphar motif,
which forms a frame for the others, occurs in the Bellerophon
story cited above and in the story of Astydamia and Peleus. The
stepmother motif, which is very widespread, is represented in
Greek by the stories of Demodice and Phrixus, Philonome and
Cycnus, and Damasippe and Hebrus.[9] The chaste hunter who
spurns womankind may be Melanion, whom Aristophanes characterizes in *Frogs* (781 ff.). And to compass Hippolytus' death by
his father's curse he uses the folk motif of the three wishes. If the
fusion of these elements is Euripides' own work, it is remarkable
that he follows the ancient pattern as closely as he does. His doing
so, when his plot does not require it, is proof that it is indeed the
ancient pattern that he had in mind.

In the Argument to our play, which bore the subtitle "Garland-
Bearer" and was presented in 428 B.C., we are told that it is a re-

vision of "unseemly things meriting castigation" in a *Hippolytus* bearing the subtitle "Veiled" which Euripides had presented a few years before. The title *Hippolytus Veiled* is Alexandrian, and proves that the text survived and was studied. It is from the earlier play, as students both of Euripides and of his imitators agree, that the latter derived,[10] and we can tell what the "unseemly things" in *Hippolytus Veiled* were by looking at Ovid's *Heroides*, 4, Seneca's *Phaedra*, and other adaptations and allusions.

Among other details peculiar to the earlier play, as for instance, that the scene was Athens, not Troezen, and that Theseus had gone to Hades with Pirithous, not on a mere festival pilgrimage, there are two of special importance for our inquiry. (1) In the earlier play, as in the Senecan and other versions, Phaedra herself, not a nurse, took the initiative in soliciting Hippolytus, and probably herself used or threatened to use some philter which might prove lethal. Phaedra's illness and the intervention of the nurse as physician and factotum were introduced to make Phaedra less reprehensible. It was probably because of the earlier and more wanton Phaedra that Aristophanes (*Frogs* 1043) makes Aeschylus charge Euripides with bringing "harlots like Phaedra and Stheneboea on the stage." It would be unfair to speak so of the pitiful Phaedra of our play, though it must be confessed that Aristophanes is capable of such unfairness. (2) In the earlier play Phaedra apparently used succession to the kingship as a bait, as she does in Seneca (*Phaedra* 617 ff.) and as her avatar, as we shall see, does elsewhere. A trace of this motif seems to have survived in the extant *Hippolytus*. In defending himself to his father Hippolytus says: "Was it because this woman excelled all other women in beauty of person? Or did I expect to rule your house, attaching myself to a woman that was an heiress?" Phaedra was no longer beautiful, so the logical alternative in Theseus' mind must have been that Hippolytus was impatient to inherit. It is of interest to note, incidentally, that a modern adaptation of the Senecan plot like Racine's *Phèdre* makes the question of succession very important.

Against a fifth-century Athenian background where both factors are inconceivable, it is reasonable to suppose that a tragedian who represents a woman as taking the initiative and offering kingship as an inducement must have consciously followed the ancient paradigm; and avowed imitators who retained the personages and the tragic conventions by which Euripides for all his innovations was still constrained propagated the paradigm. The most characteristic departure of hellenistic imaginative literature is that it descends from the heroic to the bourgeois. New Comedy and Romance are not constrained to draw their personages from the gallery bequeathed by the heroic age, but could invent characters, and therefore actions, freely, and the characters they invent are all middle class. Eventually even the bourgeois love story aspired to a heroic dignity it could never have had in the classical period. *Hero and Leander* (of the fifth century A.D.) starts like a Romance with a boy and girl meeting and falling in love at a festival and then being separated, but instead of prose and a happy ending Musaeus tells his story in hexameters and closes with tragic death.

We should expect, then, that adaptations of the Hippolytus story in the hellenistic age would involve not kings and queens but bourgeois *dramatis personae*, and also that the ending would be not only happy but edifying. Because the personages now bear different names their derivation from Euripides' cast is not obvious at first glance, but closer scrutiny will unmask their true identity under a dozen different guises. This has been shown in a brilliant and utterly convincing study by Martin Braun,[11] who centers his attention on the Joseph-Potiphar's wife story in the Testaments of the Twelve Patriarchs, which is probably the oldest surviving example of the group but which itself probably depends on some intermediate treatment.

The Testaments of the Twelve Patriarchs consists of a series of deathbed discourses imagined to have been delivered in turn by the sons of Jacob to their descendants. Whether, as the preponderance of scholarly opinion holds, the work was written in Hebrew in the second century B.C. and interpolated by Chris

tians,[12] or whether it was written in Greek in the second century
A.D. by Christians who used much older Jewish materials,[13] the
portion of concern to us is surely of pre-Christian origin.[14]

Chapters 3–9 of the Testament of Joseph is an expansion of the
story of Joseph and Potiphar's wife as told in Genesis (39.7–15).
Except for devotional parentheses the added material is derived, as
has been conclusively demonstrated by Braun, from the *Hippolytus* of Euripides, and indeed from the earlier rather than the
later version. Proof rests on the fact that motifs which belong to
the Phaedra legend are included though they are wholly inap-
propriate to the Joseph story. An ingenuous lad might initially
mistake the meaning of a stepmother's caresses, but how could
Joseph, who was adult and not a stepson, be so obtuse? And could
the Egyptian offer Joseph dominion over her establishment when
her husband (solicitous of her health, as in the later Apuleius and
Heliodorus versions) was alive and well? Could a slave threaten
to denounce his mistress when there were no witnesses to corroborate his charge? Could a woman in a polygamous society be
deterred from suicide by being reminded that her successor might
beat her children? In any case, suicide for so sentimental a reason
as disappointed love is unintelligible in the framework of Biblical
literature. And when Joseph adduces the welfare of the children
as an argument against suicide the Egyptian seizes upon his concern as proof that he really loves her, and the author supplies a
psychological observation on the propensity of the love-smitten
to believe what they wish were true—a passage as characteristic
of hellenistic erotic writings as it is unimaginable in the Bible.
With the obvious adaptations of the Phaedra legend in hand we
can surmise that other motifs not so ill-fitting also derive from the
same source; for example, the Egyptian sends Joseph drugged
food, and shams illness. The fact that these same motifs recur in
the Romances and other erotic literature merely shows how
familiar the material was, and reinforces the suggestion that some
intermediate retelling of the story was responsible for the proliferation of its motifs throughout the hellenistic world.[15]

A longer but less complete version of the Joseph story is that in

Josephus, *Antiquities* (2.39–59). Josephus expands five verses into five pages, and fills most of them with rhetorical speeches which dilute the dramatic tension. But his full use of the Phaedra material is palpable, and an earlier study by Martin Braun [16] (whose theme here is the relationship between hellenistic historiography and fiction) shows that almost every clause has recognizable affinities with hellenistic fiction. Josephus must certainly come into consideration as a transmitter of the Phaedra material to later ages.

In later adaptations of the story, particularly in the Romances, the young man's motive for rejecting the temptress is loyalty to a wife or sweetheart; in the Joseph story, whether in the Testaments or Josephus, it is loyalty to a religious principle. Hellenization doubtless brought with it such institutions as *hetairai* and a general relaxation of old standards of sexual morality which alarmed the defenders of religion and is reflected in a new concern with emphasizing the importance of sexual morality. This concern appears not only in other of the Testaments and in rabbinic writings but notably in St. Paul and all Christian teachers east and west (Jerome is a striking case) until the final victory of Christianity. Joseph was always the model of the spiritual athlete who resisted sore temptation, and these versions of his story doubtless did much to fix the plot in western civilization. But it should be noticed that even in Euripides Hippolytus is motivated not by loyalty to a sweetheart but out of religious principle. Indeed Hippolytus goes farther in insisting on total abstinence for religious reasons. In Genesis it is breach of trust, not necessarily carnality, which Joseph gives as the reason for his refusal (39.9): "There is none greater in this house than I; neither hath he kept back anything from me but thee, because thou art his wife: how then can I do this great wickedness and sin against God?"

It may well be that it was the religiously motivated chastity of Hippolytus that made him particularly attractive to Jews and Christians. In the ordinary hellenistic development of his as of other classical stories we should expect that the original religious burden would have faded and perhaps be replaced by some new ethical content; and we shall find that this is the case. But where a religious motivation of a different order is attached to the story we may legitimately suspect the effects of east-west fusion.

For a quite secular version of the complete Phaedra story reduced to a bourgeois level we turn to Apuleius (*Metamorphosis* 10.2–12). The passionate stepmother, the ingenuous stepson, the woman's solicitation during a siege of love-sickness, her vengeance for a rebuff by charging that the young man had made an attempt upon her virtue are all there. Now instead of a nurse, it is the solicitous husband or doctor who fail to diagnose the illness. Apuleius gives the story an interesting sequel. It is when the ingenuous lad is paying a duty call on his sick stepmother that she makes her shocking proposal, and in her chagrin at his eluding her she has a poison prepared for him. When her own son takes the potion by mistake she accuses the stepson of having made an attempt upon her, of having threatened her with a sword when she repulsed him, and then of having vengefully killed her own child. Instigated by his wicked wife, the unfortunate father pleads with the authorities to condemn his son unheard, and the son is saved only at the last moment by the testimony of a respected physician whom the woman had retained to prepare the poison but who had prepared a soporific instead. When the coffin was opened the boy was just awakening from his drugged sleep. The supposed death of the younger brother and the "premature burial" motif—which occurs repeatedly in the Romances [17] and survives in *Romeo and Juliet*—are added on in keeping with the new standards of erotic tales and to make a deft connection with Apuleius' next episode; they do not affect the first part, which is derived from the Phaedra legend.

Adaptations in Greek are more numerous. The completest and most artistic is the episode of Demaenete and Cnemon in Heliodorus' *Ethiopica* (1.9–14). As in the case of Apuleius the personages here are upper middle class, not royalty; and Heliodorus outdoes Apuleius in providing circumstantial detail to promote verisimilitude. But the story is that of the earlier Hippolytus with elaborations now grown customary: the ingenuous lad does not at first suspect his stepmother's affection, she feigns sickness which

wins the credulity of the solicitous husband, she threatens the boy
with mischief, she uses a trick to lend color to her charge that he
had sought to corrupt her, and (as in Apuleius) the husband begs
the authorities to condemn his son unheard. The eventual trap-
ping and punishment of Demaenete is a new touch, but this we
should expect of a moralizer like Heliodorus.

But we also have moralization expressly based on religious sanctions. The best example is Philostratus' *Life of Apollonius of
Tyana* (6.3) which, as we shall see, is our best example of a pagan
aretalogy.[18] When the stepmother whose advances he had rejected
calumniates him to his father, the chaste youth in this version
leaves home to become a boatman on the Nile, but neither preens
himself on his virtue nor descends to cynicism. Despite his experience he continues to offer daily sacrifice to Aphrodite, and
when he is introduced to Apollonius he protests that "there is no
particular credit in having abstained from wrong."

So indeed, to a lesser degree, is religion involved in the several
parallels in the Greek Romances other than the episode of Demaenete and Cnemon mentioned above; Cnemon is not Heliodorus'
hero but only a foil to make Theagenes' virtue shine brighter. But
the chaste heroes of the Romances are regularly solicited, naturally in vain, by women who have power to threaten—in Heliodorus himself Theagenes is tormented by Arsace, the viceroy's
wife (7.4, 9); in Xenophon of Ephesus Habrocomes is solicited
by one master's daughter, Manto (2.3 ff.), and by another master's wife, Cyno (3.12), who kills her husband to make way for
Habrocomes and then accuses him of the murder when he eludes
her; and there are similar episodes in Chariton and Achilles Tatius.
In most of these cases, and most notably in Xenophon of Ephesus,[19] the deliverance of the sore-tried heroine is directly connected with devout prayer offered to a tutelary deity.

One final ancient version of the story, involving the traditional
personae of stepmother, husband and father, stepson, wise physician, and even the question of succession to the throne, shows
how the religious and secular motivations might merge and in
their merged form affect history. This is the story, accepted as

historical by a number of authors,[20] of Antiochus, son of Seleucus I, who fell in love with his young and beautiful stepmother. The lady, in accordance with the refined sensibilities of the age, is completely innocent; and even the young man who is, quite properly again, the one to be affected, scrupulously refrains from transgression though the relationship affords him such opportunities as the *Heroides* 4 and Apuleius versions point out. He falls sick and is carried tight-lipped to the very brink of death when he is saved by the intervention of a wise physician, who persuades the father, through a ruse, to divorce his wife and yield her to his son, who is a more suitable mate.

It is true that Antiochus' abstinence seems to be motivated mainly by loyalty to his loving father, but his gentleness and his self-sacrificing adherence to his ideal has something of the saintly about it; and here we may recognize the same kind of influence which gave new shape to the Biblical story of Joseph. Here each of the four persons concerned shows tenderest consideration of the others; the whole story is bathed in the gentler love of understanding and benevolence. Tragic passion has been broken to harness and made serviceable to a morality which Europe has accepted as its norm. Whether any part of the new gentleness and the new esteem in which chastity was held derived from the east is problematical. The new note introduced into Greek love lyric by Meleager, it has been observed,[21] might be explained as heightened sensibility at tension with a heightened reverence for chastity, and it is precisely the same tension which gives the Antiochus story its special character. And the Antiochus version of the Hippolytus story had its own progeny. Paul Wendland has shown that the story in its entirety probably lies back of the elder Seneca's *Controversiae* 6.7, and mentions a number of Christian stories where its outlines may be discerned.[22]

The Phaedra story, in the form Euripides had given it, was particularly suited to hellenistic interests and therefore its fortunes are easy to trace, but Phaedra was by no means the only tragic heroine whose erotic adventures interested later ages. In a diatribe against women a character in Achilles Tatius lists the women of tragedy who brought calamity upon men (1.8), naming not only Phaedra and Clytemnestra, but Chryseis, Penelope, Aerope, Eriphyle, Stheneboea, and significantly the wife of Candaules, whom we have cited as the keystone of the classic triangle. Fragments of a hitherto unknown tragedy on Gyges and Candaules' wife were published in 1950; the fact that no ancient author mentions such a tragedy only goes to show how much we do not know about Greek literary history. The first editor and the early critics maintained that the tragedy belongs to the middle of the fifth century B.C., and it has been suggested that the tragedy was actually the source of Herodotus' account (1.8–13), which reads like the synopsis of a play. But sound arguments for bringing the date down as low as the third century have also been adduced.[23] If that is so, we should have a hellenistic reworking of an old story such as has been posited for the Phaedra story, and such as may be posited for other traditional stories.

Whether or not the west learned about love from the east, it seems probable that the east learned from the west not only plots of love stories but something about the literary form appropriate to discourse about love. Of this there is evidence in the Song of Songs, which is a canonical book of the Bible. The close affinity which subsists between erotic and religious lyric utterance has made it easy to allegorize the Song of Songs, and it is on the basis of allegorization (the lovers are God and Israel or Christ and the Church) that the book is made acceptable to various religious communions. But it is significant that its canonicity was disputed as late as the second century A.D., and today no critical scholar believes that it was originally intended as allegory. What it was intended as is difficult to determine. It is neither a unified lyric nor a drama, as has been maintained by various critics, but rather a congeries of lyrics, some twenty-five in number. According to the prevailing view, these are all connected with certain Semitic marriage usages, where festivities continue for a week and the bride

and groom are celebrated in song as a king and queen. Whatever
their occasion, the Song does consist of a collection of lyrics all
concerned with the theme of love.

And however ancient the usage of celebrating lovers in song
may be, it is clear from philological evidence that this collection
belongs to the hellenistic period. *Appiryon* (3.9) is the Greek
phoreion, meaning "palanquin" or "bedstead," and *pardes* is the
Greek *paradeisos*, "park," though that word may have come
directly from the Persian as the Greek word did. The relative *she-*
instead of *asher* is a sign of late date. So low a date makes hellenistic influence possible, and as early as the seventeenth century
some scholars (including the redoubtable Grotius) have thought
that the lyrics were eclogues or pastorals in the hellenistic manner.
A recent study by Dr. M. Rozelaar, an Israeli scholar,[24] provides
tangible proofs for thinking that they in fact are.

The main obstacle to perceiving literary influence is the assumption that the imagery which the Song applies to landscape or
persons is natural and inevitable, and European pastoral poets do
in fact employ similar imagery. But the European poets have
themselves consciously imitated, through Vergil's *Eclogues*, the
same hellenistic poets who may well have influenced the poet of
the Song. Actually, even if we invoke Jung's collective unconscious to explain diffusion of literary motifs, no "natural" reason
will explain the use of identical motifs in the pastoral poetry of
diverse peoples. Unlike other literary forms, where we can trace
development step by step, pastoral was an *invention* of the hellenistic age, and wholly artificial. Perhaps it was suggested by
misunderstanding of such ancient productions as the Homeric
Hymn to Demeter, which, like much in Theocritus, has the character of a masque, with a rustic landscape, country names, and a
goddess masquerading as a nursemaid. Vergil and Sannazaro and
Spenser and other later writers of pastoral present landscapes like
Theocritus' because they learned from him, directly or indirectly;
and if we find the same kind of landscapes in the Song of Songs
there is a presumption that its author too learned from the The-
ocritean tradition.

The fullest and most familiar pastoral that has come down to us is Longus' *Daphnis and Chloe*. It may be as late as the third century and it is in prose, but it is indubitably in the main line of the pastoral tradition. The description of the garden in Longus (2.3–4, cited below at p. 217) with its varied fruits and flowers and running water is a regular feature of pastoral, and the white and ruddy boy playing in the garden is familiar as the Eros who is sometimes represented against a rustic background in hellenistic sculpture.[25] In Song of Songs (4.12–15) we read:

A garden inclosed is my sister, my spouse; a spring shut up, a fountain sealed. Thy plants are an orchard of pomegranates, with pleasant fruits; camphire with spikenard, spikenard and saffron; calamus and cinnamon, with all trees of frankincense; myrrh and aloes, with all the chief spices: a fountain of gardens, a well of living waters, and streams from Lebanon.

The "white and ruddy" lover who is invited to "come into his garden and eat his pleasant fruits" is very like Longus' Eros. It is true that Longus' seems to be an actual garden whereas the garden at Canticles describes a person; but hellenistic poetry used similar imagery to describe the beloved. Here is Polyphemus' address to Galatea, adapted by Ovid (*Metamorphoses* 13.789 ff.) from Theocritus' eleventh idyll:

O Galatea, fairer than the leaf of the snow-white privet, more blooming than the meadows, more slender than the tall alder, brighter than grass, more wanton than the tender kid, smoother than the shells worn by continuous floods, more pleasing than the winter's sun or than the summer's shade, more beauteous than the apples, more sightly than the lofty plane tree, clearer than ice, sweeter than the ripened grape, softer than the down of the swan and than curdled milk, and, didst thou not fly me, more beauteous than a watered garden.[26]

Polyphemus goes on (13.811 ff.) to describe his grotto and the apples and the gold and purple grapes growing there. These he is laying up for Galatea. The swain's offer is like the lover's in Canticles (7.13): "The mandrakes give a smell, and at our gates are all manner of pleasant fruits, new and old, which I have laid up for thee, O my beloved."

In the Fugitive Love of Moschus (second century B.C.) Cypris offers a reward for the return of the runaway, and provides a description (1.6 ff.):

He is a very noticeable lad, you would know him among twenty: complexion not white but rather like to fire; eyes keen and beaming; a naughty disposition but fair spoken, for what he thinks and says are not the same—his voice is of honey, his mind gall . . . his locks are abundant, his forehead bold.

The Shunamite too complains of a fugitive (5.6): "I sought him but I could not find him; I called him but he gave me no answer." And her appeal to the daughters of Jerusalem to help her search affords an occasion, as does Aphrodite's advertisement, to describe the lover (5.9–16):

What is thy beloved more than another beloved, O thou fairest among women? what is thy beloved more than another beloved, that thou dost so charge us? My beloved is white and ruddy, the chiefest among ten thousand. His head is as the most fine gold; his locks are bushy, and black as a raven. His eyes are as the eyes of doves by the rivers of waters. . . .

And so on, till the inventory is complete. Neither of the descriptions is of a kind issued by the Missing Persons Bureau; in both the sole object of the search is to afford an occasion for celebrating the lover.

The human form being relatively constant, it is to be expected that lovers the world over would find the same features of the beloved ravishing; but the modes for expressing their ravishment need not be the same. They are not indeed the same in Canticles and in the epigrams of the *Palatine Anthology*, but their similarity seems more than accidental. Here are inventories of female charms from the *Anthology*, first by Rufinus (5.47):

Golden are her eyes and her cheeks like crystal, and her mouth more delightful than a red rose. Her neck is of marble and her bosom polished; her feet are whiter than silver Thetis'.[27]

In Canticles 4.3–5 we have:

Thy lips are like a thread of scarlet, and thy speech is comely; thy temples are like a piece of pomegranate within thy locks. Thy neck is

like the tower of David builded for an armory, whereon there hang
a thousand bucklers, all shields of mighty men. Thy two breasts are
like two young roes that are twins, which feed among the lilies.

These descriptions start at the top and move downward; in the
fuller and more detailed inventory in Canticles (7.1–7) the order
is reversed—feet, thighs, navel, belly, breasts, neck, nose, eyes,
head, hair. But an equally vivid piece by Philodemus (5.132) follows the same order and includes the same features.

From descriptions we pass to the imagery of action. It is a commonplace of Greek erotic poetry to speak of lovemaking as gathering the vintage or other fruit and of kissing as sipping nectar
or honey. Here are examples from the *Anthology* (5.227 and
5.305):

Thee, the rosy-armed, the crown of my devotion, I hold enchained in
the gentle knot of my arms, and gather the vintage of love.

A girl kissed me in the evening with wet lips. The kiss was nectar, for
her mouth smelt sweet of nectar; and I am drunk with the kiss, I have
drunk love in abundance.

More usually it is honey that the beloved's lips drop, as in 5.32 and
5.244. And so it is in Canticles 4.11:

Thy lips, O my spouse, drop as the honey-comb; honey and milk are
under thy tongue.

And surely the vintage figure underlies Canticles 5.1:

I have eaten my honey-comb with my honey; I have drunk my wine
with my milk.

There are subtler parallels in the use of tropes. When 5.270 in
the Anthology speaks of the "honeyed harmony of thy breasts,"
we are uncertain, as we are meant to be, whether the perspiration
of passion may not be intended; and it is so when the Shunamite
fumbles with her lock (4.5) "and my hands dropped with myrrh."
A word used with one meaning in one line will be repeated in the
next with new meaning, for example (Canticles 1.6) "They made
me keeper of the vineyards; mine own vineyard I have not kept";
or (2.15) "the little foxes that spoil the vines; our vines have tender
grapes." The same usage can be paralleled in the Greek (e.g.,

Palatine Anthology 5.143 and 144, both by Meleager, and 5.90).

And finally, notice should be taken of a striking parallel in structure. The song which Thyrsis sings in Theocritus' first *Idyll* uses the refrain "Begin, dear Muses, begin a country song," but at irregular intervals and sometimes with a word or two changed. The refrain does not divide the song into strophes, and is made to fit syntactically into the context. Bion's *Lament for Adonis* follows the same practice. "Weep for Adonis, the Loves are lamenting" (in Mrs. Browning's version) is repeated, with slight changes, at irregular intervals. Canticles exhibits the same phenomenon, which indeed points to the division between the separate lyrics in the poem. In the first the refrain at 2.7—"I charge you, O ye daughters of Jerusalem, by the roes and by the hinds of the field, that ye stir not up nor awake my love till he please"—is repeated verbatim at 3.5. But it is varied at 5.8—"I charge you, O daughters of Jerusalem, if ye find my beloved, that ye tell him that I am sick of love"—and again at 8.4—"I charge you, O daughters of Jerusalem, that ye stir not up nor awake my love till he please." Another series is composed of 2.16—"My beloved is mine and I am his; he feedeth among the lilies"—which is slightly altered at 6.3 and 7.10. A third series is made up of 2.17, "Until the day break and the shadows flee away," along with 4.6 and 8.14.

It may be that the physiological reactions of the lover in the presence of his beloved are always as Sappho's masterpiece describes them, that all lovers think of kisses as dropping honey, and even that all lovers strive to celebrate the features of the beloved in beautiful and striking language; but sophisticated literary devices must be learned, and it would appear the poet of Canticles learned his from the Greeks. He was not a devout man, in the ordinary sense; the only time he uses the word God is when he speaks of the heat of jealousy (8.6) as, literally, "a flame of God,"—which the Authorized Version correctly translates "a most vehement flame." But he was a Hebrew poet, not a Greek, and his knowledge of Greek poetic modes therefore indicates the degree of hellenization among people who did not hellenize in the literal sense of "speaking Greek."

If writers of Hebrew knew hellenistic erotic poetry and a devout moralist could adapt the Phaedra legend, probably in a hellenistic retelling, in order to make the Joseph story more edifying, it would be likely that original stories embodying the new knowledge might be produced, at least for edification. One example of particular interest in our context is the book of Judith in the Apocrypha, of which the extant Greek is a translation of a Hebrew original.

In brief the story of Judith is as follows. Nebuchadnezzar, angered by insubordination of subject peoples, dispatches Holofernes with numberless forces to subdue all the peoples to the west. Most submitted at once, but the Israelites, recently returned from their captivity, prayerfully prepared to resist. An Ammonite leader named Achior warned Holofernes that God would help the Israelites; Holofernes angrily thrust him from the camp, and the Israelites received him kindly into their stronghold at Bethulia. Holofernes cut off Bethulia's water supply, and after severe suffering the people made their leaders promise to capitulate if no deliverance came in five days. The rich and pious widow Judith lectures the leaders on their lack of faith, prays at length, changes her sackcloth for elegant attire, and goes to the enemy camp, taking permissible food with her in a bag. She remains as Holofernes' guest for three days, eating her own food, however, and going out to pray. On the fourth evening he arranges an elaborate feast, with transparent intentions, but when the two are left alone he is heavy with wine. Judith cuts his head off, puts it in her lunch bag, and returns to her own people. At the sight of it Achior is converted, and Judith raises a hymn of thanksgiving. Discomfited by the loss of their leader, Holofernes' host is easily defeated. Judith resumes her sackcloth, rejects many offers of marriage, and dies highly respected at the age of 105.

The efforts which have been made over the years to make Judith's hopeless chronology and geography jibe with history were foredoomed to failure; the book is plainly a romance and bears no more relation to history than do the oriental potentates and their campaigns in Chariton or Heliodorus. In date the book

cannot be older than the Maccabean period, if only because passages like 3.8 and 6.2 clearly reflect the measures of Antiochus
Epiphanes; "Who is god but Nebuchadnezzar?" could not have
been written earlier. Indeed the militant and religiously inspired
nationalism, the fact the heroine's name is the feminine of Judah,
the high importance attached to the observance of dietary rules,
and in general the resounding success won by individual prowess
and prayer against an overwhelming force, all seem to suit the
temper and needs of the Maccabean struggle. But they would suit
the struggle against the Romans as well, and it would be perfectly
natural for the author to recall the atmosphere of the earlier and
now classic struggle, as was done, for example, by the author of
IV Maccabees. Long ago Renan suggested that Judith was intended
as a criticism of Berenice, who consented to be mistress of her
people's executioner Titus, and the suggestion has recently been
developed, but with no real cogency, by E. Mireaux.[28] But the
most convincing argument in favor of Greek influence does not
depend upon a late dating.

The Greeks too had a story of a divinely favored community
which was attacked by a powerful oriental tyrant who cut their
water supply off until there was barely enough for five days, and
which was then saved by miraculous intervention. Here is the
story as it was inscribed on stone, along with other sacred records,
at the temple at Lindus: [29]

When Darius, King of Persia, sent forth a great army for the purpose of
enslaving Hellas, this island was the first which his fleet visited. The
people of the country were terrified at the approach of the Persians and
fled for safety to all the strongholds, most of them gathering at Lindus.
Thereupon the barbarians set about to besiege them, until the Lindians,
sore-pressed by a water shortage, were minded to hand over the city
to the enemy. Right at this juncture the goddess stood over one of the
magistrates in his sleep and bade him be of good courage, since she
herself would procure, by intercession with her father, the water they
needed. The one who saw the vision rehearsed to the citizens Athena's
command. So they investigated and found that they had only enough
water to last for five days, and accordingly they asked the barbarians
for a truce for just that number of days, saying that Athena had sent

to her father for help, and that if help did not come in the specified time they would surrender the city. . . . When Datis, the admiral of Darius, heard this request, he immediately burst out laughing. But the next day, when a great cloud gathered about the Acropolis and a heavy shower fell inside the cloud, so that contrary to all expectations the besieged had plenty of water, while the Persian army suffered for lack of it, the barbarian was struck by the epiphany of the goddess. He took off his personal adornment and sent it as an offering—his mantle, his necklace, and his bracelets, and in addition his tiara, his scimitar, and even his chariot, which formerly was preserved here, but was burned along with most of the offerings in the priesthood of Halius Eucles, son of Astyanactidas [probably soon after 350 B.C.] when the temple caught fire. As for Datis, he set forth on the business before him, after establishing peace with the besieged and declaring publicly, "These men are protected by the gods."

The inscription closes by citing six historians, mentioning book numbers, in which the events were recorded. The date of the inscription is 99 B.C.; the tradition it records is indubitably very much older, so that it is plainly impossible for it to have been influenced by the Hebrew original of Judith. On the other hand, it is hard not to believe that the stories are somehow connected, and if that is the case then even without the chronological factor Judith is clearly a barbarization, ethically and artistically, of the Greek story, not the other way around.

The classic paradigm for the unexpected deliverance of a small and righteous people from the attack of an arrogant and overwhelmingly powerful invader is the story of the invasion and repulse of Xerxes as told in Herodotus and repeatedly echoed in later writers. The first part of Lucian's treatise on *How History Should be Written* shows that Herodotus was much imitated by later writers who took the wildest liberties with geography (as Judith does), and there can be little question that our author too had his eye on Herodotus. The first section communicates a sense of the king's enormous wealth and power, his wrath at being crossed, his council, his long preparations which put the whole world into turmoil, and then the massive and seemingly irresistible movement of the huge armament. All of this echoes Herodotus' account of Xerxes' analogous steps in his seventh book. Some of Herodotus' phraseology—the clearest example is "earth and water" as a token of submission (2.7)—has come through even in translation. The description of the palace at Ecbatana with which Judith begins is in itself revealing. When the careful Polybius comes to speak of this structure (10.27.8) he notes specifically that it was a great favorite with writers who wished to exaggerate and astonish. Clearly the author of Judith is in the tradition of romantic historiography.

The writers of romance proper took over the practices of the hellenistic historians but made their "history" the vehicle for erotic adventure. The author of Judith does the same, except that his erotic matter is not so skillfully mortised into his history. The unevenness in the composition of Judith, and in particular in the second part where the heroine (the surrogate of the Lindian Athena) plays her role, are due to unskillful adaptation of the modes of another literature. At every turn we are reminded of familiar hellenistic motifs, and though individual instances may represent natural and universal commonplaces, their accumulation suggests literary dependence. When the heroine of a story is a widow it may be natural to speak of her as rich and wise as well as handsome and yet as being respected for her chastity, but it is nevertheless noticeable that the widowed heroines in Greek stories are praised in the same terms. Plutarch, for example, in *Amatorius* 2, has the following: "At Thespiae there lived a lady called Ismenodora, rich and well born, who had led an exemplary life, by Zeus; she had lived as a widow for no small space without reproach, though she was young and made a good appearance." [30] In the same treatise Plutarch tells of a chaste widow named Camma who used her beauty to entice an enemy to his death. Stories of chaste women who are not widows who kill their would-be ravishers are numerous, and so are descriptions of women who prink themselves out to impress a man for one reason or another. An odd circumstance in the Judith story is that Holofernes waited so long when Judith was apparently in his power. In Heliodorus Chariclea puts impetuous Thyamis off by a religious plea, and is indeed saved by divine intervention. In Xenophon of Ephesus Anthia is bedizened by her owner for the specific purpose of enticing men, but saves herself by pretending illness. Perhaps we are meant to infer, from the special mention of bath and toilette on the eve of the fateful party, that Judith had previously pleaded ritual impurity. On the other hand, in the atmosphere Judith's murder of Holofernes comes as something of a shock; in Xenophon of Ephesus, Anthia does despatch a would-be ravisher, but she was alone and helpless in her prison-cave and had not given her attacker encouragement. The model of the heroic woman who killed her people's enemy when he put himself in her power is of course the Biblical Jael, but Jael did not herself create the occasion and her story has no breath of the characteristically hellenistic erotic titillation. What makes the Judith story awkward is the mixed atmosphere of piety and license; the erotic has come in, and shows its leering face despite the author's efforts to smother it in piety. If the constraints of the religious motivation (in itself admirable) are removed, the story would spring back into the pattern of Greek romance. Yet despite the critic's sense of inconcinnity between the erotic and pious strands, Judith remains an example of fusion; certainly the Renaissance artists who painted Judith saw her in one piece.

Chapter XIII

ARETALOGIES AND
MARTYRDOMS .

IN sophisticated Roman authors the word *aretalogus* denotes a professional reciter of wordy and incredible stories. So when Augustus entertained friends at dinner, Suetonius tells us (*Augustus* 74), "he introduced music and actors or even strolling players from the circus and especially aretalogi." We learn a little more about what cultured Romans thought of aretalogi from a passage in Juvenal's Egyptian satire (15.13 ff.): "When Ulysses told a tale like this [of cannibalism] over the dinner table to the amazed Alcinous he stirred some to wrath, some perhaps to laughter, as a lying aretalogus." The passage goes on to list the impossibilities in Ulysses' narrative and then adds: "Did he deem the Phaeacian people so devoid of brains? . . . The Ithacan's tale was all his own with none to bear him witness." For his own story Juvenal provides a precise time and place. We shall see that Ulysses' narrative is elsewhere cited as a typical aretalogy by those who depreciate the form, and that the aretalogist usually supplied assurances of veracity, mock or real, in the form of oaths, witnesses, or date.

But even in the Romans there are hints that aretalogies could be serious. So Porphyry, glossing the name Crispinus in Horace (*Sermones* 1.1.20), says: "Plotius Crispinus was a student of philosophy; he also wrote poems, but so voluble (*tam garrule*) that he was called an aretalogus." The interesting point here is that a student of philosophy could also be an aretalogus. In his *On Poetry* (24, Jensen) Philodemus of Gadara, who may have been

Horace's teacher and was himself a writer of Cynic diatribes, equates the aretalogist with the writer of mimes; the mime, in the hellenistic age, was a serious study of morals, and writers of mimes were in fact called "biologists," or students of life. We learn more of the serious aspect of the aretalogist from the Bobbio Scholia on the Juvenal passage: "Aretalogi tell of miraculous deeds, which is to say *virtutes* [= *aretas*]." This is in keeping with the meaning of the word attested from the fourth century B.C. down: [1] originally an aretalogist was a kind of evangelist who proved the stature of a deity or holy man by reciting his miraculous works. So a slave in Terence (*Adelphi* 535, based on Menander) says: "I shall make him think you a god; I shall recite your *virtutes*." The original sense of the word is shown by the usage of the Septuagint, where "to speak the wonders of God" is regularly rendered by *aretas legein*, literally "to speak the virtues." [2] Aretalogus, then, is "one who (professionally) speaks the wondrous deeds of a deity," and *aretalogia* is the discourse he delivers.

It is clear that the derogatory sense which the Romans attached to the aretalogus was the development of a rationalist and aristocratic society, when many religious teachers might in fact have become charlatans and mountebanks who appealed only to the mob. One might compare the lewd and unprincipled impostors who posed as priests of Isis in the eighth book of Apuleius (24–31) with the truly reverent attitude to the genuine cult in the eleventh book. The phenomenon of the secularization of originally religious forms is common enough in Greek literature and art. Hymns or statues or drama originally religious lose their serious burden as beliefs change but their forms are retained for their aesthetic value, and those who practice these forms may be unaware that they ever had deeper meaning. From Callimachus' hymns it appears certain that he never realized that the so-called Homeric Hymns were part of a solemn ritual; the Alexandrian Pleiad and even Seneca saw only stark passion or prettiness in classical tragedy; and Theocritus apparently thought that the author of the Homeric Hymn to Demeter was only trying to offer, with less sophistication and virtuosity, the same kind of entertainment as he was himself offering in his Idylls. Actually, though the word aretalogy is probably not earlier than the fourth century, the thing it describes must be very much older; the greater Homeric Hymns are in effect themselves aretalogies.

In the classical period the thing and its name went into desuetude, and it is easy to see why; but in the spiritual chaos and searchings of the hellenistic age it acquired a new vogue, at first, doubtless, among the more susceptible lower classes, but then in the hands of people who called themselves philosophers. Their ultimate models were the genuine philosophers of the hellenistic age, Cynics and Stoics and Epicureans, who centered their efforts upon improving the spiritual welfare of men and whose teachings therefore inevitably took on a homiletic tinge. In the case of Epicurus in particular the personality of the founder became an object of special reverence. Not only were his writings cherished as a kind of scripture but for centuries his birthday was solemnly celebrated and his portrait displayed and even carried about. The attitude of convinced Epicureans towards their founder approached that of a religious communion to its first prophet,[3] and his real qualities were exaggerated to a kind of saintliness. The same tendency manifests itself elsewhere. In the literature of the Alexandrian Jews, as we have seen, Moses occupies a much more exalted position than he does in Palestinian literature, and Artapanus' account of him is in effect an aretalogy. The circumstances which produced these phenomena, and the esteem in which figures like Epicurus or Moses were held, inevitably called forth imitation. The careers of other teachers were dramatized and beatified, by themselves or by their followers, in order to enhance their credit and lend force to their teachings. They did in fact acquire large followings, at first among humbler classes but eventually among the respectable, though always there were rational minds who decried them and their works. Our best reflection of the kind of attraction the aretalogies exerted and the kind of resistance they met with on the part of rationalists is offered by a series of criticisms and parodies in Lucian.

In his *Philopseudes* Lucian professes himself baffled by the psychological and religious puzzle: Why are serious people interested in lies about miracles, why the sick yearning to invent them and to clothe them with circumstantial proofs of veracity, why is the disease so infectious? The first miraculous tale Lucian recounts is of a man bitten by a deadly snake (11–12). The man, already putrefying, was healed by a Babylonian who used an incantation, which included seven names out of a sacred book, and a splinter of stone chipped from the tomb of a virgin. The victim himself took up his bed and walked. The Babylonian summoned all the serpents in the area, including one old one who was slow to come, and then caused them to be consumed by blowing upon them. These "facts" were attested by eyewitnesses. This story probably originated with some snake charmer, but it was widely diffused and has left many echoes.[4] The *Philopseudes* contains three other tales of remarkable exorcisms, involving ghosts rather than snakes, again with circumstantial details to lend verisimilitude.

Indirectly Lucian's best-known work, his *True History*, is also criticism of aretalogies. He starts by complaining of the monstrous lies told by Ctesias in his work on India, by Iambulus in his *Oceanica*, and by other writers of travel books which, like Iambulus', were in fact utopias,[5] and then says: "The originator and teacher of this foolishness is the Homeric Odysseus, entertaining Alcinous' court with his prisoned winds, his men one-eyed or wild or cannibal, his beasts with many heads, and his metamorphosed comrades; the Phaeacians were simple folk, and so he could tell them these miraculous tales." Juvenal too had made Odysseus at Alcinous' court the prime example for his lying aretalogus, and perhaps he and Lucian derive from a common work critical of aretalogies. What the *True History* parodies is not the aretalogy proper but the utopian travel books he mentions in his preface; but the utopias were themselves a development of the aretalogy.

The most memorable episode in the *True History* is its hero's

adventures in the belly of the whale, and this inevitably recalls
Jonah in the Old Testament. The curious thing about the book
of Jonah is that it conforms so well to the pattern of the aretalogy.
Unlike the prophetic books with which it is grouped, it does not
record Jonah's discourses (except for the quoted psalmlike prayer
at 2–3.10) but tells his career. Now a Jonah, son of Amittai, is
mentioned at II Kings 14.25 as a prophet under Jeroboam II
(786–746 B.C.), and our book is placed beside those of the eighth-
century prophets; but there can be no doubt that it belongs to
the hellenistic age.[6] The eponymous hero of Daniel similarly belongs to the sixth century, but the book of Daniel is positively
dated to 164 B.C. The absolute universalism of Jonah, so directly
opposed to the particularism of Ezra, for example, gives it a definitely Stoic coloring. Jonah's career, the wonderful things that
befell him and their lesson, is exactly in the mode of the aretalogy.
Whether or not the stories of a man inside a big fish stem from a
common source, it seems that the literary modes do have a more
than accidental affinity.

Lucian has a number of wonder-working itinerant missionaries
whose marvelous careers and ultimate transfigurations he recounts,
of course with utter skepticism. One is dealt with in his *Peregrinus*.
After many adventures, including an insincere conversion to
Christianity, Peregrinus, surnamed Proteus, came to Alexandria,
where he practiced Cynic austerities, shaving his head on one
side and smearing his face with dirt. Among other mountebank
tricks, he allowed his auditors to beat his buttocks with a stick. He
went to Rome, whence he was expelled for reviling the emperor.
He closed his career by immolating himself on a lighted pyre.
Peregrinus is represented by Lucian as being a thorough hypocrite,
driven only by a lust for notoriety.

The piece on *Alexander of Abonutichos*, the oracle-monger,
is more thoughtful, for it explains how popular hopes and fears
make such an impostor possible and successful. Furthermore,
whereas we may suspect that Peregrinus was himself fooled by his
pretensions, Alexander is a hard-headed operator who studies
the psychology of his victims, skillfully uses prophecies after the

event, and tries blackmail where possible. His masquerade was exposed when in his last illness the physician had to remove his wig to treat his head.

From these and other writings of Lucian we sense widespread yearnings for certainty and salvation in a world where all land-marks had disappeared, when men felt helpless and alone and unsheltered. Charlatans and impostors to exploit men's longings there must have been in abundance, and the objects of Lucian's satire doubtless deserved his excoriation. But surely the charlatans could not have flourished if there were not also honest men who felt themselves called to help their fellows and who spent them-selves generously in their efforts to do so. One of these was Apol-lonius of Tyana, who lived in the first century A.D. Apollonius too comes in for unfavorable mention in Lucian (in the *Alexan-der*). He was attacked as a wizard and a charlatan in a lost work by a contemporary called Euphrates and his work was depreciated in a book about him by a certain Moeragenes. The extant *Life of Apollonius of Tyana* by Philostratus [7] (born A.D. 172) is intended as a defense. Philostratus wrote his work at the instance of Sep-timius Severus' empress, Julia Domna, who was of Syrian birth and interested in religious revival; it was she who reorganized the institution of Vestal Virgins. Julia Domna put into Philostratus' hands a memoir of Apollonius by his Babylonian companion and disciple Damis, and also a quantity of letters and other memo-rabilia. The exaggerations of the master's wisdom and supernatural powers found in Philostratus probably derive from Damis, who clearly made his work an aretalogy.

The life as Philostratus tells it is in brief as follows. Apollonius was born at the beginning of the Christian era at Tyana in Cap-padocia; his birth was attended by miracles and portents. At the age of sixteen he set himself to observe the Pythagorean discipline and abstained from wine, meat, marriage, leather or woolen cloth-ing, and shaving. At the town of Aegae he established himself in the temple of Asclepius, where his reputation for sanctity brought crowds of sick to be healed. At the death of his parents he gave the greater part of his patrimony to his elder brother and the rest to poor relations. He then observed five years of complete silence, and traveled through Asia Minor. His reputation for holiness was such that warring factions in Cilicia and Pamphylia made peace upon his appearance. He knew languages without having learned them, perceived the inmost thoughts of men, understood the speech of birds and beasts, and was able to predict the future. He held the Pythagorean belief in metempsychosis and remembered his former incarnation. He preached strict asceticism, condemned dancing and similar diversions, carried no money, and urged others to use theirs to relieve the poor. He visited Persia and India, where he consorted with the Brahmins, and he went up the Nile to visit the gymnosophist recluses. In Alexandria he talked with Vespasian and Titus soon after Titus had taken the temple in Jerusalem. On a visit to Rome he had incurred the wrath of Nero, but Nero's minister Tigellinus was so awed by him that he set him free. After the death of Titus he was arrested by Domitian on a charge of subversion, but again was marvelously liberated. He died as a very old man in the reign of Nerva, and according to popular tradition ascended bodily to heaven. After his death he appeared to certain persons who had entertained doubts about a future life.

In various parts of Asia Minor temples and shrines were dedicated to Apollonius, and in the second and third centuries opponents of Christianity set him up as a rival to Jesus, citing his power over spirits and demons. The emperor Alexander Severus erected a statue of Apollonius along with others of Alexander the Great, Orpheus, Abraham, and Christ in his private shrine, and a certain Hierocles wrote a book to show that Apollonius had been as remarkable a sage, wonder-worker, and exorcist as Jesus Christ. Philostratus himself never intended his work as anti-Christian, but it did give offense to Christians, and Eusebius wrote a treatise to refute it. Eusebius does not deny Apollonius' occult powers, but says merely that they were of an inferior order and possible only because Apollonius was in league with evil spirits.

An interesting point about the *Life of Apollonius* is that it shows us the aretalogy rising in dignity. Apollonius himself may have had his following only among the simple crowd, and Damis' memoir may have been, as Philostratus says, crudely written; but we can now see the man and the type he represents ascending in the scale of respectability. More thoughtful and responsible people are attracted by his teaching, and Philostratus makes his evangel the subject of a serious and polished literary work. As the aretalogies ascend in the scale of values the philosophers imitate them, and eventually become enough like them to be themselves attacked by the Lucians. And though the life of Apollonius and the book about it may be unique in quality there were surely other prophets and missionaries whose careers were recorded. The synoptic Gospels, as both defenders and enemies of Apollonius saw, are aretalogies of virtually the same type. The type is very obvious in the case of the Apocryphal Acts of the Apostles; these usually show little organization but are simply a collection of miracles, which stop with the extraordinary death of the apostle.[8]

Frequently the account of a holy man's career closes, as might be expected, with a description of the extraordinary circumstances surrounding his death and sometimes his transfiguration. At Apollonius' assumption, for example, an unseen choir of maidens sang (8.30) "and their song was this: 'Hasten thou from earth, hasten to heaven, hasten.' In other words, 'Do thou go upwards from earth.' " And when Lucian's Peregrinus was at the point of death he cried out, "I have left earth, I go to Olympus." In the case of any distinguished personage curiosity about the manner of his dying is natural, but the ancients seem more than normally concerned with recording last words and gestures, as any reader of Livy or Tacitus, to say nothing of Plutarch or Suetonius, will have noticed. Perhaps the Greek usage of heroizing the distinguished dead [9] is a factor; Sophocles' tragedies often turn on the death of the hero because they are in effect demonstrations that he merited heroization. But the obvious paradigm for the meaningful death of a holy man is the death of Socrates, as idealized by Plato.

Examples of *teleutai* or *exitus clarorum virorum*, historical and otherwise, are very numerous.[10] In the historical category one thinks of the death of Tacitus' father-in-law in the *Agricola*, or the death of Seneca in his *Histories* (15.62 f.). For an impressive idealization, mention might be made of the death of the Spartan reformer Cleomenes in 221 B.C., and what happened when his flayed body was hung. Plutarch tells the story of the apparently supernatural phenomenon and the popular reaction to it, and then, though his estimate of Cleomenes is very high indeed, he provides a rational explanation (*Cleomenes* 39):

In the last extremity Virtue cannot be outraged by Fortune. A few days afterwards those who were keeping watch upon the body of Cleomenes where it hung, saw a serpent of great size coiling itself about the head and hiding away the face so that no ravening bird of prey could light upon it. In consequence of this the Egyptian king was seized with superstitious fear, and thus gave the women occasion for various rites of purification, since they felt that a man had been taken off who was of a superior nature and beloved of the gods. And the Alexandrians actually worshipped him, coming frequently to the spot and addressing Cleomenes as a hero and a child of the gods; but at last the wiser men among them put a stop to this by explaining that, as putrefying oxen breed bees, and horses wasps, and as beetles are generated in asses which are in the like condition of decay, so human bodies, when the juices about the marrow collect together and coagulate, produce serpents.

Plutarch's group on Agis and Cleomenes and the Gracchi shows a strong Stoic coloring throughout; the Stoics were particularly interested in virtuous men who encountered death in some memorable way, as the four figures in this group did, and doubtless made collections of such *exitus*.

A favorite example was Calanus, an Indian and a gymnosophist, who immolated himself on a pyre in the camp of Alexander the Great at the age of seventy-three. The story of Calanus is told at greater or lesser length by eight different authors;[11] the passage in Philo is of especial interest because it quotes a letter Calanus wrote (*Quod omnis probus liber* 14):

Calanus was an Indian by birth, of the school of the gymnosophists. Regarded as possessed of endurance more than any of his contemporaries, by combining virtuous actions with laudable words he gained the admiration, not only of his fellow countrymen, but of men of other races, and, what is most singular of all, of enemy sovereigns. Thus Alexander of Macedon, wishing to exhibit to the Grecian world a specimen of the barbarians' wisdom, like a copy reproducing the original picture, began by urging Calanus to travel with him from India with the prospect of winning high fame in the whole of Asia and the whole of Europe; and when he failed to persuade him declared that he would compel him to follow him. Calanus' reply was as noble as it was apposite. "What shall I be worth to you, Alexander, for exhibiting to the Greeks if I am compelled to do what I do not wish to do?" What a wealth of frankness there is in the words and far more of freedom in the thought! But more durable than his spoken are his written words, and in these he set on record clear signs of a spirit which could not be enslaved. The letter he sent to Alexander runs thus: "Calanus to Alexander. Your friends urge you to apply violence and compulsion to the philosophers of India. These friends, however, have never even in their dreams seen what we do. Bodies you will transport from place to place, but souls you will not compel to do what they will not do, any more than force bricks or sticks to talk. Fire causes the greatest trouble and ruin to living bodies: we are superior to this, we burn ourselves alive. There is no king, no ruler, who will compel us to do what we do not freely wish to do. We are not like those philosophers of the Greeks who practise words for a festal assembly. With us deeds accord with words and words with deeds. Deeds pass swiftly and words have short-lived power; virtues secure to us blessedness and freedom."—Protestations and judgements like these may well bring to our lips the saying of Zeno: "Sooner will you sink an inflated bladder than compel any virtuous man to do against his will anything that he does not wish." For never will that soul surrender or suffer defeat which right reason has braced with principles firmly held.

Right reason as a brace to enable the virtuous to adhere to principle despite the compulsion of a tyrant's command is precisely the theme of the Fourth Book of the Maccabees. The attitudes and the very words of the aged sage Eleazar to Antiochus Epiphanes as represented in that book are remarkably like Calanus' attitude and words to Alexander. The exchanges between Eleazar and Antiochus are fuller and more philosophical, and it is very likely that the pattern for these exchanges is the disputation between Socrates and Callicles in Plato's *Gorgias;* but in dramatic presentation there is obvious kinship between the Calanus and the Eleazar stories. Neither has so close an analogue to the other elsewhere in ancient literature. Fourth Maccabees, in turn, became a model for Christian martyrdoms.[12] The earliest literary account of a martyrdom we have is that of Polycarp, dated to the second century. The description of the constancy of the martyrs in the second chapter of the *Martyrdom of Polycarp*[13] is remarkably reminiscent of Fourth Maccabees, and the Martyrdom of Polycarp set the tone for the numerous martyrdoms composed in the fourth century.[14] All ultimately go back to the genre *exitus clarorum virorum*.

But there were pagan martyrs too. Some dozen bits of papyri, mostly discovered and identified since 1893, contain what purport to be transcripts of quasi-judicial proceedings in which some stalwart Alexandrian defies a Roman emperor, sometimes of the first century, and is martyred in consequence. The collection of these pieces as a whole has been called *Acta Alexandrinorum* or *The Acts of the Pagan Martyrs*.[15] Scholarly opinion no longer holds that these are actual court records nor yet that they are parts of a single fictional work or even of a single compilation of works of the same class. They do have a more or less common form and are anti-Roman or antisemitic. They would appear to be based on actual events but put into a standard literary form; this would be in keeping with the hellenistic literary doctrine of the *plasma*, of which the requirements were that it must be based on truth, that its elaborations must have verisimilitude (*hos genomena*, "things as they may have happened"), and that they communicate some edifying lesson. The lesson which Father Musurillo, who has given us the best edition of the *Acta*, suggests is this:[16] "The Hellenes of Alexandria and the chora [hinterland] doubtless projected themselves into the character of their heroes, and these were idealized in an attempt to preserve their Hellenic integrity against the encroachments of a 'barbarian' civilization."

If the *Acta* are not a single work, as they obviously are not, then it is interesting to note that so many disparate writers adopted the same form. More general compilations of *exitus* we know were made, and Diogenes Laertius must have used several such.

They would seem to have been the sources of such stories as the execution of Callisthenes by Alexander (5.4), of Zeno and the tyrant (9.26 f.), and the murder of the philosopher Anaxarchus by Nicocreon of Salamis (9.59).[17] The Hermippus of Smyrna whom Diogenes quotes was apparently the author of such a collection.[18] The celebrated instances of constancy in the face of tyranny recorded in pagan writers were repeatedly invoked by the Church Fathers, especially Tertullian and Clement, as models for Christian emulation,[19] and the instances themselves, transparently disguised, were adapted to Christian worthies in such collections as the *Historiae monachorum* and the *Historia Lausiaca*.[20] It is hardly conceivable that Athanasius' *Life of St. Antony* could have been written if Philostratus' *Life of Apollonius of Tyana* were not in existence, and the *Life of St. Antony* in turn exerted its influence upon a whole series of lives of the saints.

One other possible reembodiment of the aretalogy deserves mention. In the Greek Romances Karl Kerényi has observed that certain motifs—premature burials, scourging of the hero, apparent executions from which the victim is providentially delivered, and similar matters—recur in each of our extant examples.[21] They are not then, Kerényi argues, disparate romances but disparate treatments of a single basic story, and this story he identifies as an aretalogy of the Isis-Osiris cult. Originally the extravagance of the aretalogy was plebeian and despised by the literate; the object of the writers of romance was to give it standing by clothing it in elegant literary form. Actually the Romances are no more like one another than the plays of Plautus or of New Comedy in general; Greek literary genres, like Greek architectural types, conform to established patterns. But it is true that each of the Romances shows a virtuous hero or heroine overcoming apparently insuperable hostility by virtue of a special providence which, appearances to the contrary notwithstanding, ensures his ultimate deliverance. If not the details, the general tendency may reflect the influence of the aretalogies. If that is so, then the Romances have had a large role in disseminating aretalogy over all of Europe.

Chapter XIV

CULT AND MYSTERY

WHEN the Greeks first come into our ken their religion is already a blend, compounded mainly of the beliefs of the Achaean invaders superimposed upon those of the aboriginal Aegean population.[1] The native substratum was mainly chthonic, and the religion of the newcomers mainly Olympian. The chthonic deities lived underground, were usually feminine in nature, and were much concerned with ties of family; they operated directly and according to mechanical rule, as for example in requiring the blood of the slayer or his kinsman to expiate bloodshed, regardless of the circumstances of the shedding. The Olympians dwelt on Mount Olympus, were masculine in nature (even Athena insists on her masculinity), and operated at a distance and by intelligence. Homer glorifies the Olympians and seems intentionally to ignore all chthonic elements (as when he omits the sacrifice of Iphigenia, of which he must have known, and ignores problems of ritual impurity); in consequence he has been numbered, to be sure by an enthusiast, among the world's great religious teachers.[2] But Homer's new religion, if indeed it was his, did not make the old anathema; that happens only when a new dispensation is promoted by a powerful priesthood, which the Greeks did not have. In religious as in certain other attitudes Homer represents a more advanced, or perhaps only a more aristocratic, view than do the Greeks of better-known periods, and the beliefs which he ignores persist down to the end of antiquity. Sometimes the old was refined and sublimated, as when the chthonic Erinyes, or Furies, are transformed into Eumenides, or kindly powers, but not abolished, in Aeschylus' play. A devout believer in a religion which promises blessedness to the virtuous dead should in logic rejoice when loved ones of whose virtue he is convinced enter upon eternal bliss, but the urge of ordinary humanity compels him to grieve nevertheless. Chthonic beliefs touched upon intimate and powerful urges in human life, and they too continued despite logic.

There was little room for sentimentality of any kind in the Olympian religion. Apollo, who spoke for his father Zeus and was its chief representative, stood for political conservatism and discipline. "Know thyself" means not "Brood over the nature of man," but "Realize your limitations and stay in line." The religion of Apollo and the Olympians was soon institutionalized, and by the time of the hellenistic age had little meaning for thirsty souls seeking contact with the unseen. But even in the classical period religious life was far more vital and pervasive than one would guess from the austere classics and the austere temples. Along with the intellectual Apolline element there was the emotional Dionysiac, and in time Dionysus came to share honors with Apollo in Delphi itself. The Orphic cults, as we can see from their efflorescence in the hellenistic age, continued, and there were the various mysteries, Eleusinian and other, to provide emotional satisfaction and promise. Reminders of unseen powers were everywhere; in the cities and in the countryside a man was never out of sight of some shrine or memorial to a hero who retained potency to intervene in human concerns.[3] All of life was steeped in a sense of supernatural presences. The picture of the meeting of east and west as an encounter between thoroughgoing rationalists and religious believers is therefore wholly mistaken. In the field of religion, even, as we shall see, in details of cult, mutual understanding was easy and assimilation proceeded naturally until it was stopped by outside forces.

Assimilation was effected in two ways. One was to accept a new deity or cult and adapt it, more or less, to Greek ways. Even in the classical period hospitality was shown to newcomers; Socrates, for example, is persuaded to stay overnight in the Piraeus, at the beginning of the *Republic,* so that he might attend the rites

in honor of the Thracian Bendis. Other and more important early
accessions were Cybele and Adonis and Attis. Scholars who
have been concerned to maintain the integrity of the nordic
Greeks against oriental pollution have insisted that the vogue
of the exotics was no more meaningful than the vogue for Egyptian
or Chinese *objets d'art* in Europe a century ago, or that the cults
were so wholly transformed in the Greek spirit that little but the
original names remained.[4] It is indeed true that the exotic cults
were adapted and sometimes reinterpreted—Plutarch's *Isis and
Osiris*, for example, conforms the Egyptian cult to Greek ideas—
but there can be no doubt that the eastern importations actually
functioned as religions in the west.

The other mode of assimilation was by syncretization, and for
this too there was ancient precedent; at the first arrival of the
Achaeans, alien deities were identified with native. When their
expansion introduced the Greeks to new deities the process was
greatly accelerated, so that the hellenistic age became the great
period of religious syncretism. The Greek Zeus becomes Zeus-
Amon-Re in Egypt, Zeus Hypsistos or Zeus Baal Shamayin in
Syria, Zeus Jupiter in Italy. Syncretism was easy in Italy because
Greeks and Italians derived from a common origin and their gods
were identical until a relatively late period; but they were no
longer so in the hellenistic age, and it was by the process of syncretization that they were identified.

There was no rivalry between Zeus and Jupiter, and neither
was there rivalry between Zeus and his syncretized forms in the
east. The Greeks could readily understand that Zeus might bear
another epithet and require special usages in a different region
—as he did in different regions in Greece itself—and the hellenized natives were pleased rather than otherwise to see their
deity identified with Zeus. Antiochus IV clearly thought he was
conferring a favor upon Jerusalem when he introduced the cult of
Zeus Baal Shamayin there, and when he erected his "abomination
of desolation" at the altar he did not expect the violent reaction
on the part of the pious—who alone did react violently. So much
is indicated by the fact that the officials despatched over the

THEOPHRASTUS SKETCH OF
SUPERSTITIOUS MAN

countryside to introduce the new cult were not attended by armed forces; Mattathias and his sons were able to refuse obedience, after some of their coreligionists had accepted the cult, and put Antiochus' emissary to death.

It is important to realize that cultic usages among the peoples concerned were not so discrepant as to make fusion impossible. The Syrian cult did involve practices that were repugnant to puritanical religion—that is the meaning of the "wanton women" mentioned in connection with it—but to the non-theologically minded the new observances might seem no stranger than observances at another locality in one's own country. The Greeks were not only as continuously aware of the supernatural as any other people, but expressed their awareness in similar ways. Here, for example, is Theophrastus' sketch of the Superstitious Man, which must have been recognizable in the fourth century B.C.:

The superstitious man is one who will wash his hands at a fountain, sprinkle himself from a temple-font, put a bit of laurel-leaf into his mouth, and go about for the day. If a weasel run across his path, he will not pursue his walk until someone else has traversed the road, or until he has thrown three stones across it. When he sees a serpent in his house, if it be the red snake he will invoke Sabazius, if the sacred snake he will straightway place a shrine on the spot. He will pour oil from his flask on the smooth stones at the cross-roads as he goes by, and will fall on his knees and worship them before he departs. If a mouse gnaws through a meal-bag, he will go to the expounder of sacred law and ask what is to be done; and if the answer is, "give it to a cobbler to stitch up," he will disregard this counsel, and go his way, and expiate the omen by sacrifice. He is apt also to purify his house frequently, alleging that Hecate has been brought into it by spells; and if an owl is startled by him in his walk he will exclaim 'Glory be to Athene!' before he proceeds. He will not tread upon a tombstone, or come near a dead body or a woman defiled by childbirth, saying that it is expedient for him not to be polluted. And on the fourth and seventh days of each month he will order his servants to mull wine, and will go out and buy myrtle-wreaths, frankincense, and smilax; and on coming in will spend the day crowning the Hermaphrodites. When he has seen a vision he will go to the interpreters of dreams, the seers, the augurs, to ask them to what god or goddess he ought to pray. Every month he will repair to the priests of the Orphic Mysteries to partake in their rites, accompanied by his wife, or (if she is too busy) by his children and their nurse. . . .[5]

A corrective to the impression that Greek religion was sheerly intellectual, and a corrective also to the impression that the eastern cults, and especially the Jewish, were uniquely stringent in their requirements of ritual purity is provided by cultic regulations at various Greek sites, preserved chiefly in inscriptions.[6] Here, for instance, are the rules for the priestess of Demeter Olympia at Cos; their date is unknown, but presumably they continued in force through the hellenistic and Roman periods: [7]

The priestess must be pure from the following: She must in no wise come in contact with anything unclean; she must not participate in a hero meal for the dead; she must not touch a grave; she must not enter a house where a woman has given birth to a child, whether a live birth or a still one, during the preceding three days; nor during the three days following a burial shall she enter the house in which someone has died; and she must not eat carrion [i.e., meat of an animal that has perished or been suffocated].

Here are rules for persons about to be initiated in the mysteries at Lycosura; primitive as they obviously are, they doubtless continued in force throughout antiquity: [8]

It is not permitted to enter the temple of the Lady Goddess with any object of gold on one's person, unless it is intended for an offering; or to wear a purple or bright colored or black garment, or shoes, or a finger ring. But if one enters wearing any forbidden object, it must be dedicated to the temple. Women are not to have their hair bound up, and men must enter with bared heads. No flowers are to be brought in at the mysteries; no pregnant women or nursing mothers are to have any part. If anyone wishes to make an offering, let it be of olive, myrtle, honey, grains of barley clean from weeds, a picture, a white poppy, lamps, incense, myrrh, spice. But if anyone wishes to offer the Lady Goddess sacrificial animals, they must be female and white. . . .

Stories of humble piety are numerous and universal. Here is one cited by Porphyry (*De abstinentia* 2.16) from Theopompus, doubtless the historian of the fourth century B.C.[9] A rich man whose custom it was to bring lavish offerings to the gods was told by the priestess that it was Clearchus (otherwise unknown) who lived at Methydrion in Arcadia (a notoriously poor region) who honored the gods best of all.

He was amazed at this and desired to see the man and meet him personally in order to learn in what manner he offered sacrifice. Having soon arrived at Methydrion, he was full of scorn for the tiny, poverty-stricken place; for he could not believe that even the whole town itself, let alone a single man in it, could be in position to offer the gods nobler or more magnificent honors than he. Nevertheless he sought out the man and begged him to explain in what way he honored the gods. Then Clearchus said that he performed the offerings with great care at the appointed times; that every month on the day of the new moon he crowned and decorated the pillars of Hermes and of Hecate, and the other shrines which his forefathers had erected, and that he honored them with incense and crushed barley and offering cakes; and that year by year he held public sacrifices, not neglecting any of the festivals.

These three examples are from places thoroughly Greek, and aside from the lesson of discipline which is a by-product of ritualism their burden is purely formal and institutional. There was no yearning for righteousness, no missionary zeal, nothing like the phenomena we call conversion and apostasy, which imply an exclusive loyalty. When a Greek traveled abroad, therefore, he might properly share in the religious observances of whatever people he was visiting, with no sense of disloyalty to the gods of his own place. And strangers coming to a Greek city from elsewhere were similarly expected to participate in the religious observances of the place of their sojourn without apostasy from their native gods. Occasionally foreigners would remember their native deities by some observance in a strange land, as did the group of Egyptians (probably actually Greeks who had lived in Egypt) who made a dedication to Isis in Eretria in the third century B.C.[10]

When foreign-born groups settled in a hellenistic center in considerable numbers they naturally brought their own cults; such was the origin of the worship of Isis and of the Jewish synagogues in Rome. But it must be remembered that these exotic forms would be found only in great commercial centers, and that their membership, at least in the beginning, would be confined to socially inferior groups.[11] Of both groups mentioned we know that eventually they engaged in missionary activities. Of one regular missionary campaign, that of the Indian King Asoka early in the third century B.C. we are told by the king's own inscriptions, though we do not know how effective his mission was, nor indeed the precise nature of his religion. Here is what Asoka himself said: [12]

King Priyadarsi [Asoka] considers moral conquest the most important conquest. He has achieved this moral conquest repeatedly both here and among the peoples living beyond the borders of his kingdom, even as far away as six hundred *yojanas* [about three thousand miles], where the Yona [Greek] king Antiyoka rules, and even beyond Antiyoka in the realms of the four kings named Turamaya, Antikini, Maka, and Alikasudara [Ptolemy Philadelphus, Antigonus Gonatas, Magas of Cyrene, and Alexander of Epirus, all early third century], and to the south among the Cholas and Pandyas [in the southern tip of the Indian peninsula] as far as Ceylon. . . . Everywhere the people heed the king's instruction.

An admirable illustration of several developments characteristic of religious life in the hellenistic age is afforded by the regulations for a private cult in Philadelphia, in Egypt, inscribed on a marble stele of the late second century B.C.[13] The regulations were drawn up, on the basis of divine inspiration, by an individual named Dionysius, who owned the house in which the communicants met; the house itself had once been a shrine of the Phrygian goddess Agdistis. The cult was not properly a mystery, but a private religious association which persons of quite humble position might join; it had no official character and was not part of a state apparatus. Some dozen deities, including such "useful" figures as Prosperity, Wealth, Health, the Graces, and Victory were given a common worship. The combination of disparate deities in a single cult is a clear indication of the hellenistic tendency towards syncretization. But even more significant of the new religious climate are the ethical requirements for admission (though all social classes are welcomed) and the high moral standard, particularly in sexual conduct, which the communicants are pledged to maintain. Communicants are bidden to report derelictions of their fellows which come to their attention. Divine requital is promised for conduct good or bad: "To those who obey the gods will be gracious and will always be giving them everything good, such as the gods are wont to give to men whom they love. But if any transgress they will hate such persons and will lay upon them great penalties."

The most interesting and the most successful of the fabricated, or at least refurbished, cults was that of Sarapis.[14] This was introduced, allegedly from Sinope or Seleucia, by the first Ptolemy, and consciously combined the characters and functions of the more potent and "useful" Greek deities with those of Osiris and Apis. All the men named as having had a hand in shaping the cult of Sarapis or designing its magnificent temple are either Greek or, like the priest Manetho, thoroughly hellenized Egyptians. The face of the god was that of a bearded and benevolent Zeus, but his head was surmounted by a wheat-container as an emblem of fertility and his left hand grasped a rod like Asclepius' to show that he was a god of healing. At his right knee was the three-headed dog Cerberus to show that, like Osiris, he was a god of the underworld. He was similarly identified with other deities, Greek and Egyptian, so that his cult is some such epitome of hellenistic religion as the Arch of Constantine is of Roman sculpture. And the cult of Sarapis was widely propagated in the commercial centers of the Mediterranean, including Rome, until it was supplanted by that of Isis, which could give greater emotional satisfaction.

At Delos in particular, which was a great commercial center, the cult of Sarapis flourished. A column in the first of the Sarapea at Delos, dating from the latter part of the third century B.C., bears an inscription recording the circumstances of the introduction of the cult to Delos: [15]

The priest Apollonios made this record on the god's order. Our grandfather Apollonios, an Egyptian of the priestly class, brought his god with him when he came from Egypt and continued to serve him in accordance with tradition. He is believed to have lived ninety-seven years. My father Demetrius succeeded him and continued in the service of the gods, and for his piety was honoured by the god with a representation in bronze which is dedicated in the god's shrine. He lived sixty-one years. When I inherited the sacred things and devoted myself busily to the observance of piety, the god gave me an oracle in my sleep. He said that he must have a Sarapeum of his own dedicated to him and that he must not be in hired quarters as before, and that he would himself find a place where he should be set and would show us the place. And so it was. Now this place was full of dung, and it was advertised as for sale on a notice in the passage through the market-place. As the god willed it, the purchase was completed and the temple was built quickly, in six months. But certain men rose up against us and the god and laid a public action against the temple and me, for the infliction of punishment or fine. And the god made me a promise in my sleep: *We shall win*. Now that the trial is over and we have won in a manner worthy of the god, we render due thanks and praise the gods. Here is the poem of Maiistas on this theme.

The poem, in sixty-five hexameters, recounts the miracles worked by the god and the circumstances of the building of the temple. The story then proceeds on the same theme. The priest prays Sarapis to ward off death, and the god replies:

"Cast care from thy mind. No human vote shall destroy thee, for this action affects me myself and no man shall say that it prevailed against me: so be no longer downcast." And when the time for the trial came, the whole city hastened to the temples, yes, and all the multitudes of strangers from many lands to hear justice. Then did thou and thy spouse perform that dread wonder. Thou didst paralyse the wicked men who were bringing the action, making their tongues speechless within their mouths, so that no one praised their ability or the evidence which they had to give in support of their case. In truth by divine operation they stood like heaven-struck phantoms (*or*, idols) or stones. *And all the people in that day marvelled at thy power*, and thou didst bring great glory to thy servant in heaven-established Delos. Hail, blessed one, thou and thy consort who are the gods of our temple: hail much hymned Sarapis.

We see from this account that the cult claimed immemorial antiquity, though it was in fact a new creation, and that it met with a certain hostility upon its introduction at Delos. But presently we find a second Sarapeum at Delos, and then a third, and that about 180 B.C. the cult became public and its income equaled that of Apollo and far surpassed the incomes of Asclepius, Artemis, and Aphrodite.

Rich archaeological and epigraphical remains and skillful interpretation have made the course of events at Delos clear.[16] The progress of Sarapis at other centers must have been similar, and indeed there is scattered evidence to indicate that this was so. So also the progress of lesser cults must have been analogous; the opposition to the introduction of the cult of Sarapis at Delos, mentioned in the inscription, is reminiscent, for example, of the opposition which St. Paul encountered as described in Acts. The process of fusion was easy and natural. Even the Jews were willing to listen to St. Paul when he preached in their synagogues until they were made to realize that his doctrine involved a danger to their own traditions.

In simple terms the process involved drawing elements from various sources into a combination which would have the widest general appeal. In the Sarapis example, for instance, the worshiper bred to the Egyptian tradition would find enough that was familiar to satisfy the conservative propensity of religious observance, and so be able to assimilate the Greek elements easily, and the Greek could similarly assimilate the Egyptian. And the resulting amalgam could in turn assimilate still other elements more easily, and, more important, new and spiritualized interpretations of the old. The general tendency of such a process is in the direction of monotheism. The process was understood and put into words by Plutarch in *Isis and Osiris:*

There are not different gods in different nations, barbarians and Greeks, southerners and northerners. Just as sun and moon and sky and earth and sea are common to all though named differently by different people, so the one Reason ordering this world, the one Providence governing it, and the subordinate powers set over all have different honors and titles among different peoples according to their customs. Some men, whose lives are sanctified, use faint symbols, others use clearer ones; these guide the mind towards things divine, but not without danger, since there are those who go completely wrong and slip into superstition, and again there are others who avoid superstition as though it were a marsh and then fall unawares over the precipice of godlessness.[17]

If this process may be styled centrifugal and expansionist, a centripetal and particularizing force was exerted by another development in consonance with the religious temper of the hellenistic age, and that is the efflorescence of mystery religions.[18] The mysteries known in classical times, of which those at Eleusis were the most highly regarded, doubtless go back to pre-hellenic times. Their vogue continued because they offered their initiates a more intimate communion with a deity and higher promises for the future; and it was natural therefore that mysteries should proliferate in the hellenistic age. The essential character of a mystery is defined by Professor Nock [19] as follows: "A *mysterion* is a secret rite, in which the individual participates of his own free choice, and by which he is put into closer relation with the deity honoured; normally he must undergo ceremonies of initiation (not usually capable of repetition) conferring a new and indelible spiritual condition and commonly giving assurance of happiness hereafter." "Initiates," Aristotle tells us (*On Prayer* Frg. 45: 1483a19), "do not need to learn something but to experience something and be put into a certain frame of mind." If the Synoptic Gospels are in the nature of aretalogies, the Fourth is in the nature of a mystery.

Initiation into a mystery was a matter of individual choice, subject of course to more or less rigorous scrutiny of qualifications by the authorities of the mystery and frequently involving very considerable expense. When religion was detached from its old ties there was greater incentive for adhesion to a mystery, and towards the end of paganism individuals often sought initiation into several mysteries. The most popular in the hellenistic and Roman periods were those of the Great Mother, Attis, Isis and Osiris, Mithras. The adherents of a given cult, especially one of foreign provenience, would unite to form an association, which would sometimes be headed by a professional priest; this is a peculiarly oriental touch. The precepts to be observed were more detailed and more binding than they had previously been, and they included purifications, asceticism, baptisms, and sacraments, along with the use of sacred symbols and rites which possessed special efficacy. Participation in the mysteries assured salvation and even deification. The myth in each case was a symbolic representation of the suffering, dying, and resurrected god, and the initiate might expect to recapitulate the same history.

Elaborate rules of asceticism and a special connection with the supernatural had been characteristic of Pythagoreanism,[20] which, like the classical mysteries, had been influenced by pre-hellenic Orphism. We know that Pythagoras founded a kind of religious order whose rule of life was premised upon an expectation of lives to come. In the first century B.C. Pythagoreanism underwent a vigorous revival, perhaps in part as a "native" response to the challenge of the exotic mysteries. It was naturally the religious aspects of the Pythagorean doctrine which Neopythagoreanism emphasized and elaborated;[21] it will be remembered that Apollonius of Tyana professed himself a Pythagorean. Two features of Neopythagoreanism are of especial interest. For one thing the members formed a fraternity for admission to which the postulant must undergo rigorous tests; the rule of life within the fraternity was austere and subject to strict discipline, and it involved a considerable degree of communism. For another thing, there was a special reverence for and dependence upon the authority of the founder; that is why so many apocrypha were fathered on him. Exaltation of the founder was a common phenomenon in hellenistic philosophical and religious movements; we have noticed it in the cases of Epicurus and of Moses, and in both cases, as in Neopythagoreanism, the writings of the founder, genuine or supposititious, acquire a special sanctity. The doctrine of Epicureanism prevented it from becoming a cult in any but a figurative sense, and indeed ensured the hostility of both Neopythagoreanism and Judaism. But the Neopythagorean and Jewish (and subsequently Christian) traditions were bound to interact upon one another, whether by antagonism or assimilation or both. On the basis of the explicit literary tradition we can see that Neopythagoreanism influenced Neoplatonism directly and was in fact virtually subsumed in it, and we can see also that it influenced Jewish thought through Philo and Christian thought through Clement of Alexandria. But the subliterary influence of Neopythagoreanism was much greater than this inventory suggests; it is possible that the doctrine touched not merely individual thinkers in the Judeo-Christian tradition but substantially affected the main stream of that tradition.

Possible avenues for the invasion of Neopythagoreanism are suggested by two books with significant titles: Isidore Lévy's *La Légende de Pythagore de Grèce en Palestine*,[22] and Jérôme Carcopino's *De Pythagore aux Apôtres*.[23] Both are extremely learned and extremely ingenious, but Lévy's deals with an earlier period and is more fundamental. Stripped of its elaborate argumentation and documentation, his thesis is as follows. The various biographies and biographical details concerning Pythagoras which have come down from the Roman period clearly derive from a single source, which must have been a legendary life of a miraculous character—in fact, an aretalogy. An important element in this legendary life which the more formal lives omitted but which has left traces in Vergil and in Lucian was a descent to the underworld. The legendary life of Moses which was used by Philo and Josephus, and before them and in particular by Artapanus, contained elements adapted from the legendary life of Pythagoras. Scattered stories of a descent to the underworld undertaken by Moses are adaptations of Pythagoras' descent. Jewish borrowings of Pythagorean materials are not limited to miraculous tales, however, but show profound influence of Pythagorean religious thought. Alexandrian Judaism, Pharisaism (whose first appearance Lévy dates to the age of Herod), and Essenism, in the respects in which they differ from Old Testament religion, all show the marked effect of ideas of which the legendary life of Pythagoras was the vehicle. And finally Lévy attempts to demonstrate that the Gospel itself represents the final triumph of the legend and of hellenistic Pythagoreanism.

Inferences based on other inferences cannot suffice to support so large and complicated a structure, and Lévy's thesis has been generally ignored. But latterly it, and Josephus' detailed account of the Essenes (*Jewish War* 2.122–61) which it both used and supported, have received unexpected corroboration from the documents associated with the Essene-like community whose conventicle was situated at Qumran near the Dead Sea. The evidence is contained in the so-called Manual of Discipline, discovered in 1947, taken together with an earlier document found in the lumber room of the ancient synagogue at Cairo in 1897 and ascribed, until its affinity with the Manual of Discipline was recognized, to an unknown Zadokite sect.[24] The documents, supported by the archaeological remains, introduce us to a religious brotherhood with strict requirements for admission, a term of probation, and an austere and rigid communal discipline. The connections with traditional Judaism in outlook and specific precepts as well as in the use of Biblical phraseology are obvious; and yet some of the doctrine was sufficiently unlike traditional Judaism for scholars to attribute it to a heterodox sect for half a century. Similarly, the regimen of the Manual is virtually identical with the usages of the Essenes as described by Josephus. Now the Josephus passage is so like a description of the Pythagorean tenets that it is used in accounts of Pythagoreanism, and its validity as a description of the Essenes has been regularly denied on the grounds that in keeping with his apologetic aims Josephus regularly made the Jewish religious sects look like Greek philosophic schools to woo the sympathy of pagan readers. But the Manual does much to rehabilitate Josephus' credit in these passages, and if Josephus is right then the Qumran brotherhood was in fact very like a Neo-pythagorean fraternity. The communal organization and the strict rules for its administration can hardly be explained otherwise than as direct influences of Pythagoreanism. Of the many good scholars who have discussed the Qumran community it is significant that Professor Dupont-Sommer, whose high competence covers general hellenistic as well as theological literature, should be the first to recognize the organizational affinity between the Qumran community and the Pythagorean brotherhoods.[25] His suggestion has been rejected in some quarters but it has much to recommend it. And if the notion of an elaborately organized and disciplined religious brotherhood did not derive from the Pythagoreans it derived from other hellenistic practices.

The connection of the Manual of Discipline, in turn, with the literature of the New Testament is beyond question. It is not a matter of an anticipation of Jesus and his Passion, as early enthusiasts claimed, but of a common climate of language and imagery, a common basic store of beliefs and aspirations, and a common attitude toward the secular authorities. An impressive list of parallels in what might be called technical phraseology can be drawn up,[26] but similar and similarly significant parallels, though not so numerous, exist between such a book as Fourth Maccabees and the New Testament. Nor were the Essenes or the Qumran community the only channel by which Pythagorean teachings reached Christian teachers. An erudite and subtle analysis, too remote and much too involved to rehearse here, of the representational motifs of Pythagoreanism, especially of the Leucadian Leap, of literary allusions, and in particular of the newly uncovered early Christian monuments in Rome, leads Professor Carcopino to the conclusion that early Christian evangelists in Rome endeavored to retain their loyalty to both Christianity and Pythagoreanism simultaneously.[27] In their own minds, in that case, they must have achieved some fusion between the two.

What has been said of the relationship between the Neopythagoreans and Christianity may be said of the mysteries and other religious manifestations of the hellenistic age. In an earlier generation the devout were disturbed when indubitable parallels with Christianity were pointed out; but it has come to be realized that no derogation of the peculiar quality of Christianity need be involved and that it is natural for a new faith to show the coloring of the age into which it is born. St. Augustine himself wrote (*Retractationes* 1.12.3): "The very thing which is now called the Christian religion existed among the ancients also, nor was it wanting from the inception of the human race until the coming of

Christ in the flesh, at which point the true religion which was already in existence began to be called Christian."

Indeed, it was not from the farther pagan environment that Christianity borrowed, but as the Qumran evidence combined with the findings of archaeology and philology show, from a Judaism already hellenized. The bitter animosity of the young Church towards the ultimate source of some of its central institutions is not an example of filial ingratitude. The Greek elements had become so thoroughly assimilated into hellenistic Judaism and hence into Christianity that these very elements came to be regarded as a native possession which must be protected from alien rivals.[28]

Chapter XV

PRAYER AND CONFESSION

THE most obvious area of fusion, and the most momentous in its effects, is religion; when earlier writers addressed themselves to distinguishing the strands in the hellenistic skein it was natural and right for them to make religion their point of departure and their goal. But usually it has been through Christian lenses that the Greeks have been regarded, and even today books are written in the unconscious assumption that the classical Greeks must be judged by Christian standards. The result has usually been that Greek religion has been deplored as childish (which is an inexplicable anomaly in view of their high intelligence in other areas) or patronized for its occasional approaches to the acceptable standard.[1] Even when the pagan system is admired, as by early nineteenth-century romantics and by a number of German scholars in the thirties, the gauge of Christianity is still implied and the pagans are used as a stick with which to belabor Christianity. It is very difficult, whatever the observer's commitments may be, to shake off two millennia of a tradition which has shaped every aspect of his culture. We have glanced at some of the ways in which that tradition took shape, in the area of religion, but a truer index to a people's religion than the ritual of cults and mysteries and the speculations of philosophers is what men seek from their gods, and accordingly we must turn to prayer.

Because men are reasonably homogeneous the things they seek, at the elementary level, are much of a kind, and so are the means they employ for persuading the deity; from the beginning, therefore, there is considerable common ground between pagan prayer and Judeo-Christian prayer. In both cases there may be traces of a mechanical approach, where the deity could be constrained by magic or bribed by gifts, and this approach persisted, at least vestigially, in both groups. But at the higher levels the mechanical approach was transcended, so that by the gauge of profundity and nobility of utterance there is common ground at the higher levels also. The temptation to which apologists for either side are susceptible and which must be avoided is to confront the higher level on one side with the lower on the other. It is a fault easy to commit because the texts which are inevitably the first to be invoked, Old Testament and Homer, each represents several strata of thought. If we choose very early Old Testament prayers we might consider first the petition of Hannah (I Samuel 1.10 f.):

And she was in bitterness of soul, and prayed unto the Lord, and wept sore. And she vowed a vow, and said, O Lord of hosts, if thou wilt indeed look on the affliction of thy handmaid, and remember me, and not forget thine handmaid, but wilt give unto thine handmaid a man child, then I will give him unto the Lord all the days of his life, and there shall no razor come upon his head.

For all its touching humility and trust this is a *quid pro quo* arrangement, such as can be abundantly paralleled in both literatures. For a prayer without either the personal or contractual element we may consider this from Amos 7.2 (repeated at 7.5):

I said, O Lord God, forgive, I beseech thee: by whom shall Jacob arise? for he is small.

And finally, for a grand specimen of a formal, public prayer, we may look at Solomon's, at the dedication of the temple (I Kings 8.23 ff.) which begins:

Lord God of Israel, there is no God like thee, in heaven above, or on earth beneath, who keepest covenant and mercy with thy servants that walk before thee with all their heart.

Solomon reminds God of his promises to David and hopes that the pledge will be kept.

Yet have thou respect unto the prayer of thy servant, and to his supplication, O Lord my God, to hearken unto the cry and to the prayer, which thy servant prayeth before thee today: That thine eyes may be open toward this house night and day, even toward the place of which thou hast said, My name shall be there: that thou mayest hearken unto the prayer which thy servant shall make toward this place. And hearken thou to the supplication of thy servant, and of thy people Israel, when they shall pray toward this place: and hear thou in heaven thy dwelling place: and when thou hearest, forgive.

There follows a long list of transgressions which might be expected and the hope that they will be forgiven upon adequate prayer at the temple. This is a model for later liturgical prayers, as at Ezra 9, Nehemiah 1–9, and Daniel 9.4–20.

In all of these specimens and in their numerous parallels there is of course a common factor which sets them apart from Greek prayer. Hebrew prayer, whether a private petition for miraculous intervention or a communal plea for the nation's welfare or for purity of heart, is addressed to a sole and omnipotent deity whose relationship with mankind is in the nature of a covenant. Hebrew prayer is therefore permeated by a consciousness of sin, need for repentance, and the conviction that man's sole hope is in divine forgiveness. The Homeric gods are not susceptible to intimate, almost familial, pleading. They were indeed nearer to man, for their contours and passions were the same, but they were farther too, and their immortality made an unbridgeable difference. They could in any case not interfere with the course of nature and had other things to do than keep book on the doings of mortals. "You would have no respect for me," Apollo says to Poseidon (*Iliad* 21.462), "if I were to fight you about a pack of miserable mortals, who come out like leaves in the summer and eat the fruit of the field, and presently fall lifeless to the ground." "It will be intolerable," says Hephaestus to Zeus and Hera (*Iliad* 1.573), "if you two fall to wrangling and setting heaven in an uproar about a pack of mortals."

If we look aside from certain extraordinary interventions in Homer, as when Aeneas is wafted away from danger in a cloud or when a deity guides a spear to its billet, it may be said that there are no miracles in Homer. The apparent exceptions may be explained in part as unrevised primitive materials—like the unrevised bit about the sons of the gods looking upon the daughters

of men in Genesis 6.2—or better as a poetic description of the
effect of an action upon the onlookers.[2] The typical Homeric
prayer is not for some external and miraculous intervention but
for a surge of the powers already inherent in a man to meet some
crisis. When a god appears to a human the poet regularly remarks
that none but the individual concerned noticed him. The most
striking case is when angry Achilles is drawing his sword to attack Agamemnon in the council in the first book (193 ff.). Athena
seizes Achilles by his golden hair, "visible to him alone, no man
else could see her," and under her gaze Achilles returns his half-
drawn sword to its scabbard and decides to use words instead. It
is the same when Odysseus is mastering the fleeing Achaeans
(2.169 ff.) or when Diomedes' spirit flags (5.125, 364, 482). No
miracles are involved; the heroes merely bethink themselves of the
resources already in them and lift themselves, as it were, by their
own bootstraps. Ajax does once pray for an unnatural darkness
to be dispersed (*Iliad* 17.645)—but only so that he can see to do
his own fighting. This stalwartness is rather like Samson's (Judges
16.28): "And Samson called unto the Lord, and said, O Lord
God, remember me, I pray thee, and strengthen me, I pray thee,
only this once, O God, that I may be at once avenged of the
Philistines for my two eyes."

A different, and to us more familiar, view of prayer is to be
found in the *Iliad* itself (notably in Phoenix' speech at 9.490 ff.)
and in other writers, but in general the attitude outlined prevails.
In matters religious Aeschylus seems always to stand alone, and
the prayer of the maidens in the *Suppliants* (for which we have
noticed a Hebrew analogue, to be sure some centuries later) is a
petition for peace and prosperity for their generous hosts; but
even here no miracle is involved—only an uninterrupted continuance of a normal situation—and no *quid pro quo* offered.

Along with their detachment the Homeric gods have a near-
ness for mortals who have qualities like their own. But this near-
ness results only in the efflorescence of powers already active in
the mortal, as in the cases of Achilles and Diomedes and Odysseus.
The best illustration is Sappho's famous prayer to Aphrodite:

Throned in splendor, deathless, o Aphrodite
child of Zeus, charm-fashioner, I entreat you
not with griefs and bitternesses to break my
        spirit, o goddess;

standing by me rather, if once before now
far away you heard, when I called upon you,
left your father's dwelling place and descended
        yoking the golden

chariot to exquisite doves, who drew you
down in speed aslant the black world, the bright air
trembling at the heart to the pulse of countless
        fluttering wingbeats.

Swiftly then they came, and you, blessed lady,
smiling on me out of immortal beauty
asked me what affliction was on me, why I
        called thus upon you,

what beyond all else I would have befall my
tortured heart: "Whom then would you have Persuasion
force to serve desire in your heart? Who is it,
        Sappho, that hurt you?

Though she now escape you, she soon will follow;
though she take not gifts from you, she will give them:
though she love not, yet she will surely love you
        even unwilling."

In such guise come even again and set me
free from doubt and sorrow; accomplish all those
things my heart desires to be done; appear and
        stand at my shoulder.[3]

"Stand at my shoulder"—but the crisis is my own to solve. From
this the transition to prayer for inward strength of another kind
is natural. Socrates' prayer at the end of the *Phaedrus* (279 B.C.)
is essentially a spiritualization of a Homeric warrior's:

Beloved Pan, and all ye other gods who haunt this place, give me
beauty in the inward soul; and may the outward and inward man be at

one. May I reckon the wise to be the wealthy, and may I have such a quantity of gold as a temperate man and he only can bear and carry.[4]

This is no petition for a miracle, nor yet for union with the divine; the gulf between man and his gods is unbridgeable.

The logic of the hellenistic philosophies virtually precluded the possibility of prayer. The Stoics believed in a divine providence which regulated all things, and nothing could therefore be changed by prayer. In any case, the ordinary blessings for which men pray are now all declared to be "things indifferent" and therefore not specially to be desired. Men must follow providence in any case, and all that is left to pray for is that he follow willingly. Thus Cleanthes prays (527, von Arnim):

> Lead me, O Zeus, and lead me, Destiny,
> Whether ordained is by your decree.
> I'll follow, doubting not, or if with will
> Recreant I falter—I shall follow still.[5]

It is good for the broom to sweep, whether or not the floor is made cleaner. The Stoic prayers express awareness of the divine and aspiration towards it without regard to any external result. So the beautiful hymn of the same Cleanthes:

Thou, O Zeus, art praised above all gods: many are Thy names and Thine is all power for ever.

The beginning of the world was from Thee: and with law Thou rulest over all things.

Unto Thee may all flesh speak: for we are Thy offspring.

Therefore will I raise a hymn unto Thee: and will ever sing of Thy power.

The whole order of the heavens obeyeth Thy word: as it moveth around the earth:

With little and great lights mixed together: how great art Thou, King above all for ever!

Nor is anything done upon earth apart from Thee: nor in the firmament, nor in the seas:

Save that which the wicked do: by their own folly.

But Thine is the skill to set even the crooked straight: what is without fashion is fashioned and the alien akin before Thee.

Thus hast Thou fitted together all things in one: the good with the evil:

That Thy word should be one in all things: abiding forever.

Let folly be dispersed from our souls: that we may repay Thee the honour, wherewith Thou hast honoured us:

Singing praise of Thy works for ever: as becometh the sons of men.[6]

If prayer was futile for the Stoics because providence is unalterable, it was as least as futile for the Epicureans because there is no providence. It is no part of piety, their spokesman Lucretius says (5.1196 ff.), to turn towards a stone with veiled head, to approach every altar, to prostrate oneself on the ground, to spread one's hands out before the shrines of the gods, to sprinkle altars with torrents of animal gore, to add prayer on prayer; it is much better to regard all things with mind serene. But it was only the devotee's agitation that the Epicureans deprecated; their doctrine not only acknowledged the existence of the gods but advised that the customary observances in their honor be maintained. So far from being atheists, as their opponents through the ages have alleged, the Epicureans taught, at least by implication, that men must love the gods without expectation of being loved in return and without hope of reward either in the present or the future. Actually the main stream of Greek literature, from Homer to Epicurus and beyond, reflects the same impersonality on the part of the deity; and hence the function of prayer is aspiration for a flowering of resources, whether physical or spiritual, which are inherent in man himself.

From Maximus of Tyre, who lived in the second century A.D., we have an essay (the fifth) entitled "Whether one should pray." Like his contemporary, the Syrian Lucian, Maximus was concerned to maintain the "pure" Greek tradition, and in his remarks on prayer, especially as contrasted with those of the Neoplatonists we shall presently glance at, we must agree that he does stand in the main line of the classical tradition. Here is a précis of his essay: Should men pray or not? Midas' prayer was granted but brought him only regrets; the gods heeded neither the entreaties of Priam nor the sacrifices of Croesus. But such stories aside, can man really persuade the deity? Will the deity change his will at our entreaty? The truth is, God will neither give any-

thing beyond their deserts to those who pray nor fail to give those
who do not exactly what they deserve. Not one of the four
powers to which prayers relate—providence, fate, fortune, skill—
is influenced by petition. Asking and entreating have no place.
God is a strict judge and gives what is right. But we do remember
that Socrates ("Socrates' life was full of prayer"), Pythagoras,
and Plato prayed; the point is that the prayer of a philosopher is
not asking but communion with the god. There are only few who
make this high use of prayer but they benefit the world; "in the
great darkness we need a little light."

In its attitude to prayer Jewish tradition was as consistent as
Greek. The form and spirit for which the Bible provided authority were further hallowed by long use in liturgy which, outside the temple at Jerusalem, was the central feature in worship.
The received forms of prayer (though probably not the style of
worship) were therefore less susceptible to external influence
than other genres of literary and even religious expression. It is
noticeable that in books like III and IV Maccabees and Wisdom
of Solomon which date near the Christian era and are manifestly
influenced by Greek ideas and Greek forms, the prayers which
are attributed to various personages show no Greek influence
whatever in form or content but are wholly in the Old Testament
tradition. Though the prayers in these books are represented as
extempore and uttered by individuals, they are in fact public and
communal and uttered by authorized personages; but prayers presumably private show the same form. The same principle is continued in the New Testament; however novel the surrounding
matter may be, formal prayers like the Magnificat or the Pater
Noster retain much of the traditional forms.

In Ecclesiasticus, which is possibly the oldest book in the Apocrypha, there are numerous prescriptions for prayer,[7] and all imply
a covenantal relationship with a deity who is omnipotent but yet
has a special concern for the faithful. In the book of Tobit, like
Ecclesiasticus of the early second century B.C., both Tobit himself
and Sara, whose seven several bridegrooms had died, pray for

death. Each is a *cri de cœur*, but each maintains the correct form in glorifying God in the invocation and in appealing for a just execution of the contractual relationship. The prayer of Tobit, as becomes a sage elder, is more restrained (3.1–6):

Then I being grieved did weep, and in my sorrow prayed, saying, O Lord, thou art just, and all thy works and all thy ways are mercy and truth, and thou judgest truly and justly for ever. Remember me, and look on me, punish me not for my sins and ignorances, and the sins of my fathers, who have sinned before thee: For they obeyed not thy commandments: wherefore thou hast delivered us for a spoil, and unto captivity, and unto death, and for a proverb of reproach to all the nations among whom we are dispersed. And now thy judgments are many and true: deal with me according to my sins and my fathers: because we have not kept thy commandments, neither have walked in truth before thee. Now therefore deal with me as seemeth best unto thee, and command my spirit to be taken from me, that I may be dissolved, and become earth: for it is profitable for me to die rather than to live.

Sara's, as becomes a young woman, is more emotional (3.11–15):

Then she prayed toward the window, and said, Blessed art thou, O Lord my God, and thine holy and glorious name is blessed and honourable for ever: let all thy works praise thee for ever. And now, O Lord, I set mine eyes and my face toward thee. And say, Take me out of the earth, that I may hear no more the reproach. Thou knowest, Lord, that I am pure from all sin with man, and that I never polluted my name, nor the name of my father, in the land of my captivity: I am the only daughter of my father, neither hath he any child to be his heir, neither any near kinsman, nor any son of his alive, to whom I may keep myself for a wife: my seven husbands are already dead; and why should I live? but if it please not thee that I should die, command some regard to be had of me, and pity taken of me, that I hear no more reproach.

Tobit is, like Judith, a romance, based on the oriental story of Ahikar but influenced in form by hellenistic practice.[8] It is interesting that in the Greek romances, too, young women who were sore tried by having their virtue threatened or impugned pray for death.[9]

In the world of the New Testament the conception of the omnipotent personal deity who answers petitions continues—"Ask and it shall be given you" (Matthew 7.7, Luke 11.9); "Ask and ye shall receive, that your joy may be full" (John 16.24)—but the covenantal tends to give way to the father-son relationship (Galatians 4.4–7), and the Deity does not require an enumeration of man's desiderata: "For we know not what we should pray for as we ought: but the Spirit itself maketh intercession for us with groanings which cannot be uttered" (Romans 8.26 f.). These conceptions are naturally echoed in the Christian writers of the first centuries,[10] but there is also a new note of spiritual aspiration, reminiscent of the Greek's effort to lift himself by his bootstraps through prayer. Philo, who, as has been observed, was one of the principal catalysts for fusing the Judeo-Christian and Greek religious traditions, says (*De somniis* 1.23): "Strive thou, O soul, to become the house of God, his holy temple, his loveliest abode."

A later Alexandrian with broad secular learning and deep religious feeling who was influenced by Philo was Clement of Alexandria (c. 150–214). Clement was born and educated a pagan, and is himself a key illustration of fusion, as his remarks on prayer show.[11] The orthodox Gnostic, Clement says, prays with understanding, for his conception of God is true and his standard of things desirable rests on reality. He therefore prays not for illusory advantages but for such spiritual gifts as forgiveness, freedom from sin, indifference to things indifferent, independence of the flesh, knowledge of the will of God. He will share the common petitions of the faithful, but better, he will pray silently, communing with God in his heart. He understands that though God knows our wants before they are uttered, and unasked gives every good gift to those fit to receive, even so prayer and even petition is right and has its spiritual uses. Prayer may indeed be a return of providence upon itself: man's will may be so identified with God's that what we suggest to God is really his own purpose.

Origen (185–253), again an Alexandrian, combines Clement's and the traditional conceptions of prayer. On the one hand he accepts Clement's intellectual mysticism, "but on the other hand, Origen does not, as Clement seems to do, forget the needs of Christians who are less advanced." [12] Origen is perfectly aware of such objections to prayer as we saw adduced by Maximus of Tyre (*On Prayer* 5.6): "First, if God foreknows the future, and if this must needs come to pass, prayer is vain; secondly, if all things come to pass by the will of God, and his counsels are fixed, and none of the things he wills can be changed, prayer is vain." Origen's answer, to which he devotes the main part of his treatise *On Prayer*, is that God's foreknowledge takes into account man's prayers or his failure to pray. He does insist that the objects of prayer must be "great things" and "heavenly things," but prayer is objectively efficacious, not merely a subjective conditioning of man's own mind.

Neither Philo nor Clement interrupted the traditional usages in their respective communions, but their effects, derived from their secular education, remain clearly perceptible. As increasing stress is placed on aspiration, the covenantal relationship, even in Jewish prayer, recedes into the background, though the personal relationship and the sense of utter dependence continue. Formulas like "Our father in heaven" become normal, petitions for material goods tend to open with a formula like "May it be thy will," and instead of enumerating desiderata the prayer uses an expression like "What is good in thy sight do." Public prayers which were part of a liturgy were more tenacious in retaining traditional forms; the effect of the new modes of thought on modes of expression is more perceptible in individual petitions. Here are two specimens out of a number recorded in the Talmudic treatise *Berakhot:* [13] "The needs of thy people are many and their wit is scant. May it be thy good pleasure, O Lord our God, to give to each one all his needs, to each several person the supply of his lack" (60b). Or more simply: "Do thy good pleasure in heaven above, and give composure of spirit to those who revere thee here below, and what is good in thy sight do" (29b).

Except for its personal note this is not far from the kind of prayer prescribed by Maximus or practiced by Apollonius, who said (*Life* 4.40): "My prayer, ye gods, is this: May ye give me what I should have." In view of the manifest influence of Greek views on other aspects of Judeo-Christian religious thought we may hazard the surmise that the alteration in form and content of prayer may be due to the influence of Greek humanism. But the conception of the holiness of God and his concern for the spiritual welfare of his children continued undiminished, and we may surmise with no less probability that they affected the form and content of prayer in the west. The effect may best be illustrated by the Neoplatonists, who were outside the Judeo-Christian tradition. Here is Porphyry (a Greek adaptation of his Semitic name Malchus) on the proper attitude to the divine (*To Marcella* 18):

The chief fruit of piety is to honor God according to the laws of our country, not deeming that God has need of anything, but that He calls us to honor Him by His truly reverend and blessed majesty. We are not harmed by reverencing God's altars, nor benefited by neglecting them. But whoever honors God under the impression that He is in need of him, he unconsciously deems himself greater than God. 'Tis not when they are angry that the gods do us harm, but when they are not understood. Anger is foreign to the gods, for anger is involuntary, and there is nothing involuntary in God. Do not then dishonor the divine nature by false human opinions, since thou wilt not injure the eternally blessed One, whose immortal nature is incapable of injury, but thou wilt bind thyself to the conception of what is greatest and chiefest.[14]

And here is Iamblichus, another Syrian, on prayer (*On the Mysteries of the Egyptians* 5.26):

To spend a long time in prayer nourishes our spiritual understanding, makes a far wider room in our souls for the reception of the Gods, opens the things of the Gods to men, gives us familiarity with the flashings of the Light, little by little perfects us internally for the Divine contact, till it leads us upward to the highest height, gently uproots the habits of our own minds and plants instead those of the Gods, awakens trust and communion and indissoluble friendship, creates the Divine Love, kindles what is Divine in the soul, purges away from the Soul everything of contrary quality, eliminates so much of the shining aether-stuff round about the Soul as disposes us to physical reproduction, perfects good hope and faith in the Light:

in sum, Prayer makes those who employ it, if I may use the word, familiars of the Gods.[15]

Elements recognizable alike from their disparate antecedents and from their echoes in all the subsequent literature of prayer appear in the prayer with which Simplicius, the commentator of Aristotle, closes his commentary on the *Encheiridion* of Epictetus:

I beseech Thee, O Lord, our Father and Guide of our reason, make us mindful of the dignity of which Thou hast deemed us worthy. Grant unto us moral freedom, that we may be cleansed from the contagion of the body and of all irrational passions; may we overcome and master them, and, as is fitting, use them properly as our instruments. Assist us to a proper direction of the reason within us and its harmony with all Reality by means of the light of Truth. Thirdly, I beseech Thee, my Saviour, remove completely the mist from our eyes that, as Homer says, we may know God and man.[16]

Simplicius was the last pagan professor of philosophy; he was driven from his chair at Athens when Justinian's edict closed the pagan schools. But Simplicius himself shows how completely hellenism had been fused with hebraism.

Confession is normally thought of as a concomitant of prayer, and it is stressed as such not only in Origen's but also in Cyprian's and Tertullian's treatises on prayer. In the case of confession, as in prayer, we find kindred phenomena east and west and an ultimate fusion, but here the influences are of a different character and move in a different direction. Confession is indeed mentioned and its ritual described in a number of pagan authors but it is noticeable that the deities involved are all oriental—Isis, the Anatolian Mother, and the Dea Syria.[17] Ovid (*Ex Ponto* 1.51–8) describes a confession to Isis, apparently in the presence of a priest, and Juvenal (6.535–41) speaks of women confessing to Isis whenever they had had conjugal relations on forbidden days. Juvenal speaks of confessions to the Great Mother which involve immersions, dragging oneself across the Campus Martius on his knees, and large gifts (6.511–26). Plutarch (*On Superstition* 168c) draws a vivid picture of the confessing penitent: "He seats himself on the road with a sack, clothed in rags, and often he rolls naked in the mud and confesses some sin of his, such as having eaten or drunk this or that thing, or having gone along a road not permitted by the divinity." From 170d of the same treatise we see that the divinity involved is the Dea Syria: "The superstitious man believes that if anyone eats herrings or sardines the Dea Syria devours his shins, inflames his body with ulcers, and consumes his liver." On the basis of *Aeneid* 6.567 ("Rhadamanthys enforces confession") it has been argued [18] that confession was an Orphic requirement—on the premise that Book VI of the *Aeneid* is much influenced by Orphism. But the confession which Rhadamanthys enforces is after death, which is different from confession of the living. It has also been suggested that the cult of the Cabiri on Samothrace required confession, on the basis of a story in Plutarch, *Laconian Apophthegms* 217d, but the story seems to prove the reverse. Antalcidas on being initiated was asked what sin he had committed, and answered, "If I have committed any the god must know," which is to say, "I do not need to confess." In any case, what the priest wished to elicit was whether the candidate was polluted by blood guilt, which would require a cathartic procedure.

It is of interest to observe that the authors who respected the classical tradition (and Clement must be counted in their number) speak disparagingly of confession when they mention it at all. It is clear that they did not consider it part of that tradition, and clear that they were right. If then the east refined its conceptions of prayer by what it learned from the west, the west refined its conception of confession by what it learned from the east.

Chapter XVI

BLESSED LANDSCAPES

AND HAVENS

EVEN in describing the person of his beloved, as we have seen, the poet is apt to conform to literary tradition, sometimes without being aware of his own conventionality. It is the same with descriptions of landscapes. Here the tradition is not so exigent, because natural scenery offers wider possibilities than even the most richly endowed human frame, but for the same reason where the tradition is followed it is unmistakable.

The Greeks were susceptible to natural as to other beauty, but their anthropocentric literature makes little room for it. When a tragic poet has a character or a chorus apostrophize natural scenery, as in the *Philoctetes* or the *Hippolytus*, it is almost tantamount to a declaration that humanity is despaired of and the speaker wishes to dissociate himself from it. In Plato's *Phaedrus* (229) Socrates is sensible of the charms of the shaded grass and gentle breezes along the babbling Ilissus, but then he explains that he seldom leaves the city because he is "a lover of knowledge, and the men who dwell in the city are my teachers, and not the trees or the country." [1]

The description of landscape exhibits the same alteration in motivation as characterizes the history of other Greek art forms, plastic as well as literary: the origin is in the service of religion; then when the religious motivation has faded the form is retained, frequently without realization that it ever carried a religious burden, for the aesthetic satisfaction it provides; and finally it is endowed with a new meaningfulness. In literature this is notably true of drama and hymnody; and it is no less true of what the ancient critics called *ekphrasis* ("literary description") of landscape. The oldest and most memorable is the description of the Elysian Fields in the *Odyssey*, in Proteus' prophecy to Menelaus (4.563 ff.):

As for your own end, Menelaus, you shall not die in Argos, but the gods will take you to the Elysian plain, which is at the ends of the world. There fair-haired Rhadamanthus reigns, and men lead an easier life than anywhere else in the world, for in Elysium there falls not rain, nor hail, nor snow, but Oceanus breathes ever with a West wind that sings softly from the sea, and gives fresh life to all men. This will happen to you because you have married Helen, and are Jove's son-in-law.[2]

The fact that kinship is sufficient to insure salvation is in itself evidence that this passage belongs to an older stratum of thought which Homer here retained; elsewhere the only post-mortem blessing that he acknowledges is immortality of fame. The landscape is clearly the same as is attributed to Olympus, which the earlier conception must have connected with the Elysian fields (*Odyssey* 6.43 ff.):

Here no wind beats roughly, and neither rain nor snow can fall; but it abides in everlasting sunshine and in a great peacefulness of light, wherein the blessed gods are illumined for ever and ever.[2]

Homer's modernizations, as we know from numerous examples, did not efface the older view, and both Hesiod and Pindar, who expressed devotion to early religious ideals, teach that the islands of the blest are the eternal reward of heroes. Hesiod specifies their location along the shores of Ocean (*Works and Days* 166 f.):

They live untouched by sorrow in the islands of the blessed along the shore of deep swirling Ocean, happy heroes for whom the grain-giving earth bears honey-sweet fruit flourishing thrice a year, far from the deathless gods, and Cronos rules over them; for the father of men and gods released him from his bonds.[3]

Pindar speaks of the bright flowers, the shade, the fragrance, the serenity, and also tells us how the blessed heroes amuse themselves (Frgs. 129–130):

For them the sun shineth in his strength, in the world below, while here 'tis night; and, in meadows red with roses, the space before their city is shaded by the incense-tree, and is laden with golden fruits. . . .
Some of them delight themselves with horses and with wrestling; others with draughts, and with lyres; while beside them bloometh the fair flower of perfect bliss. And o'er that lovely land fragrance is ever shed, while they mingle all manner of incense with the far-shining fire on the altars of the gods. From the other side sluggish streams of darksome night belch forth a boundless gloom.[4]

Clearly this is the model (though Pindar was probably not his source) which Vergil used for his picture of the Elysian fields and the pastimes of its denizens (*Aeneid* 6.637 ff.):

They came to a land of joy, the green pleasances and happy seats of the Blissful Groves. Here an ampler ether clothes the meads with roseate light, and they know their own sun, and stars of their own. Some disport their limbs on the grassy wrestling-ground, vie in sports, and grapple on the yellow sand; some trip it in the dance and chant songs. There, too, the long-robed Orpheus matches their measures with the seven clear notes, striking them now with his fingers, now with his ivory quill.[5]

The supernal light and fragrance and balminess of the scene are frequently and unmistakably echoed in other Greek writers, such as Aristophanes (*Frogs* 448 ff.), Euripides (*Hippolytus* 732 ff.) and Theocritus (22.36 ff.), and persisted in pagan writers to the second century and beyond. Plutarch's pendant to Plato's Vision of Er describes the place of the blessed (*On the Delay of Divine Retribution* 22, 565 f.) as "painted with verdure and every color of flower and breathing forth a soft and gentle breeze which perfumed the ambient air with an odor marvelously delightful."

One final pagan example of what may be called a religious application of the story must be cited, and that is the Pseudo-Platonic *Axiochus* (371 c) which dates from perhaps the first century B.C.:

The heroes are given a dwelling in the place of the pious where in endless springtide foison of every fruit burgeons and fountains of pure water flow and meads spangled with flowers of every kind and hue are at their prime, and there are discourses of philosophers and theaters of poets and round dances and recitals of music and agreeable banquets and feasts self-catered and serenity unmarred and sweet pastime. Never does harsh cold or heat occur but an atmosphere always well moderated suffuses them, tempered with the gentle rays of the sun.

Now the denizens of the happy place are not doughty warriors but scholars and artists and those that understand their works. The new heroization of the intelligentsia, which was carried over into Judaism and Christianity, we have discussed in another context.[6]

Even before Pindar we see indications that the picture could be put to secular use. A poem of Sappho previously known from two slight fragments and made more intelligible by a Ptolemaic ostrakon published in 1937 obviously echoes the traditional picture of the Elysian fields. Here is the translation presented in Professor Alexander Turyn's excellent study of the poem: [7]

. . . descending from the mountaintop come hither for my sake, to the holy temple of Crete, where is a lovely grove of apple trees, and altars censed with frankincense, and there cold water rustles through the apple boughs, and the whole place is shaded by roses, and the drowsy quiet of the quivering leaves reigns over the sacred shrine. And there a horse-nourishing meadow blooms with vernal flowers, and the dills breathe a mild odor. . . . There, o Cypris, give me benevolently nectar, which mingled with joy thou pourest out gracefully in golden cups.

So faithful is this description to the pattern that the doubtful reading "horse-nourishing" (*hippobotos*) can be supported by Vergil's *per campum pascuntur equi* (*Aeneid* 6.652). Turyn suggests that Sappho was moved to adapt a hieratic text because she was describing a sacred precinct—Aphrodite's in Crete. This, then, may not be a complete secularization of the motif, particularly if Sappho herself, as there is reason to believe, was officially associated with Orphism. The Leucadian leap, which is connected with her name, was regularly employed by the Orphics to denote translation to immortality. Another poem of Sappho (Frg. 58) is relevant at this point. Addressing a rich but uneducated lady, Sappho says that she will have no share in immortality but will descend to Hades, whereas her own immortality is assured. The contrasting fates of poets and philistines seems to have been part of the Orphic tradition. Thus Vergil too places "the pious bards whose utterance was worthy of Apollo" (6.662) in Elysium, whereas "those who crouched over wealth found in earth" (6.610) were condemned to hell.

A more purely literary use of the picture, and the fullest treatment of it which has come down, is in Lucian's *True History* (2.5–12):

As we drew near the island, a marvellous air was wafted to us, exquisitely fragrant, like the scent which Herodotus describes as coming from Arabia Felix. Its sweetness seemed compounded of rose, narcissus, hyacinth, lilies and violets, myrtle and bay and flowering vine. Ravished with the perfume, and hoping for reward of our long toils, we drew slowly near. Then were unfolded to us haven after haven, spacious and sheltered, and crystal rivers flowing placidly to the sea. There were meadows and groves and sweet birds, some singing on the shore, some on the branches; the whole bathed in limpid balmy air. Sweet zephyrs just stirred the woods with their breath, and brought whispering melody, delicious, incessant, from the swaying branches. . . . We came upon the guardians of the peace, who bound us with rose-garlands—their strongest fetters—and brought us to the governor. As we went they told us this was the island called of the Blest, and its governor the Cretan Rhadamanthus. . . . There is no night, nor yet bright day; the morning twilight, just before sunrise, gives the best idea of the light that prevails. They have also but one season, perpetual spring, and the wind is always in the west. The country abounds in every kind of flower, in shrubs and garden herbs.[8]

If there is no faith here neither is there parody; the picture justifies itself as a work of art.

In the case of the Phaedra story, it was observed that it became a part of the general literary stock when those who used it, Apuleius for example, altered names and circumstances so that the source was not immediately recognizable. So the pleasance appropriate to Elysium becomes the pattern for any delightful garden, as in Longus' *Daphnis and Chloe* (2.4):

Whatever the seasons bring my garden produces. In the spring it has roses, lilies, and hyacinth, and both kinds of violets; in the summer poppies and pears and all varieties of apple; now it has vines and figs and pomegranates and green myrtles. To this garden troops of birds make their way together each morning, some for food and some to sing, for it is over-arched and shady and abundantly watered by three springs; if one would remove its hedge he would fancy he was looking at a natural wood. When I entered my garden about noon today I espied a little boy under my pomegranates and myrtles, some of which he was holding in his hands. His complexion was as white as milk, his hair bright as fire, and he shone as if he had just been bathing.[9]

The shade and the water, the flowers and the music, and in particular the red and white coloring of the extraordinary occupant of the garden are all regular motifs in the descriptions of the Elysian fields and of the Christian paradise which derive from them.

If Greek literature is concerned with words and deeds rather than scenic backgrounds, Biblical literature is even more so. Only in the Song of Solomon does landscape play a considerable role, and then we have to reckon with alien influence. Even the Garden of Eden contains nothing but what is essential for the tremendous action which was to take place there (Genesis 2.8–10):

And the Lord God planted a garden eastward in Eden; and there he put the man whom he had formed. And out of the ground made the Lord God to grow every tree that is pleasant to the sight, and good for food; the tree of life also in the midst of the garden, and the tree of knowledge of good and evil. And a river went out of Eden to water the garden; and from thence it was parted, and became into four heads.

This is little enough basis for the picture which was elaborated by Milton and which has informed men's imagination of Paradise. And it is the Greek tradition of Elysium which Milton expanded to make his picture. Tertullian was acute enough to recognize that there was an interdependence between the Greek and Christian pictures of rewards and punishments in a future life, but maintained that the pagans were the borrowers (*Apologeticus* 47):

We are laughed at when we preach that God will sit in judgment; but so do poets and philosophers also premise a tribunal among the deceased. We are met with guffaws if we threaten Gehenna, which is a store of arcane fire for punishment beneath the earth: but they have the river Pyriphlegethon among the dead. And if we mention Paradise, a place of divine pleasance destined to receive the spirits of the saints, separated from the notice of the ordinary world by a certain station in the fiery zone, they hold to a belief in the Elysian fields. Whence, I ask you, did philosophers or poets derive notions so similar?

The scoffers scoffed, it is plain to see, because to them the pictures of the other world had become mere belles-lettres, as it was for Lucian. As a serious article of faith it had been taken over by another tradition. The seriousness of the new believers, and also the derivation from paganism, is set forth by Josephus. Speaking of the Essenes he says (*Jewish War* 2.155):

Sharing the belief of the sons of Greece, they maintain that for virtuous souls there is reserved an abode beyond Ocean, a place which is not oppressed by rain or snow or heat, but is refreshed by the ever gentle breath of Zephyrs coming in from Ocean; while they relegate base souls to a murky and tempestuous dungeon, big with never-ending punishments.[10]

There is not the slightest reason to question Josephus' veracity at this point. He is indeed capable of coloring truth to aggrandize his own credit or to flatter his Roman patrons, but where these considerations do not apply he is a reliable historian. And in this point Josephus has received unexpected support from the so-called Manual of Discipline which governed the Essene community at Qumran near the Dead Sea. The organization of that community, it has been pointed out, shows marked affinities with that of Pythagorean brotherhoods which also followed Orphic beliefs. Josephus' language is not merely his own or his literary ghost's decorative reminiscence but surely the language the Essenes themselves employed.

From the Essenes to Christianity the path is notoriously level and open. The document which, for our purposes, affords the clearest evidence for the effectiveness of this path is the Apocalypse of Peter, which is contained in a parchment codex found in a grave at Akhmim in Upper Egypt toward the end of the last century.[11] The influence of Orphic beliefs in regard to rewards and punishments is clear and has been acknowledged by very conservative theologians. The Elysium passage, which is our present concern, is demonstration enough (§ 15):

And the Lord showed me a spacious place outside this world suffused with supernal light. The air there was permeated with the rays of the sun, and the earth itself blossomed with unfading flowers and was filled with perfumes and shrubs which were fragrant and imperishable and bore blessed fruit. So powerful was the aroma that it carried from that place to us.

It is no part of our present purpose to follow the tradition in subsequent Christian literature (where it can be carried to Dante and beyond) or to isolate the sources of its various increments, or to show how punishments as well as rewards derive from Orphic tradition.[12] But the recurrence of the "pleasance" theme in the secular literature of the west [13] is a model for the persistence of cultural motifs, as two or three specimens will show.

Frequently the scenery of Elysium, as painted in the sixth *Aeneid*, is transposed to a lover's bower, as in a poem of Petronius (131):

> A noble plane spread leafy shade
>   Against the summer glare,
> And Daphne too made cool the glade
>   With berries in her hair,
> And all around the trim pines swayed
>   Their high tops in the air;
> A stream with vagrant ripples played
>   And plashed the pebbles there.
>
> Place made for love! The nightingale—
>   A woodland witness she—

And the swallow from the city's pale
   Played on the grassy lea,
And there amid the violets frail
   In tuneful revelry
They practised in this peaceful vale
   Their wonted minstrelsy.[14]

But frequently the pleasance is described for its own sake, as in this epigram of Luxorius, a North African poet of the sixth century:

Garden whose beautiful foliage never grows thinner, whose spring balsam is always fragrant, whose delicate fountain of clear water gives rise to a spot well-watered by mossy streams, garden where the sweet singing of birds resounds . . .[15]

Perhaps the lushest pleasance of all is that of Tiberianus, who belongs to the fourth century:

O, the Stream was flowing coolly through the meadows of the pass,
smiling with a glint of pebbles, painted with the flowers and grass.
Over dark-blue leaves of bay and over green of myrtle trees
slid with whispering caresses pleasantly a little breeze.

Underneath, with fullblown blossoms, grass had lushly made a lair.
Gilt the crocus-spikes had littered it and lilies glittered there.
Through the grove there softly went the breath of violets sweetening.
Tall amid the jewelled graces and the bounty of the spring
goldenly the flower that Venus loves was rising in the rows,
Lucifer of colour-fires and Queen of scented things, the Rose.
Wetted were the forest dews upon the richly-streaming ground
as the rivulets from bubbling springs made music all around.
Shining with the spray they gushed and rushed and wound about and
   crossed.
Myrtle thickly spread about a cave, and all the cave was mossed.

There, along the shade more birds than you can fancy whirred and
   sang.
Songs of spring among the branches with a rustling sweetness rang.
Murmur of the babble-stream in all the gossip-leaves was heard
as the zephyr-muse was woken and the lyre of wind was stirred.
Whosoever through the lovely green, the scent and music, strayed,
found a pleasure in the stream and breeze, the birds and flowers and
   shade.[16]

The remarkable thing here is that though the poet's fancy seems completely unfettered he is in fact working with the six recognized "charms of landscape" which were formulated by Libanius (1.517, 200): "Causes of delight are springs and plantations and gardens and soft breezes and flowers and bird voices." The formulation might have been constructed on the basis of the classic description of the Elysian Fields. The tradition of the pleasance or *locus amoenus* (at *Aeneid* 6.638 Vergil had called his Elysium *amoena virecta*) persisted through the Middle Ages and was prescribed by writers on style and the art of poetry.[17] We need only look at Spenser's *Faerie Queene* 3.6.29 ff. and the analogues which the commentators cite to see how both pagan and Christian elaborations of the Orphic tradition were incorporated into a picture which has been assimilated into the western store.

When the King of Argos in Aeschylus' *Suppliants* finds himself cornered by the plea of the Danaids he says (47): "It is a sea of ruin, fathomless and impassable, that I have launched upon, and nowhere is there a haven from distress." Commenting on the frequency of such imagery in Aeschylus, Wilamowitz remarks that it is unusual in Germanic literature but natural for seafaring peoples like the English ("to take arms against a sea of troubles") or the Greeks. It is indeed common in Greek literature, where adversity is very commonly spoken of as a storm-tossed sea, relief as bailing bilge water, and release as reaching harbor.[18] When the release is the attainment of some desirable objective the harbor is a "haven." The notion of death as a haven after the long and troublesome voyage of life becomes a commonplace in such authors as Cicero and Seneca.

The notion of a deity piloting an actual ship safely through perilous seas is very old. In *Odyssey* (9.142 f.) we read: "There we sailed, and some god guided us through the dark night, for nothing could be seen." And in *Agamemnon* (661 ff.) the messenger reports:

Ourselves and our ship, its hull unshattered, some power, divine not human, preserved by stealth or intercession, laying hand upon its helm: the Saviour Fortune willed to sit aboard our barque so that it should neither take in the swelling surf at anchorage nor drive upon a rock-bound coast.

A religious note of a subtler kind appears in a choral ode in Euripides' *Bacchae* (902 ff.):

Happy (*eudaimon*) is he who has escaped the tempest at sea and found harbor. Happy is he who has risen triumphant over his toils. . . . I call blessed (*makarizo*) the man whose life is happy day by day.

Here the religious note is more profound, as the blessing is less tangible, than in the earlier passages; *eudaimon* and *makarizo* become regular elements in the vocabulary of religion. In Philo the use of "haven" in a religious sense is very common; "wisdom" is a "windless harbor" in *De fuga* (50), "truth" is in *De decalogo* (67), and "virtue" in *De somniis* (2.225). The "haven" image was soon applied to Christ, as in Odes of Solomon (38):

The Truth [i.e. Christ] took me and led me, and carried me across pits and gullies, and from the rocks and waves it preserved me; and it became to me a haven of salvation and set me on the arms of eternal life.

And in Lactantius (*Divine Institutes* 6.8.5) we have:

The celestial light will so guide and steer you that it will pilot you to the supreme haven of wisdom and virtue with no going astray.

The image of the desired haven becomes a recurrent theme in all religious literature, and is a favorite in hymns and homilies to this day—even among landlocked peoples with no experience of the sea. The proliferation of the marine image, more clearly than that of the blessed landscape, is a manifest result of fusion.

Chapter XVII

ART

INFORMED taste prefers the archaic Apollo in the Metropolitan Museum to the elaborate and theatrical Apollo Belvedere in the Vatican. The great Wilamowitz said that it was nothing short of blasphemy to think of a Roman Venus as the deity to whom Sappho addressed her prayer. The best work of the classical period fills the spectator with awe; its grandeur, its serenity, its remoteness, is humbling and a little terrifying, and our relationship to it must remain as impersonal as our relationship to a Grand Canyon or a white lily. The great innovation in hellenistic art is that it does engage our more immediate emotions. The archaic Apollo is content to symbolize vitality by putting one foot forward, to symbolize soul by smiling. In other respects he is, like the more developed art of the classical period, idealized. The classical portraitist, for example, gives us a statesman or philosopher nearly as idealized and detached as a god, with only a minimum of physical likeness to make recognition possible. Men we know were old when they were portrayed are represented in their ideal prime. In hellenistic art we see even women old and sick, people with tortured bodies and anguished expressions, people with protruding ears and realistic warts—such people as constitute the *dramatis personae* of New Comedy. To speak of hellenistic decadence in any sphere of culture is meaningless; with reference to the plastic arts it is wrong. We may ideally prefer and as ordinary humans be flattered by the high dignity of the classic, and if dignity be the gauge then the hellenistic age shows a degeneration. But hellenistic art embraces a much wider range, and granted the change in spiritual climate, hellenistic artists were as masterly as their predecessors and achieved effects beyond those of their predecessors.[1]

In art as in other cultural activity Greek interaction with the east, notably, in this case, with Egypt, began early. The archaic Apollo figures were influenced by the archaistic Saite statues, and the simper on the late Saite statues seems to be an unintelligent imitation of the more meaningful smile on the archaic Apollos. Gem cutting was always a Greek specialty, but the Greeks took over the scarab and gave it a new lease on life after it disappeared in its own country. The satyrs of the Greek vase painters are surely adaptations of popular Egyptian representations of the dancing god Bes. The Egyptians themselves had probably derived the form from the Mesopotamian region, where the Sumerians represented the demon Lakhamu or Enkhidu, the half-animal companion of the hero Gishdubar in similar form.[2]

In the hellenistic age interaction is enormously accelerated and multiplied, and its product is perceptible in a wide variety of expressions and in widely separated regions.[3] The range of distribution and something of the character of this art is indicated by Walter Otto: [4]

Wherever we turn our glance, whether to early Ptolemaic tombs like the grave of the Egyptian high priest Petosiris near El Amarna or the much later necropolis of Kom-esh-Shukafa at Alexandria, the Artemisium of Magnesia, the pavilion of the second Ptolemy, the sanctuary of Antinous at Antinoupolis, the temples at Baalbek or the buildings of the first Herod, the Jewish synagogues in Galilee and the Syrian Christian churches, the mausoleum of Hadrian, the monument of Antiochus I of Commagene on Nerudh-dagh, and the late monument of Philopappus on the Greek mainland or the rock structures of Petra, the castle of Mshatta and the mansion of the Kalif in Mesopotamian Samarra, the Buddhist Gandhara sculptures of India, the paintings at Tufan and the frescoes of Salihijeh or Christian sarcophagi and the pictures of the catacombs at Rome, the palace of Diocletian at Spalato, the monumental arches of the west and the great baths in North Africa or the great dome structures so familiar to us from the Pantheon and Hagia Sophia—wherever we turn our glance, whether to the monuments mentioned or to numerous others,

the picture is always the same. From the remains of the art of hellenism
we can read as out of a picture book its two basic elements—the
Greek and the oriental. And not only that: we can also read the trans-
formations in hellenism.

In art as in other fields the Greek spirit developed and vitalized its
increments, but it was also constricted by the rigidity and formal-
ism of the east. On the other hand, the striving for the infinite, the
gigantic scale, magnificence for its own sake, the eventual victory
of the general over the particular, which characterize late antique
art have been ascribed to the influence of the east. The pioneer in
recognizing the enormous influence of the east in artistic conceptions and expression was Josef Strzygowski, one of whose works
is significantly entitled "Hellas in the Embrace of the East"; and
it was the eastern element in late antique art, according to Strzygowski, which determined the character of European art.[5] Later
scholars have discounted Strzygowski's extremer claims, but his
fundamental position is recognized to be sound.

To follow the course of development we turn first to the beginnings of the hellenistic period and to a form in which the
classical period had left a high and vigorous tradition. In sculpture
hellenistic techniques appear to be a natural development out of
what went before. Whether or not the differences in mood, the
soft and relaxed air which some critics call Alexandrianism and
the intensity and flamboyance they call Asianism, were inspired
from without it is difficult to say. We do know that Greek craftsmen received commissions from eastern potentates and worked in
the east from an early date, as they later worked in Rome, and
that under direction or otherwise they introduced into their work
eastern motifs, which were then given a new life.

Perhaps the best known early example is the admirable Alexander sarcophagus,[6] so called because it includes a likeness of Alexander akin to that in the famous Alexander mosaic, now in the
museum at Istanbul. This was made for the Syrian Abdalonymus,
whom Alexander appointed king of Sidon in 332 B.C. The sarcophagus is in the form of a temple, and has a gabled roof with

simulated tiles. In the vault burials at and near Marissa in Palestine which we shall presently consider, the gabled roof was intended as a symbol of immortality, as being a form appropriate to a god's temple, and so it probably is here. The lions which serve as akroteria at the corners, the palmettes and griffins which flank the akroteria at the center, and the vine tendril molding on the frieze all carry the same sort of symbolism. The lively coloring of the whole is again reminiscent of eastern practice.

The pediment as well as the sides of the sarcophagus are covered with reliefs depicting vigorous action, four battle scenes and two of hunting. One long side represents the battle of Issus (333 B.C.) which is also the subject of the celebrated Alexander mosaic, and it is plausibly conjectured that both are adaptations of a painting by Philoxenos of Eretria. The scene is filled with wild action, and yet the grouping is carefully designed to make a harmonious composition. In the hunting scenes on the other long side and one of the short, Greeks and orientals are no longer fighting but helping each other against attacking beasts. The chief personage is in Persian dress, probably Abdalonymus himself. The other battle scenes, in the remaining short side and the two pediments, are more favorable to the Persians than to the Greeks. The features and dress of the Persians are carefully studied and presented with dignity.

The Alexander sarcophagus illustrates the beginnings of fusion at several levels. There is actual cooperation of Greeks and natives, and though the carving is unmistakably Greek, the symbolism, in design and color, suggests the simultaneous use of disparate alphabets destined eventually to fuse into one. The pace was, of course, very different. In the frescoes in the synagogue at Dura, to which we shall come presently, the Greeks are distinguished from the orientals in posture and composition as well as in costume, and the two kinds of symbolism have gone only a short distance on the way to coalescence.

In wall decoration an eastern element is easier to recognize.[7] The simulated marble incrustation, especially in the lower parts of walls, which became common all over the hellenistic world, is an imitation of eastern building practice, where walls of unbaked brick had to be faced with glazed tiles or stone slabs which were made to form a design as decorative as possible. At the center of a slab there might be an inlay of stones of different color or colors to form a geometrical pattern, which might have its own symbolic significance. The first and most impressive use of this technique known to the west was the fourth-century palace of the famous King Mausolus of Caria (for whom his wife subsequently erected the celebrated Mausoleum), and it came into general use, most familiarly in the so-called first style at Pompeii. The so-called carpet design of wall decoration, involving patterns of flowers realistic or stylized, also derived from the east and probably from Egypt. The inspiration was doubtless from textiles actually used for floor coverings and perhaps sometimes used as wall covering. The best illustration of this technique is in the vaults at Kertch, in southern Russia, though it too is widespread. Our own wall decoration of paper in floral patterns may be considered a remote descendant of this technique.

The hellenization of Palestine is a topic of special interest, and among the hundreds of tombs in that area there are a number whose elaborate decorations throw light on the process. The group at Marissa (Mareshah), some twenty-five miles southwest of Jerusalem and dating from the late second century B.C., possesses particular interest.[8] Corridor and stairs lead down to a square hall which is flanked by two oblong chambers and which leads in turn to the main and much longer hall, at the far end of which is an elaborate niche holding a couch. Behind the niche were burial places, apparently the most important in the entire complex. Set into the three free walls of the flanking chamber and the two of the main hall are deep openings each of which could hold two bodies at a perpendicular from the wall. A bench runs around the three chambers underneath the openings. The entire complex is filled with painted decoration, most elaborate in the niche and the main hall. Here there was an elaborate animal frieze. On one wall, beginning at the far end, a man is blowing a trumpet and a mounted hunter with two dogs is fighting a leopard.[9] There follow in order a tree, a male lion, an animal cut away for a burial recess, a bull with blood gushing from its mouth being attacked by a huge snake, a preposterous giraffe, a boar, a griffin, an oryx, another tree, a rhinoceros, an elephant, and a Negro attendant. All of the figures are labeled; the Negro is "Aethiopia." On the other wall the frieze runs in the opposite direction and includes two fish, a crocodile with an ibis on its back, a hippopotamus, a wild ass trampling and biting a serpent, two unidentifiable animals, one with a large red tusk, a porcupine, a lynx with enormous ears, and finally a lion with a human face. The hunting scene is reminiscent of the Alexander sarcophagus. The Persian costume and saddle cloth of the hunter are the same: dark red breeches, a short tunic belted at the waist, a yellow chlamys with long sleeves, and Phrygian cap. The prevailing colors are red and yellow. The heavy festoons which tie all the decoration together are of red and dark brown dots against a neutral background. The technique is like that of Greek vase painting: the design was lightly incised, the contours then freely drawn in gray, and then the color added. The animals have given rise to some quaint theories, as for example that the owner was an animal dealer or curator of a zoo. There can be no doubt that, as Professor Goodenough suggests, they carry religious symbolism. They occur frequently in the art of the Near East, though the preponderance of Egyptian specimens here is odd. The ruins of the "palace" of Hyrcanus at Arak el-Emir (c. 175 B.C.) also show an animal frieze.[10]

From the point of view of symbolism the niche at the end is the most interesting, as it was the most important, part of the tomb. It was painted in red, in the form of a gabled temple. On either side of the doorway are Panathenaic vases of hellenistic shape, one black with a red band and top and the other red with a pink band and top. In the spandrels at either side of the gable is an eagle with scrawny neck and outspread wings. These are outlined in black and painted a bright red. Underneath one of the eagles (and originally probably under the other also) is a round yellow table supported by ornate lion's feet, and on the table is an elaborate vessel spouting fire.

What the symbolism of these various elements may be is questionable, but that they do carry symbolism and are not mere decoration is certain. As Goodenough points out, similarly elaborate decorations have been found in underground tombs which were permanently covered, where mere decoration would be meaningless. And their symbolism, like their techniques, is clearly a mixture of Greek and various exotic elements. Peters and Thiersch, whose book on the subject is fullest (though newer theories have been advanced in the interval), summarize the matter by ascribing the necropolis to "a Phoenician settlement on Jewish-Idumaean soil under Egyptian-Syrian rule, with a culture which, with the exception of some Persian influences, is chiefly Greek." [11] The various elements listed are undoubtedly present, but one possibility which scholars writing in 1905 naturally excluded can now be mentioned. From other indubitably Jewish archaeological remains in Palestine, where even synagogue decoration plainly shows pagan symbolism, we now know that until the lines of demarcation were hardened by the rabbis the Jews were as syncretistic as the prophets had charged them with being. We shall find that the Dura synagogue, half a century later, displayed decorations lineally descended from the sort of thing we see at Marissa. The Marissa necropolis may indeed not have belonged to Jews, but it is altogether possible that it did. An insulation so indifferent as not to exclude hellenistic erotic poetry and hellenistic diatribes from its literature would be open to other forms of symbolism also.

The Greek towns of South Russia present a series of painted vault tombs dating from the fourth century B.C. to the fourth century A.D.[12] These enable us to see the development of the incrustation style, which originated in Mesopotamia, together with the floral carpet style, which came possibly from Egypt. At Kertch, in the tomb called Stasov's Catacomb after its discoverer, the lower part of the wall imitates slabs of colored marble inlaid with slabs of another variety in geometrical patterns, and the upper part has conventionalized floral designs. Against this background are horsemen wearing pointed caps and carrying long spears riding to meet one another in battle, and behind them are foot soldiers with shields. The colors are bright to the point of garishness and the drawing is childish, but the picture of action derives from the Greek. Here too, then, we see a mixture of elements, though not quite the macedoine of the Marissa tombs.

Perhaps the most dramatic example of artistic fusion and the most far-reaching, for it influenced Buddhist art in Tibet and China and Japan, is that afforded by the art of Gandhara in India.[13] Gandhara became part of the Persian empire under Cyrus the Great and supplied a contingent for the invasion of Greece under Xerxes in 480–479. It was conquered by Alexander in 327–326, but was ceded by Seleucus I to Chandragupta. Chandragupta's grandson was Asoka (272–232), whom we have encountered as an ardent proselytizer; under him the people of Gandhara were converted to Buddhism. After his death and through the second century Gandhara was under the rule of Greeks from Bactria. Early in the first century B.C. the Greeks gave way to the Sakas, who in turn gave way to the Kushans: both these peoples were of Scythian origin. In A.D. 250 the Sassanians won control of Gandhara, and held it till 390, when the White Huns swept over the country. Gandharan art shows traces of all its occupiers, but by far the most meaningful is the influence of the Greeks.

In the first place the figure of Buddha himself is a product of Greek influence. It was fashioned by a man who, as Foucher put it, was "artiste par son père grec et bouddhiste par sa mère indienne." [14] Greek, and specifically hellenistic, technique is put at the service of Indian spirituality. That Greek influence is present is beyond question, if only because contemporary reliefs from Gandhara show Corinthian columns and women in Greek dress. There are no earlier Buddhas, and the oldest figure (in the Museum für Völkerkunde in Berlin) provides a curious kind of evidence. The drapery on the upper part of the seated figure is perfectly hellenistic, but on the thighs the folds go down perpendicularly as they could never do on a seated figure; the explanation is that a sculptor used only to standing figures was baffled by the new problem, and merely continued the folds on the trunk.[15]

The type that was followed on the draped Buddha was the familiar Greek orator type, and it was this type that the earliest representations of Christ followed. Ezra reading the law in the Dura frescoes may well *represent* (it is much too late to *be*) an intermediary. Mr. Rowland has recognized the essential kinship between the Christ and Buddha figures; his explanation is that each was an incarnation of a *logos* and that it was therefore natural for Greek artists to represent each by the orator type.[16] This conception of the Buddha has touched the peoples of the east as widely and as deeply as that of Christ touched those of the west.

With regard to the reliefs, in many from the risers of the stairs of stupas or relic shrines, the Greek influence is more unmistakable. Some exhibit the career of Buddha from his earlier lives to his last incarnation, and show very great skill in combining compression with clarity. They possess the easy grace and attention to detail of the best Alexandrian genre pieces, together with profound spirituality. As an illustration of fusion achieved one can think of no apter parallel than Christianity itself.

A curious manifestation of secular Chinese art is worth mention as an illustration of the devious paths influence may sometimes take.[17] In the latter half of the first century B.C. Chen Tang, acting without royal authority, had captured the city of Jzh-jzh, far on the western frontier, which was fortified by the Hun "emperor" Shan-yü. Though his victory was a great and useful achievement Chen Tang had committed a capital offense in forging his orders, and it was important for him to conciliate his king before he arrived home. He endeavored to do so by sending ahead paintings of the crucial moments in his battle, in nine scenes. The paintings have of course disappeared, but they are described in the account of Chen Tang's campaign found in Ban Gu's *Han-shu* (*History of the Former Han Dynasty*). The first scene showed the city well at a distance, with shouting defenders and colored banners on top, and the attackers below, "arranged like fish" at either side of the gate. Succeeding pictures show stages of the attack, through the night and the morning following, until in the ninth the wall has been breached and the palace set afire. The eminent sinologist J. J. L. Duyvendak, who first translated and discussed the text, noted that "pictorial representation of a historical event, of a complex nature, of which the various elements seem one by one to have been analyzed and combined to form a composite picture" was altogether unprecedented in Chinese art.

The fish-like formation at the gates of the beleaguered city is indubitably the Roman *testudo*, also unprecedented in China, and the individuals who taught Chen Fang that Roman tactic also told him that in order to conciliate good will at home Roman generals sent ahead pictorial representations of the crucial moments in their victory and that such pictures were carried in the triumphal processions. In the triumph of Vespasian and Titus, for example, Josephus tells us (*Jewish War* 7.142) that "the war was shown by numerous representations, in separate sections, affording a very vivid picture of its episodes." Painstaking investigation by Professor Homer H. Dubs has shown that Chen Tang probably had in his employ Roman veterans who had survived Crassus' debacle at Carrhae in 53 B.C. and had made their way five hundred miles to the east. And if these Romans taught Chen Tang the technique of the *testudo* and the propaganda uses of pictures, they doubtless also told him how such pictures should be painted. Perhaps they even had a hand in the actual painting; the pictures used in the Roman triumphs were usually painted at the scene of action. To present historical event by a series of chronological panels, as in the column of Trajan, was a Roman specialty; here is a romantic and spectacular episode showing that the specialty could be transplanted on the opposite side of the world.

If the art of the hellenized areas of India shaped religion in the far East, that of hellenized Mesopotamia shaped religious art in Byzantium. The art of Palmyra too is naturally influenced by hellenistic work, but it retains a somber hieratic quality which is native. The Palmyrenes called a portrait *naphsha* or "soul"; we have spoken above of the fortunes of its Hebrew equivalent *nephesh*. In keeping with this concept is the "strict frontality, far-reaching linearity, and intense spirituality" which Rostovtzeff mentions as the characteristics of Palmyrene art. The Palmyrenes symbolized their city by its Gad, which is Semitic for Tyche or Fortuna. The Gad of Palmyra in the Yale University Art Gallery figured as a stately seated woman is like the Tyche of Antioch in the Vatican, except that she is supported not by a river god but by a nude woman pressing her right breast and so symbolizing the springs which provided Palmyra's water.[18]

Palmyra and Gandhara exhibit the process of fusion at an advanced stage. A specimen of the beginnings of the process, where the disparate elements are little more than juxtaposed, may be more instructive. Such a specimen is offered by the frescoes in the synagogue at Dura Europus, uncovered by archaelogists of Yale University and the French Academy in 1932.[19]

Dura was a completely undistinguished frontier town in Mesopotamia, on the caravan route to Palmyra. It was the seat of a Roman garrison, posted there against the threat of Sassanian invasion from Persia. The Jews in Dura lived by providing supplies to this garrison; the design and decorations of their synagogue buildings and the inscriptions in Greek, Aramaic, and Iranian show that they had connections both with the east and the west. About A.D. 245 they enlarged and refurbished their old synagogue. In its new form the synagogue complex, which occupied part of a residential block, included a pillared forecourt where various communal activities, education among them, were carried on, a dwelling house to serve as a hostel for transients, and the synagogue proper. This was a boxlike structure, of a type indigenous to the region, measuring 15.47 meters by 9.65 meters and almost 7 meters high.

At the center of the solid long wall on the west (and therefore facing Jerusalem) was an elaborate apsidal niche to contain the ark for the scrolls of the law. In the long wall on the east were two doors, an imposing one near the center, and a smaller one, for women, near the short wall on the south. Around the interior, and interrupted only by the two doors and the niche, ran a masonry bench with a footrest; at the southern end, where the women sat, the footrest was omitted for reasons of modesty. The floor near the benches was well worn; its center and the benches (as shown by droppings of paint from the frescoes) were covered with mats. Holes in the floor in front of the niche show where a lectern was removed; holes at the top of the niche had held supports for the curtain before the ark.

The west wall of the synagogue was separated from the city wall by only a narrow street, and on the occasion of an impending Sassanian attack this street was packed with mud to buttress the city wall, and to support the strain the interior of the synagogue was also packed with an earthen ramp, rising from the floor on the east to the full height of the structure on the west. This ramp has left its mark on the wall decorations. When the danger grew more critical the ramp was extended eastward, so that the whole synagogue was filled with earth. The city fell nevertheless, in A.D. 256, and was abandoned, but the packed earth protected the wall decorations from sun and rain, just as the ashes from Vesuvius protected Pompeii and its lava Herculaneum in A.D. 79.

These decorations included some five hundred large tiles bearing pictures or inscriptions on the flat ceiling and five horizontal bands of frescoes covering the walls. The band next the ceiling, which is lost, was probably simulated architectural detail. The dado above the bench consisted of panels showing heraldic animals mostly of an oriental type, masks of familiar New Comedy types, and simulated marble incrustation. The three middle bands represent fifty-eight Biblical episodes in twenty-eight panels. The subjects include such themes as the infancy of Moses, the Exodus, the loss of the ark at Ebenezer and its recovery, Elijah at Carmel, David and Saul, Ezekiel and the valley of dry bones, Ezra, Mordecai, and Esther. The stories are told in the "continuous" style, like a comic strip: a woman in mourning dress carries a limp child; Elijah on a couch handles the child; a woman in a bright dress holds a living child in her arms. The pictures are two-dimensional, without perspective or foreshortening, and the poses tend to be rigidly hieratic. Artistically the paintings hardly rise to mediocrity and are far inferior to those of Pompeii, but aside from their importance as the richest collection which has survived from their period they tell us much about the processes of cultural history.

As in the Pompeian analogue it is clear that the craftsmen who executed these pictures worked from a well-established repertoire, which was doubtless repeated, and with higher skill, in many other places. As in the pagan analogies, it is clear that two or more originally separate designs have frequently been combined in a single panel; the famous painting of the sacrifice of Iphigenia, for example, combines originally distinct pictures of the prophet Calchas, the mourning Agamemnon, and the reluctant Iphigenia.[20] We can even surmise the source which the craftsmen used. Because the paintings follow specific books of the Bible, starting with the first chapter and continuing episode by episode, it is likely that they derive from manuscript illustrations of the Bible. But though the general movement of the pictures is from right to left, which is the proper direction for Hebrew or Aramaic, the individual panels are oriented from left to right, which suggests Greek.[21] It is quite possible that the models went back to the Maccabean era. The same models doubtless influenced Christian illustrations also, for these are of kindred type and deal almost exclusively with the Old Testament figures.

But if the text the illustrations accompanied was Greek, the interpretations they suggested rested rather on native Hebrew sources than on the Septuagint. At the Exodus a file of the Israelites is armed, because the enigmatic Hebrew hamushim (Exodus 13.18, "harnessed" in the Authorized Version) is translated "armed men" in the Aramaic version of the Bible called Targum; the Septuagint has "in the fifth generation," and the hellenistic Jewish authors stress the unarmed helplessness of the Israelites. Again in the Carmel scene (I Kings 18) a little man is hiding in an aperture of the altar while the priests of Baal are praying for fire to descend, and a serpent is approaching. This represents a midrashic elaboration; the little man was to light the fire surreptitiously from below, but a serpent was providentially dispatched to kill him before he could do so.

Disparate elements similarly ill digested are shown by the costumes, the poses, and, most significantly, the grammar of representation. In his posture as in his dress the magnificent Ezra reading a scroll is clearly a Greek orator, and David playing his harp is an Orpheus. But these figures form part of compositions where the dress, posture, color, and arrangement of the other figures are as clearly oriental. The simultaneous use of disparate alphabets is more baffling when a kind of symbolic shorthand is involved. At the top of some of the panels a large hand appears; this is the hand of God and indicates miraculous intervention. Surely the congregation of Dura was sophisticated enough to understand that the picture was not a representation of a literal hand; and yet the spectator bred to the legacy of Greece is puzzled if not repelled— as he is repelled by the seven arms on an otherwise charming picture of the Sita of the Ramayana.

What gives these frescoes special interest for the student is the very obviousness of the mingling. In the scale of fusion they are at the opposite pole from the Buddhas, which the western eye, because it can see them with complete objectivity, finds completely integrated. They show hellenistic influence, to be sure, but profound religious feeling has endowed them with a combination of vitality and serenity which is reminiscent of the best classical work.[22] They are themselves classic because the process of fusion has been consummated. There are other monuments where diverse elements are juxtaposed but no more. The Arch of Constantine at Rome [23] may serve as an example; it has spirited tondi of Trajan's age and delicate rectangular reliefs of Marcus Aurelius' and a continuous frieze of Constantine's own time, crowded with what partisans of the classicizers call wretched little men (very like the little men on the Dura frescoes, incidentally) but filled with an energy which makes the earlier and showier work look effete. The Arch is an anthology, not a composition. The Dura frescoes were produced at the same time by a single company of craftsmen

for a homogeneous audience to convey a homogeneous burden.
The Greek and the Hebrew have disparate modes of thought and
disparate alphabets for expressing that thought—the external ex-
plicitness of the Greek and the concentrated inwardness of the
Hebrew, the invitation to expansion implicit in Hebrew parataxis
and the closed self-sufficiency of the elaborate Greek syntaxis, the
Greek "aoristic" indifference to distinctions of time and the close
attention to relative chronology characteristic of the Hebrew.
In the Dura frescoes the two modes have not yet coalesced, but
they have clearly begun to act upon one another.

Chapter XVIII

ROMAN EVANGELISTS

WHEN Statius meets Dante and his guide in Purgatory he says to Vergil (22.66 ff.):

Thou first didst direct me on the way toward Parnassus to drink in its grots, and then, on the way to God, thou didst enlighten me. Thou didst like him, who goes by night, and carries the light behind him, and profits not himself, but makes the persons following him wise, when thou saidst, "The world is renewed; Justice returns, and the primeval time of man, and a new progeny descends from heaven." Through thee I became a poet, through thee a Christian.[1]

The quotation is from Vergil's Fourth or "Messianic" Eclogue, which, from the time of Constantine,[2] had been accounted a proof text, almost on a level with Old Testament prophecy, testifying to the advent of the Christ. Here are the significant portions of the Eclogue:

The last age of the Sibyl's poem is now come. The great circuit of the ages is born anew. Now the Virgin returns, the reign of Saturn returns. Now a new offspring is sent down from high heaven. Do thou, chaste Lucina, favor the birth of the child under whom the iron breed will first cease and a golden race arise throughout the world. Now shall thine own Apollo bear sway.

And in thy consulship, Pollio, yea in thine, shall this glorious age begin, and the mighty months commence their march; under thy sway, any lingering traces of our guilt shall become void, and release the earth from its continual dread. He shall have the gift of divine life, shall see heroes mingled with gods, and shall himself be seen of them, and shall sway a world to which his father's virtues have brought peace.

But for thee, child, shall the earth untilled pour forth, as her first pretty gifts, straggling ivy with foxglove everywhere, and the Egyptian bean blended with the smiling acanthus. Uncalled, the goats shall bring home their udders swollen with milk, and the herds shall fear not huge lions; unasked, thy cradle shall pour forth flowers for thy delight. The serpent, too, shall perish, and the false poison-plant shall perish; Assyrian spice shall spring up on every soil.

But soon as thou canst read of the glories of heroes and thy father's deeds, and canst know what valour is, slowly shall the plain yellow with the waving corn, on wild brambles shall hang the purple grape, and the stubborn oak shall distil dewy honey. Yet shall some few traces of olden sin lurk behind, to call men to essay the sea in ships, to gird towns with walls, and to cleave the earth with furrows. A second Tiphys shall then arise, and a second Argo to carry chosen heroes; a second warfare, too, shall there be, and again shall a great Achilles be sent to Troy.[3]

The principal Old Testament proof texts, in Isaiah, are the following:

Behold a virgin shall conceive, and bear a son, and shall call his name Immanuel (7.14).

For unto us a child is born, unto us a son is given: and the government shall be upon his shoulder: and his name shall be called Wonderful, Counselor, the mighty God, the everlasting Father, the Prince of Peace (9.6).

And there shall come forth a rod out of the stem of Jesse, and a Branch shall grow out of his roots: And the Spirit of the Lord shall rest upon him, the spirit of wisdom and understanding, the spirit of counsel and might, the spirit of knowledge and of the fear of the Lord; and shall make him of quick understanding in the fear of the Lord: and he shall not judge after the sight of his eyes, neither reprove after the hearing of his ears: but with righteousness shall he judge the poor, and reprove with equity for the meek of the earth: and he shall smite the earth with the rod of his mouth, and with the breath of his lips shall he slay the wicked. And righteousness shall be the girdle of his loins, and faithfulness the girdle of his reins. The wolf also shall dwell with the lamb, and the leopard shall lie down with the kid; and the calf and the young lion and the fatling together; and a little child shall lead them. And the cow and the bear shall feed; their young ones shall lie down together: and the lion shall eat straw like the ox. And the sucking child shall play on the hole of the asp, and the weaned child shall put his hand on the cockatrice' den (11.1–8).

The parallels are sufficiently striking to suggest that Vergil might actually have read the Septuagint, but the more immediate source, indicated by the reference to the Sibyl in his opening and suggested by Lactantius, was the *Sibylline Oracles*.

According to ancient legend the *Libri Sibyllini* were brought to Rome by Tarquin and deposited in a stone chest under the temple of Jupiter Capitolinus. When the temple was burned in 83 B.C. a commission collected all the oracles it could find, and these were deposited in the new Capitol. In the time of Augustus nearly two thousand books of oracles were extant. These were scrutinized, those considered genuine deposited in coffers under the statue of the Palatine Apollo, and the remainder burned. They were again scrutinized in A.D. 19 and A.D. 32. In A.D. 363 they were still in the temple on the Palatine, but were finally destroyed by Stilicho soon after 400. The extant collection of Sibylline Oracles has little to do with the official collection. But the prestige and secrecy which surrounded the official collection made the form a favorite for religious propaganda. Since the Sibyl was a prophetess, any prophecy could be safely ascribed to her without fear of disproof, and her eminence assured ready acceptance for any prophecy which could gain currency under her name.

The twelve books of Sibylline Oracles which have come down to us, numbered 1 to 8 and 11 to 14, are largely of the character of propaganda. They date roughly from 100 B.C. to A.D. 100. Books 3–5 are so clearly of Jewish and Christian origin that they are regularly included in the body of noncanonical writing on the periphery of Scripture.[4] The relevant portion of Book 3 (which Rzach dates to the first century B.C.) are verses 619–23 and 789–91:

And then shall God give great joy to men; for the earth, the trees, and the full flocks of sheep shall give their proper fruit for men, wine and honey and white milk, and corn which is the best of all gifts to mortals. . . . He shall dwell in thee, and thou shalt have everlasting light. The wolf and the lamb shall feed together on the mountains, the leopard shall eat grass with the kid: the bear shall lie down with the herds of calves, and the devouring lion shall eat chaff at the stall as the ox, and little children shall lead them with a halter, for He shall make the wild beast harmless (*lit.* helpless) upon earth. And the babe shall lie down with the dragon and the asp, and shall suffer no hurt: for the hand of God shall be on them.

These passages, obviously based on Isaiah, are only the most salient parallels with Vergil's Eclogue. There are numerous other touches, and in other books of the Oracles as well as the Third.[5] Where parallels are so striking and where antecedent classical literature provides none so apt it is natural to assume that Vergil did in fact draw on the Sibylline Oracles, and the preponderance of scholarship agrees that he did.[6] The importance of his doing so goes far beyond the Eclogue. That piece, it has aptly and correctly been said,[7] is a blueprint for the *Aeneid*. The solemnity and the other-worldliness which made the *Aeneid* sympathetic to Christians and a force in shaping European ideas may well derive from Isaiah.

It is altogether likely if one member of an intimate circle of poets was preoccupied with an exotic book that his friends knew it also, and there is evidence that Tibullus and Horace also knew and used our Sibylline Oracles. Tibullus 2.5, written on the occasion of Messallinus' appointment to the commission which had custody of the Sibylline books, is unique among the poet's works for its solemn and religious tone. The poem invokes Apollo, praises the veracity of the Sibyl and cites as an example her predictions to Aeneas, and then proceeds to another prediction (2.71–78):

These told that a comet should appear, the evil sign of war, and how that thick on earth should fall the stony shower. And they say that trumpets and the clash of arms were heard in heaven, and sacred groves rang with the coming rout. From the images of the gods poured the warm tears; and kine found tongue and spake of the coming doom. Yea, from the very Sun ebbed the light, and the clouded year saw him yoke dim horses to his car.[8]

Immediately following the lines of the Sibylline Oracles previously cited we have the following (3.793–806):

I will tell thee an unerring sign, whereby to know when the end of all things shall come on earth. When by night in the starry heaven swords are seen westward and eastward, then shall a dust fall from heaven over all the earth and the light of the sun shall fail from heaven in his mid course, and suddenly the moon-rays shall shine out and come upon the earth; there shall be a sign of dripping of blood from the rocks; and in a cloud ye shall see a warring of footmen and horse.

To be sure, this refers to the end of the world whereas the Tibullus passage refers to the end of a civil war, but the similarity is marked enough to convince scholars that Tibullus is here drawing from the Sibylline Oracles.[9]

The affinity of Horace's Epode 16 with the Sibyllines has been recognized, but Franz Dornseiff offers the ingenious and plausible theory that here Horace is consciously replying to Vergil's Eclogue on the basis of another passage in the literature from which Vergil had drawn.[10] Vergil had hoped that the birth of the child would mark the end of the miseries of civil and foreign war; Horace sees the only escape in flight to some happy region in the west.

"Already a second generation is being ground to pieces by civil war," Horace begins, "and Rome through her own strength is tottering. . . . The savage conquerors shall stand, alas, upon the ashes of our city, and the horseman shall trample it with clattering hoof, and (impious to behold!) shall scatter wantonly Quirinus' bones that are now sheltered from wind and sun." It has been pointed out that this is like the apostrophe in Sibylline Oracles 3.464–69:

Upon thee, Italy, no warfare of foreign foes shall come, but civil bloodshed lamentable and of long continuance shall ravish thee, thou famous land, for thy shamelessness. And thou, stretched prone among the burning ashes, shalt slay thyself, in thy improvident heart. Thou shalt be no mother of good men, but a nurse of wild beasts.

The solution Horace offers is "to go wheresoever our feet shall carry us" and swear an oath never to return before the course of nature is reversed so that

tigers shall love to mate with deer, and the dove shall pair with the kite, the trustful herd fear not the tawny lion. . . . Let us seek the fields, the happy fields, and the Islands of the Blest, where every year the land, unploughed, yields corn, and ever blooms the vine unpruned, and buds the shoot of the never-failing olive; the dark

fig graces its native tree; honey flows from the hollow oak; from
the lofty hill, with plashing foot, lightly leaps the fountain. There the
goats come unbidden to the milking-pail, and the willing flock brings
swelling udders home; nor does the bear at eventide growl 'round
the sheepfold, nor the ground swell high with vipers. . . . Hither
came no ship of pine with straining Argive oarsmen, nor here did
any shameless Colchian queen set foot; no Sidonian mariners hither
turned their spars, nor Ulysses' toiling crew. No murrain blights
the flock; no planet's blazing fury scorches the herd. Jupiter set
apart these shores for a righteous folk, ever since with bronze he
dimmed the lustre of the Golden Age. With bronze and then with
iron did he harden the ages, from which a happy escape is offered
to the righteous, if my prophecy be heeded.[11]

Horace appears to be countering the Eclogue point by point. The
last age has *not* begun, for we are continuing in our misery through
two ages. The blessed peace between naturally hostile animals is
made into a series of impossibilities (*adynata*) familiar in ancient
rhetoric. It is not in Italy where figs and honey and milk are produced effortlessly but in some remote island. The blessing of the
Golden Age will visit that remote island, not Rome. A connection
between the two poems has long been recognized, and so perceptive a critic as Bruno Snell explains the echoes in the Epode as an
intentional mark of homage to Vergil.[12] To explain it as refutation, to be sure, good-natured, seems closer to the truth.

Escape from a disagreeable society by flight to a blessed region
is a theme strange to classical literature, unless we are willing to
classify Aristophanes' *Birds* in that category, or the chorus in the
Hippolytus which wishes it might turn into a bird and soar away
to the Adriatic. But Jeremiah, after describing scenes of bloodshed
and distress, cries out (9.1): "Oh that I had a lodging in the wilderness, that I might leave my people and go from them, for they
be all adulterers, an assembly of treacherous men." Curiously, the
preceding chapter of Jeremiah has a parallel to the singular motif
of the bones of Romulus, which had hitherto been sheltered from
sun and wind, being scattered (8.1 f.):

At that time, saith the Lord, they shall bring out the bones of the
kings of Judah, and the bones of his princes, and the bones of the
priests, and the bones of the prophets, and the bones of the inhabitants

of Jerusalem, out of their graves: And they shall spread them before
the sun, and the moon, and all the host of heaven, whom they have
loved, and whom they have served, and after whom they have
walked, and whom they have sought, and whom they have worshipped:
they shall not be gathered, nor be buried; they shall be for dung upon
the face of the earth.

If these parallels have any validity they suggest book knowledge rather than strange doctrines or turns of phrase that may
have been in the air. Horace makes a number of specific allusions
to Jews,[13] and a number of scholars have dealt with his knowledge
of Jews and Judaism.[14] W. H. Alexander, for one, concludes that
Horace's mother, whom the poet never mentions, was a Jewess.[15]
Franz Dornseiff goes further; he states categorically: "Horace'
father, it seems, was at the least a proselyte. The son was well
read in the Septuagint as in Greek literature." [16] He bases this on
motifs in various parts of Horace's poetry (especially *Satires* 2.3
and *Odes* 4.4) which have more direct analogies in the Bible than
in antecedent classical literature, and while none of these is convincing in itself this cumulative effect is impressive. Horace's
influence on European lyric poetry, especially in "Augustan"
ages, was greater than any other poet's, and he may then be an
agent for the assimilation of eastern modes in the west. But
Horace's mediation, it must be noted, was of a different order
than Vergil's. What he borrowed were literary motifs; his outlook on life was informed by the tradition of Greek philosophy.
Vergil's knowledge of eastern literature was more limited, but
he was more deeply affected by what he learned and made it
a central element in his chief work.[17]

The kind of borrowings that have been suggested so far imply
knowledge of books, but books are not the only means for com-
municating ideas. For one thing there were respected teachers
from the east, and we have seen that Philodemus of Gadara was
perhaps the teacher of all the poets in Maecenas' circle.[18] For
another we must reckon with influences from below which gradually became part of the intellectual climate and sometimes
proved particularly attractive to certain temperaments. The Cam-
pania, where Vergil sojourned for considerable periods, was filled

with men from the eastern Mediterranean. Graffiti in Aramaic written in Latin characters have been found on house walls in Pompeii,[19] and the realistic conversation of the upstarts at Trimalchio's dinner shows that the speakers had been bred to speak Greek or Aramaic. Some of their expressions are direct translations of Aramaic, and some of their strange words are only intelligible when transliterated into Aramaic.[20] A keen ear like Petronius' would have caught nuances of thought as well as speech, and a writer more concerned with preaching morality than with criticizing bad taste might well have assimilated some of these nuances for his sermons.

Seneca, like Petronius a victim of Nero's ruthlessness, was such a writer. Seneca reflects the moralizing element in the climate of his time, and his works do indeed contain dozens of parallels to Scripture, and especially to the New Testament. Many of these, to be sure, may derive from Stoic sources by which the New Testament itself was influenced,[21] but not all; and sometimes the formulation comes remarkably close to the language of the New Testament. Here are some specimens, arranged for convenience under separate rubrics:

Divine omniscience:

We should live as though our lives were open to inspection, our thoughts should be so framed as if there were someone who could look into our inmost heart. And there is someone who can. For what avails it that something is hidden from man? Nothing is shut off from the sight of God. He is witness to our souls and is present in the midst of our thoughts (*Epistles* 83.1).

Shall not God search this out? For he knoweth the secrets of the heart (Psalms 44.21).

All things are naked and opened unto the eyes of him with whom we have to do (Hebrews 4.13).

The divine in man:

God is near you, he is with you, he is within you. This is what I mean, Lucilius: a holy spirit indwells within us, one who marks our good and bad deeds and is our guardian (*Epistles* 41.1).

Know ye not that ye are the temple of God, and that the spirit of God dwelleth in you? (I Corinthians 3.16.)

Divine mercy:

How many are unworthy of the light and yet the day dawns. . . . If you imitate the gods you will confer benefits even on the unthankful, for the sun rises even on the wicked, and the seas are open to pirates (*On Benefits* 1.1, 4.25).

He maketh his sun to rise on the evil and on the good, and sendeth rain on the just and on the unjust (Matthew 5.45).

Self-examination:

So far as possible make inquisition of yourself, accuse yourself; play the part first of prosecutor, then of judge, and lastly of intercessor (*Epistles* 81.10).

Examine yourselves, whether ye be in the faith; prove your own selves (II Corinthians 13.5).

The golden rule:

This is the kernel of what I would prescribe: Treat your inferiors as you would be treated by your betters (*Epistles* 47.12).[22] You must live for your neighbors if you would live for yourself (*Epistles* 48.3). A man must stretch his hand forth to the shipwrecked, point his way to the wanderer, share his crust with the hungry (*Epistles* 95.51).

Whatsoever ye would that men should do unto you, do ye even so unto them (Matthew 7.12).

Liberty:

To obey God is liberty (*On the Happy Life* 15.6).

Where the spirit of the Lord is, there is liberty (II Corinthians 3.17).

Sinfulness:

There is no one who can acquit himself; any man calling himself innocent is concerned for the culprit, not his conscience. . . . To be upright judges in all things we must first persuade ourselves that not one of us is without fault (*On Anger* 1.14.3, 2.27).

If we say that we have no sin we deceive ourselves, and the truth is not in us (I John 1.8).

Chastisement:

Those whom god approves and loves, them he hardens, he chastises, he disciplines (*On Providence* 4.7).

For whom the Lord loveth, he chasteneth (Hebrews 12.6).

Foolish expectations:

How foolish it is to make plans for the future when a man does not own tomorrow! To say, I will buy and build, loan and call in money, win titles of honor, and then old and full of years I will surrender myself to a life of ease (*Epistles* 91.4).

And he said, This will I do: I will pull down my barns, and build greater; and there will I bestow all my fruits and my goods. And I will say to my soul, Soul, thou hast much goods laid up for many years; take thine ease, eat, drink, and be merry. But God said unto him, Thou fool, this night thy soul shall be required of thee; then whose shall those things be which thou hast provided? (Matthew 12.7.19.)

Life as warfare:

Life, Lucilius, is warfare (*Epistles* 96.3).

Fight the good fight of faith (I Timothy 6.12).

If these and a hundred other parallels to Scripture of equal plausibility or implausibility in the works of Seneca, the tragedies as well as the philosophical writings, are merely fortuitous, they are no less valid testimony to the presence of the same freshened conglomerate in both east and west. But no one can assert with confidence that Seneca and men of similar intellectual interests did not know the Septuagint directly. It is true that in all pagan literature there is only one specific reference to the Bible, the passage which Longinus (*On the Sublime* 9.9) drew from Caecilius of Caleacte, a highly regarded writer on rhetoric:

The lawgiver of the Jews, no ordinary man, having formed a worthy conception of divine power, gave expression to it at the very threshold of his *Laws* where he says: "God said"—what? " 'Let there be light,' and there was light. 'Let there be earth,' and there was earth."

It is unlikely that Caecilius would use a quotation which he knew was alien to all his readers, and unlikely that a man so bred to rhetoric as Seneca did not read Caecilius.

There is another bit of evidence which might indicate that

Seneca knew Bible stories—the dramatic device he uses at the end of his *Phaedra*. In Euripides' *Hippolytus* Theseus is made aware of Hippolytus' alleged dereliction through the awkward device of a letter. Seneca (and Racine after him) improves on this by having Hippolytus leave his sword, which Theseus of course recognizes. The suggestion for the improvement may have come from the parallel story of Joseph, where Potiphar is apprised of Joseph's alleged dereliction by the coat he had left behind. Seneca's form shows that he knew the diatribes, which were themselves a vehicle for eastern ethical teaching, and his matter that he knew the spirit and direction of that teaching.

Of all the classical Roman authors Seneca gives amplest expression to the world of hellenistic thought which was the product of three centuries of fusion between east and west, and of all pagan writers Seneca is surely the broadest channel to Europe. He was praised and admired by all the Fathers of the Latin Church, and was called *"Our* Seneca." [23] His authorship of the supposititious correspondence with St. Paul was not questioned until modern times. At the Council of Trent he was himself referred to as a Father of the Church; Calvin wrote a commentary on one of his treatises. It is hard to love Seneca the man, because of the discrepancies in his character—which may be due to the preparturitional struggle between Esau and Jacob within him. But it is harder to think of an individual who exemplifies more fully the processes with which this book is concerned.

Chapter XIX

AN ELECT,
WITH SOVEREIGNTY
AND WITHOUT

WHEN Deioces, who was a commoner, made himself king of the Medes, he built a magnificent palace surrounded by seven strong walls and introduced an elaborate ceremonial, as we read in Herodotus (1.99):

He allowed no one to have direct access to the person of the king, but made all communication pass through the hands of messengers, and forbade the king to be seen by his subjects. He also made it an offense for anyone whatsoever to laugh or spit in the royal presence. This ceremonial, of which he was the first inventor, Deioces established for his own security, fearing that his compeers, who were brought up together with him, and were of as good family as he, and no whit inferior to him in manly qualities, if they saw him frequently would be pained at the sight, and would therefore be likely to conspire against him; whereas if they did not see him, they would think him quite a different sort of being from themselves.[1]

Kings in the ancient Near East who had inherited their power needed no such elaborate precautions, for age-old tradition accepted them as gods or authorized agents of gods;[2] but rulers who institute a new and authoritarian regime have always had to surround themselves with a mystique, religious in nature or with religious overtones, Mussolini and Hitler no less than Deioces. Perhaps the most spectacularly successful example that history affords is the inauguration of the Roman empire. The second Caesar chose the title Augustus for its religious connotations and promulgated the doctrine that he was the providentially ordained leader of an elect which was to be bound together in the service of the special destiny to which it had been called.

The classic pattern for the process by which authority is centralized, given religious sanction, and made binding upon an elect appointed to follow a high destiny is provided by the Bible, and specifically by the reforms initiated in the reign of King Josiah of Judah in 621 B.C. We shall deal more fully with these reforms in the chapter following; here it may be said that their most notable objective was to concentrate authority in a single central sanctuary and to suppress rival or divergent elements. The "book of the law" (II Kings 22.8) which was the instrument of the reform, scholars agree, was substantially our book of Deuteronomy, and the influence of the Deuteronomist eventually informed every portion of the Biblical narrative, so that all history, from the Creation onwards, was made to point to and corroborate the exclusive authority of the central sanctuary.

The inevitable corollary of the doctrine of the central sanctuary which the Deuteronomist and all who followed him insisted upon was that its communicants constituted an elect, which could fulfill itself only by submission to the destiny for which the central authority was spokesman. Where the object of loyalty is a religious aspiration rather than a person, friction is bound to be generated between a strong-minded or a weak secular ruler and the religious authority; the Biblical accounts as we have them regularly show the dominance of the religious authority, whether prophetic or priestly. It could not be otherwise where the secular and religious authorities were separate (as they were not in the eastern monarchies and in the Augustan system) and where religious motivation was strong. When Ezra reorganized the state, after the Babylonian exile, authority was clearly centered in the high priest, and this situation apparently continued during the two centuries following; when the curtain of history is again raised,

after Alexander the Great, we find the high priest in sole authority
and his state, like others in the contemporary world, what the
Greeks called a temple state. When the Maccabees assumed rule
they did so in the quality of high priests, not kings, though they
were not of high priestly family.

In Egypt the Pharaoh himself had been a god, and the Ptolemies
adopted the position that they were the legitimate successors of
the Pharaohs. There is of course a difference between being ruled
by a god in human shape and being under the direction of a
transcendental God whose will is interpreted by intermediaries.
The Egyptians were docile possessions of their ruler; the Hebrews
participants in an enterprise to fulfill God's will. In the Seleucid
kingdom the situation was more complicated. The rulers acquired
their title, in the Greek view, by the right of conquest; their
dominions were "spear-won." But they could maintain their position only through a devoted following, which they made every
effort to enlarge, and soon adopted the expedient of deification,
which the climate of the hellenistic world had made normal.
Philosophers of the various Greek schools were much exercised to
find a rationale for the (to them) unexampled authority of the
kings, and arrived, as we have noticed, at the doctrine that the
king was *nomos empsychos*, law incarnate. In essence hellenistic
kingship was unqualifiedly autocratic; the king was master and
his subjects chattels.

But the Stoics had been advocating a different conception.
All men alike were equally members of the cosmos, and so equally
a part of a divine plan. There needed to be a ruler, they saw after
the first flush of revolutionary enthusiasm, to keep house for and
protect a great empire, but the housekeeper, like those he ministered
to, was a servant of the grand plan, not a master. We have seen
how this trend of thought was elaborated by Posidonius, whatever
its original impulse may have been, with direct reference to the
government of the Roman possessions. It was plainly under the
influence of Posidonius' teachings that the men around Augustus
formulated the program under which the empire was established. Their conceptions of Rome's place in the world were

crystallized into something like a creed, whose articles, briefly, were these: all of history is the working out of a divine plan; the objective of this plan, and the culmination of history, was the establishment and growth of Rome, and the destiny of Rome continues to be the central concern of providence. The mission of Rome, providentially ordained, is to pacify and civilize the world. The Romans, then, are an elect, with high privileges but equally high responsibilities. The instrument of destiny for guiding the Romans in the prosecution of their mission are their lawful rulers, who are divinely chosen and at least figuratively descended from the son of Venus. To deny the mission or, what amounts to the same thing, withhold obedience from its authorized administrators, is not merely criminal but sinful.

The Greeks too had been convinced of their superiority to "barbarians," but for one thing they did not invoke a theory of divine election, and for another, they were in fact very obviously superior to the barbarians they knew. But the Romans were very ready to acknowledge their cultural inferiority to the Greeks they ruled; since their professions forbade them to justify their rule on the bald basis of superior might, as the Athenians justified their destruction of Melos, they could only have recourse to claiming a mission. The doctrine of election as it appears in Augustan Rome is in fact a precise parallel to that in the Old Testament, and we shall see presently that the similarity may not have been accidental. It is plain to see that the entire Augustan system, with its rationale, was not a haphazard growth but a carefully constructed organism; the basis was Stoic political theory, though in practice deviations were as great as Cominform deviations from Marxist socialism. Stoic universalism required a leader for its implementation, and for practical reasons the leader's authority had to be acknowledged; so far Augustan propaganda could justify itself. The difficulty came when the ruler no longer regarded himself as the minister of a Stoic ideal—as Marcus Aurelius, for example, did—and became a master instead. Augustan propaganda is obvious in the works of all the major writers of the period, who were pensioners of Maecenas, a sort of minister of public information. This is not to suggest for a moment that Vergil and Horace and Livy were insincere or that their works were a perfunctory performance to gain livelihood. Any sensitive man might have very willingly done his sincere best to help realize a program which promised peace and civilization after a century of civil war, and might indeed have found his prime inspiration in such a program.

Let us look first at Vergil's *Aeneid*.[3] As in the case of all Roman poets, who regarded the Greek models in their respective genres as canonical, we can sense Vergil's own convictions by his conscious deviations from his Homeric models. Whereas Homer is concerned with heroic individuals, then, who make their own tragic choices and abide by the consequences, Vergil is concerned with an institution and a mission. Achilles not only withdraws from the fighting at a critical juncture, but prays for the defeat of his own people, and no one thinks the worse of him; Aeneas must constantly suppress his private wishes for the sake of the mission which has been imposed upon him and must school himself and his men to disciplined subordination to the destiny which has been outlined for them. His followers are called Aeneadae, children of Aeneas—the Greeks are never called children of Achilles or Odysseus—and Aeneas himself must subsume all the virtues his descendants are to show and must prove the worthy progenitor of the family which will bear rule when the Romans renew allegiance to their mission.

Here is one way to tell the story. Troy had been founded by the Latin Dardanus, and so the Trojans were in fact Italians who had sojourned for some centuries in what was to prove a temporary domicile; their true home, their promised land, was Italy. After a national humiliation a leader divinely appointed (Aeneas was the son of Venus, who had preserved him, alone of the greater Trojan chieftains, through the Trojan war) receives a mission to carry the national religious emblems back to Italy and found a state there. He conducts his people by a roundabout route, in the course of which they are subjected to many trials and to the temptation to give their mission up; but after a hard struggle

Aeneas succeeds in establishing his people in Italy and so in fulfilling the divine promise.

If the story so told suggests the exodus from Egypt and the
conquest of Canaan, another element in Vergil not found in the
Greek authors upon whom he modeled his work is even more
suggestive of eastern influences. In the course of the wanderings
and the conquest Aeneas receives repeated divine directions and
promises, which employ what may be called an apocalyptic technique. The device is common in intertestamentary writings on the
periphery of Scripture, and is represented by two examples in the
canon, Daniel and Revelation. In its typical form the apocalypse
assumes as its author some personage of the remote past who had
special opportunity to learn the divine plan; Enoch, of whom it
is written (Genesis 5.24), "And Enoch walked with God, and he
was not, for God took him," has several apocalyptic works
ascribed to his authorship, and Daniel himself belonged to the
Babylonian exile while his book was written under the Maccabees.
The alleged author, thus favored, writes his prophecy down, to
be discovered at a time of need. Because he places himself in the
remote past, the real author can "prophesy" events up to his own
day with great accuracy, and the credit for veracity thus established carries the reader forward to believe the encouraging
promises made for the actual future. Daniel can be dated to the
month, when its author left history behind—and guessed wrong.
Vergil's fictive standpoint is the twelfth century B.C., to which
date the Alexandrian scholars assigned the Trojan War. Since
Vergil himself lived in the first century B.C. he is able to "prophesy" events between the two dates quite accurately; and even a
critical reader who is aware that Vergil lived *after* the events he
prophesies is carried on to trust his picture of the actual future.
After his impressive recital of the great muster role of historical
Roman heroes and their achievements, the ghost of Aeneas pro-
claims Rome's mission (6.847–53):

> Let others fashion from bronze more lifelike, breathing images—
> For so they shall—and evoke living faces from marble;

Others excel as orators, others track with their instruments
The planets circling in heaven and predict when stars will appear.
But, Romans, never forget that government is your medium!
Be this your art:—to practise men in the habit of peace,
Generosity to the conquered, and firmness against aggressors.[4]

The conclusion, every reader must feel, is as unquestionable as its antecedents. Aeneas is clearly the instrument of destiny; Augustus, his descendant, can be no less so.

If Troy fell and Latium was taken in 1184 B.C., and Rome was established in 754 B.C., as Roman tradition held, the interval had to be accounted for. This is done in the fullest prophecy of all, that given by Jupiter to Venus when, at the beginning of the poem (1.257–96), he reassures her that her people's destiny remains unmovable. Ascanius, now to be called Iulus, will remove the kingdom to Alba Longa where it will remain for three hundred years. Then Ilia, of Trojan blood, will give birth to Mars' twin sons, and Romulus will establish Rome and give his name to the Romans.

To these I set no bounds, either in space or time;
Unlimited power I give them. Even the spiteful Juno,
Who in her fear now troubles the earth, the sea and the sky,
Shall think better of this and join me in fostering
The cause of the Romans, the lords of creation, the togaed people.
Thus it is written. An age shall come, as the years glide by,
When the children of Troy shall enslave the children of
    Agamemnon,
Of Diomed and Achilles, and rule in conquered Argos.
From the fair seed of Troy there shall be born a Caesar—
Julius, his name derived from great Iulus—whose empire
Shall reach to the ocean's limits, whose fame shall end in the stars.
He shall hold the East in fee; one day, cares ended, you shall
Receive him into heaven; him also will mortals pray to.
Then shall the age of violence be mellowing into peace:
Venerable Faith, and the Home, with Romulus and Remus,
Shall make the laws; the grim, steel-welded gates of War
Be locked; and within, on a heap of armaments, a hundred
Bronzen knots tying his hands behind him, shall sit
Growling and bloody-mouthed the godless spirit of Discord.

The problem of chronology which is here harmonized is very like the problem in early Hebrew history, and the solution (presented in much greater detail in Livy's parallel account) is like that in the historical books of the Old Testament. Joshua and Judges divide the interval between the exodus from Egypt and the establishment of the monarchy under Saul, roughly between the fourteenth and ninth centuries B.C., into periods which are multiples of forty years, and the added circumstance that the reigns of Saul, David, and Solomon are each given forty years suggests an artificial schematization. In itself this parallel need indicate nothing more than that similar problems evoke similar responses. But Vergil's use of a hero and pattern unexampled in antecedent pagan literature but very like the story of Moses, combined with the apocalyptic technique which looks forward to a kind of salvation, does suggest Scriptural influence; and we have seen above [5] that the Sibylline Oracles may well have served as the channel of that influence.

Livy's history, which has been called own sister to Vergil's *Aeneid*, starts with the same premises and moves to the same goal.[6] In many details, as in its over-all effect, it is much closer to the historical books of the Old Testament than to Herodotus or Thucydides. Both these historians show Athenian sympathies, but neither regards Athenian superiority as something to be naturally assumed by author and reader. Livy's Romans are in the natural order of things children of destiny, lords of creation, fated to prevail over all other peoples. Livy cannot marvel at Roman expansion as Polybius does any more than he could marvel at water running down hill. From the beginning heaven guided Rome to its destiny (1.4.1): "It was to fate, I hold, that the founding of this great city, the beginning of this empire, mightiest next after heaven's, is due." Rome's first king, immediately upon his translation to heaven, sends word (1.16.7): "Go and declare to the Romans the will of heaven that my Rome shall be the capital of the world; so let them cherish the art of war, and let them know and teach their children that no human strength can resist Roman arms." From the circumstances of its occurrence it is no exaggeration to say that this quotation is intended to serve as a sort of text for Livy's whole enterprise. It is made to apply to Roman expansion, as at 26.37.5: "Fortune had already engaged, as it were, to grant the Roman rule over the east." It is made to apply to the Roman habit of rising to victory after defeat, as at 26.41.9: "Fate has so ordained our lot that though we are overcome in our great wars we yet prevail."

Here are some practices of Livy which are nearer to the Old Testament than to Livy's Greek predecessors. The persistence of Rome's enemies is divinely ordained either to try the Romans, to punish them for backsliding, to provide means for keeping them alert, or to give public testimony to their superiority. Speaking of the Gallic invasion of 390 B.C. Florus (who follows Livy) says: "So great was the disaster that it must be reckoned a trial set by the gods to show whether Roman fortitude deserved world empire." Of the same disaster Camillus, who is the voice incarnate of Roman idealism, is made to say (Livy 5.51.8): "Conquered, captured, and redeemed, we were punished so severely by gods and men that we might serve as an example to the whole world." This is not very different from the concept of Assyria as the rod of Jehovah's anger and the staff in their hand as his indignation against the backsliding children of Israel (Isaiah 10.5), or of the Canaanites being left in Palestine after the conquest to prove Israel by them (Judges 3.1).

Such moral qualities as *fides*, *pietas*, *clementia* are represented by Augustan propaganda as virtually Roman monopolies. Every war, especially where there might be reason to suppose otherwise, is represented as a *bellum iustum*. Apparent Roman violations of treaty obligations, as in the Caudine surrender (9.5.2) or the Campanian alliance (7.31.1), are justified on legal grounds. Gabii is indeed taken by a ruse, but that was done by an irresponsible Tarquin, *minime arte Romana, fraude ac dolo* (1.53.4). When Camillus returned to the Faliscans their children whom the schoolmaster would have betrayed, they yielded voluntarily, not merely out of gratitude but because they recognized the worth of Roman *fides* (5.27.13). By corollary the lesser breeds without the law are assumed to be not only deficient in these traits but generally inferior. Not only are Syrians "a vile species of humanity, born for slavery" (36.17.5), but even Athenians are "good only for words and letters" (31.44.9). An account like that of the duel between Titus Manlius and the Gaul (7.10) is clearly intended to point the contrast between the sober, restrained Roman, with confidence resting on assured competence, and the gaudy undisciplined Gaul, who emphasizes his childishness by putting his tongue out at his opponent. *Fides* is not to be expected of non-Romans; *Punica religio* is a proverbial oxymoron, which ingenuous Romans sometimes, but always to their regret, accept at face value.

The gauge of truth which determines what stories should be told or what version of a given story should be preferred is frankly the extent to which the story or version documents the Augustan ideal. A similar principle is involved in the etiological stories so frequent in the early books of Livy. Places holy and accursed, institutions religious and secular, formulaic expressions, are given authority by reference to some hallowed event in antiquity. Particularly in the treatment of hallowed personages is Livy's history a kind of hagiographa. Numa, Camillus, even Scipio Africanus are hedged about with a kind of sanctity alien to their Greek counterparts. Horatius Cocles, Mucius Scaevola, Cloelia, to take characters from a single episode (2.10 ff.), are not credible human beings but bloodless embodiments of the Roman ideal. Polybius (6.55) has Horatius die in the Tiber, and Dionysius of Halicarnassus (5.33) has Cloelia and her companions effect their escape by prevailing upon their Etruscan guards to turn their backs while the girls bathe; such human possibilities as baths and drowning are somehow not to be thought of in connection with Livy's beatification of these heroes.

Not only are these figures from the remote and possibly legendary past transfigured, but even in the case of approved leaders in familiar periods of history their merits are exaggerated and their failings glossed over. This tendency appears, for example, in the characterizations of the three heroes of the Second Punic

War, Fabius Cunctator, Marcellus, and Scipio Africanus, for each of whom, however, Livy incidentally provides enough unfavorable information to render suspect the wholly favorable picture it is his manifest intention to give. Conversely, unsuccessful generals are shown to have been impiously negligent in ritual observances. In the same war Flaminius and Varro are the scapegoats. The principal charge against Flaminius (and the exculpation for the disastrous defeat at Trasimene) was his mad godlessness, illustrated by his taking up the consulship at Ariminum instead of Rome (21.63); but that he did so is plainly disproved by Polybius 3.77.1. And if Varro were really responsible for the disaster at Cannae the thanks he received (22.61.4) would have been unthinkably ironic, and he would surely not have been continued in important commands year after year (25.6.7, 27.35.2).

In all these cases, indeed, and for the whole republican period the intention seems to be that the stature of the great personage be documented by the historical events, not that the events be illuminated by the character of the participants. Thucydides, for example, provides telling characterizations of an Alcibiades, a Nicias, a Cleon, but only in order to make the events in which they participated intelligible. Livy provides a gallery of saints for their own sake, because it is a good thing for Romans to bear their saints in mind. The same hagiologic purpose is served by the thundering roll of heroes recited by Anchises' ghost in the sixth *Aeneid*. And Augustus himself put before Vergil's and Livy's readers an actual gallery of all Roman triumphators from Aeneas down, done in bronze and placed in a double row of niches in the walls of his magnificent new Forum, with the name and distinctions of each hero engraved on the plinth and his achievements summarized on a marble slab fixed to the wall below.

Of all this line of worthies the natural consummation was Augustus himself. In terms of the republican constitution which he claimed to have restored, his position was anomalous; he himself insisted that his preeminence rested only on his greater *auctoritas*, which, as we shall notice, had virtually a religious force. But that he consciously employed the associations of religion to enhance his position is put beyond question by the title he chose: "Augustus" definitely carries a religious connotation. He associated the worship of his own *genius* with the cult of the Lares Compitales in each of the fourteen regions into which he divided Rome, and he identified worship of himself and worship of Rome in the numerous temples to "Rome and Augustus" throughout the empire. In these temples the *Res Gestae Divi Augusti*, to which reference will be made, was engraved on the inner or sacred wall in the original Latin, and on the outer wall, where the colonials could read it, in the colonials' own Greek. Augustus considered himself a kind of avatar of Romulus, the founder of Rome, and it is indicative of Livy's attitude that in his account of Romulus' death he makes the people complain (1.17.7) "that their servitude was only multiplied, for now there were a hundred masters instead of one." In the whole account of the regal period the benefits conferred by the "good" kings are emphasized; the institution of monarchy is criticized only in its abuse.

Whether the Romans had arrived at their conceptions of Rome's place in the universe and of the Roman's duty to Rome independently as the most practical response to the challenge which confronted them, or whether Posidonius who adumbrated the doctrine and Vergil who gave it currency had learned from the east, the Roman and Jewish ideas in this area are so close as to approach identity. That is why Christianity, which inherited the idea from the Jews, alone of the new cults which came in from the east was unable to come to terms with Rome. Christians cherished a loyalty to another kingdom, more exigent even and less capable of being shared than loyalty to Rome. No compromise was possible, one or the other must give way. And therefore when Christianity prevailed it *became* Rome.

But before Christianity became strong enough to challenge Rome, what did Christians, and what did men with other loyalties who accepted Rome's domination perforce, do? One answer is provided, not specifically to be sure, but by easy implication by Plutarch. On the surface Plutarch's career is puzzling. Here is a

man who had made a brilliant success in the world capital, who
had friends there powerful enough to make him an honorary
consul (as we know, significantly, not from himself but from
epigraphical evidence), and who, instead of remaining at Rome
to enjoy his position, as a hundred other Greek "philosophers"
did, returned to his native Chaironea, a small and bookless town,
as he himself admits (*Demosthenes* 4) "but it would be even
smaller if I moved away." A man who had been entrusted with
important embassies in his youth becomes market inspector of a
provincial town, a man who knew all the philosophies priest of an
obsolescent cult at Delphi, a man at whose feet the intelligentsia
of Rome had sat collects the youth of Chaironea around a table
and discourses to them of literature and mathematics and music.
The answer is plain. Plutarch was doing the things a Greek was
expected to do. He must participate in public life, and if he could
not be archon at Athens he would be market inspector at Chaironea. A Greek must cherish Greek tradition, and Delphi was the
traditional hearth of Greek tradition. A Greek must be alert to
the intellectual quest, and he initiated Greek youth to that quest.
In the *Parallel Lives* he wrote we miss the great poets and artists
and find only generals and statesmen. That was because he was
not, as has been held, introducing Greeks to Romans or Romans
to Greeks, but Greeks to Greeks, to prove to his own people that
Greece had produced generals and statesmen to equal the Roman
—even Romans would admit that Greek poets and artists were
preeminent. If we find it absurd to think that anyone should think
Cato superior to Aristides or Fabius Maximus to Pericles we must
remember that Greece had been under Roman domination for
two centuries and might be inclined to accept their rulers' estimate of their heroes. That we think otherwise is proof of Plutarch's success.

What Plutarch was doing was making the Greek way of life
into a cult,[7] which could command and receive loyalty even when
sovereignty was lost, and which could therefore find adherents
without regard to national boundaries. It has been said that Plutarch syncretized religion, but the statement must be qualified.

The plain fact is that his syncretism never involves mingling but the assimilation of an alien God to Greek ideas. This was notably the case with the Egyptian religion, for whose antiquity he had a reverent regard and to whose identity with the Greek Herodotus had already pointed. Exotic religions which were incapable of assimilation to the Greek he looked upon as barbarous superstitions. Here is his opinion of the Jews, for example (169C): "Because it was the Sabbath day the Jews sat in their places immovable while the enemy were planting ladders against the walls of Jerusalem and capturing the defenses, and they did not get up, but remained there, fast bound in the toils of superstition as in one great net." And here is his judgment of another non-assimilable people (799D): "The Carthaginians are bitter, sullen, subservient to their rulers, harsh to their subjects, most abject when afraid, most savage when enraged, stubborn in adhering to decisions, disagreeable and hard in their attitude towards playfulness and urbanity."

It is an odd coincidence—surely nothing more—or a demonstration that like situations evoke like responses that another articulate people who cherished a cultural tradition offered the same response to Roman domination. The zealots who defended Jerusalem against Titus so desperately did so because they shared the universal conviction that loss of sovereignty meant the loss of all communal identity, including the communal religion. Its gods were believed to desert a falling city forever, and in speaking of the fall of Jerusalem Tacitus said that the departure of its god was signalized by a whistling sound (*Histories* 11). But before Jerusalem fell Johanan ben Zakkai had himself spirited out of the doomed city in a coffin, gathered young men about him at provincial Jabneh, and transformed what had been a sovereignty into a way of life depending upon the study of a literature.[8] So far the parallel with what Plutarch was doing is very close. The great difference was that whereas Plutarch's was only metaphorically a cult, Johanan's was one in fact. Eventually the successors of his school achieved a kind of para-governmental authority over their communicants within the sovereignty of the Roman Empire, prescribed religious requirements in detail, sent official emissaries abroad to carry their decisions and collect tribute, and used the power of excommunication to enforce obedience upon such as recognized their authority. The pattern for a spiritual brotherhood among men independent of national boundaries has been salutary, and may be of even greater usefulness in the years to come.

Chapter XX

AUTHORITY AND LAW

OF the various factors which give civilization its character, perhaps the most persistent and pervasive and indeed the most indispensable for making a social continuum possible is the concept of law and of the authority which gives law its sanction. So essential is law to the human condition that, like love, we tend to accept the manifestations of it with which we are familiar as "natural"; actually, as we have seen to be the case with love, what we have are conventions, so deeply rooted that they are no longer recognizable as such. In the east, with certain important qualifications which we shall presently notice, law was clothed with supernatural sanctions, so that deviation would amount to religious transgression. In Greece the most characteristic index of fifth-century enlightenment is Protagoras' doctrine of "man the measure." The authority of law, in this view, is based not on "nature" (*physis*) and hence immutable, but on "convention" (*nomos;* the word means both "law" and "accepted usage"). What is formulated by human society is susceptible to change.[1] Even in Greece this position, associated with the Sophists, was vigorously opposed, and it is significant that where an authoritarian system was advocated, as in Sparta's practice or Plato's theory, supernatural sanction was involved.

For the shaping of European civilization the emergence of unified conceptions of law and authority is the most meaningful consequence of interaction between east and west in the hellenistic age. In this area remoter origins are especially significant, and we shall therefore start with a brief survey of non-hellenic theory, including India and China also for the useful comparisons they offer.[2] In Egypt, as the following exposition by John A. Wilson shows, the situation was very simple:

Egypt

The basic proposition with regard to authority and the source of law in ancient Egypt is that the king of Egypt was a god. This may have been expressed in different ways in the course of Egyptian history, and this official dogma may have been imperfectly carried out in different periods, but there is abundant evidence from the beginning of the dynasties down to the Roman emperors that the ruler of Egypt was no representative or servant of the gods, did not rule by a divine right which came to him with his throne, but ruled because he was born a god, with the divine function of rule inherent in his physical and spiritual being.[3]

Though he continued to be a god, the king eventually ceased to function as such but became the tool of priests, whose principal concern was the preservation and extension of their own prerogatives. It was this that caused the mummification and eventual disintegration of Egyptian culture.

Mesopotamia

In ancient Mesopotamia the king was not a god but merely the god's trusted agent and himself subject to the god's law. But to interpret the wishes of the god required expertise, so that in fact the king was subject to the discretion and manipulation of the priests.[4] Not being himself a god, morever, the king was to some degree limited by a consultative body of elders, and this makes the Mesopotamian picture more sympathetic to European eyes. But the concept of divinely ordained law with its concomitant of a powerful priesthood remains. The situation in the Hittite kingdom was much the same. A Hittite text reads: "The land belongs to the Storm-god, heaven and earth with the people belong to the Storm-god. And he made the Labarna, the king, his deputy and gave him the whole land of Hattusa. The Labarna shall govern the whole land."[5] Again the authority of the king was to some degree limited by elders and priests. But from the circumstance that the Hittite king's person was sacrosanct and that elaborate rules were set up to protect him from contamination we can surmise that priests played a dominant role.

LEGAL AUTONOMY OF DISPARATE SOCIAL GROUPS (handwritten)

Indian law, in its earliest period, was virtually autonomous within the disparate social groups, and the king was invoked only in cases of dispute between groups or when the normal institutions of society broke down. As society grew more complex the legal authority of the king increased, until, in the kingdom of Magadha in northeast India, which had conquered all northern India about 500 B.C., a thoroughly totalitarian regime was introduced. Every aspect of life was regulated with a sole view to the interest of the king, who maintained a most elaborate bureaucracy with spies and counterspies, agents provocateurs and assassins, to see that his interests did not suffer. "The chief end," it was baldly stated, "is material advantage, for the other aims of life, both religion and pleasure, depend upon it." Amusement places, musicians, and actors were forbidden, "for then the men will take pleasure only in their fields; and the king's revenue, forced labor, goods, and crops can be increased." Invasion and foreign rule brought the expanded Hindu state to an end, and the kings of later dynasties reverted to the old religious law, which remained dominant throughout the rest of Indian history. But if the king renounced much of his secular power, his claims to religious sanctity were higher than ever, and here again the manipulation of the priesthood is evident. His principal duty, indeed, was to preserve the fourfold nature of society, to see to it that no brahmin plowed or traded and that no sudra or tradesman entered the nobility or assumed brahmin functions.[6] In effect authority came to be centered on maintaining the prerogatives of a caste, as in Egypt, and as in Egypt the result was mummification.

CHINA (handwritten) The most nearly secular of the non-hellenic systems would seem to be the Chinese, at least during the Chou dynasty (11th to 3rd centuries B.C.), which is the period relevant to our interests.[7] There was no universal church and no significant priesthood; instead there was a cult of ancestors and an elaborate but unwritten code of politeness and honor known as _li_. Society was organized as a feudalism, with the king at the apex of the pyramid. The king did possess a religious sanction in that he held the _t'ien ming,_ or "mandate of heaven," but he was himself definitely

not a divine being. Heaven shows its approval of a king by conferring the mandate (*ming*) upon him; but heaven may withdraw
or transfer the mandate for sufficient reasons. The conception of
the *ming* was very like that of the *imperium* in Rome; the *imperium*, as we shall notice, was abstract sovereignty which might
be transferred or shared. About the fourth and third centuries B.C.
the group of statesmen and theorists known as the Legalists attempted to exalt law as the sole sanction of human conduct; *li*,
in their view, was not a sufficient curb on human selfishness. This
phase was transitory, however, and Confucianism, which is in effect *li*, took its place. Of this system Bodde writes:

The Confucian theory that has since prevailed has been democratic in
the sense that it has consistently emphasized the ideal of government
for the people, has tried to counter absolutism by the weight of a
morally-educated non-hereditary bureaucracy, and has sanctioned occasional political change as an escape from tyranny. It has been un-
democratic, however, in the sense that it has never recognized the need
of government *by* the people as a whole, has always regarded such
government as the particular preserve of a small ruling elite, and has
sanctioned political change only in terms of shifting personalities, not
of basic change in the political and social order.[8]

From this survey it would appear that the most absolute authority is that which bases its sanction upon religion, and that
even when the sanction of religion is slight the people is still without a voice. When, as in Israel, it does acquire a voice, of equal
or even greater weight than the rulers', it is again upon the sanction of religion, when the whole people is conceived of as "a
kingdom of priests and a holy nation." In Israel kings could never
be supreme autocrats because the sovereignty belonged to God
acting through the people.[9] Kingship had grown out of the institution of "judges," and had been inaugurated for the specific purpose of military defense; its only claim was that it had received
divine approval, which, however, was given with reluctance (I
Samuel 10.17 and elsewhere). Nor was the king an intermediary
between God and his people; that function was reserved to the
prophets, who were consistently antimonarchical and insisted on

their priority in time and authority. King and people alike were responsible to the law.

Their willing subjection to the law made of the Israelites a polity which was conditioned neither by a sovereign ruler nor territory, which was why the polity could continue after territory and sovereign were lost. To attach the polity to a particular territory and administration required a special and vigorous effort, and we can point to the precise date when a central apparatus asserted a claim to total and exclusive authority, placed the whole body of its own legislation under religious sanctions, and suppressed rival or divergent practices. The date was 621 B.C., when the Kingdom of Judah had undergone a series of attacks like those which had destroyed the kingdom of Israel a century before, and, according to II Kings 22, the high priest Hilkiah "found," the prophetess Huldah corroborated, and King Josiah promulgated "the book of the law." This book, scholars agree, is substantially our book of Deuteronomy. The teachings which were embodied in Josiah's reforms had been elaborated by a prophetic party, mainly the disciples of Isaiah and Micah, but the formulation of their program was laid down by a master mind and has affected history to this day.[10]

The main body of the legislation was, of course, systematization and ethical refinement of usages and laws long current, many adapted from the Canaanites and going back to the code of Hammurabi, which had been reduced to writing in Babylonia more than a millennium before. Nor is the genuineness of biblical materials anterior to 621 to be impugned. Not only are the texts of certain prophets and isolated Psalms authentic, and the tradition of the Patriarchs, the Judges, and the Conquest ancient, but the data on the establishment and the division of the monarchy and the succession of kings are thoroughly historical. What is revolutionary and essential in the Deuteronomist view is the exclusive and paramount authority reposed in the single central sanctuary. All antecedent history was made to serve the new doctrine; none of the historiographical portions of the Old Testament, whether referring to the period before or after 621, is untouched by Deu-

teronomist influence. Though the Old Testament books anterior
to Kings are based on sound tradition and in large part transcribe
ancient sources, the *form* in which we have them are redactions,
sometimes compounded of a number of ancient documents, made
after 621, and calculated, by selection and distribution of emphasis, to reenforce the reforms of 621. The process is easiest to
notice in the lists of kings, where, regardless of his effectiveness
as warrior or administrator, each king is assessed solely on his attitude to the worship of the central shrine or of the Baalim. By
ordinary historical reckoning the two most celebrated kings of
Israel would be Omri (886–875) and Jeroboam II (784–744); of
Omri King Mesha of Moab tells us on his monument that he conquered the whole East Jordan country, and the Assyrians called
Israel the House of Omri a hundred years after the downfall of
his dynasty. But by the Deuteronomist's gauge these kings were
negligible, and are dismissed with the remark that they did *not*
suppress Baal worship.

The tone thus set was maintained. Ezekiel preached that the
exiles of 586 would be restored forever if the new sanctuary they
would build would be kept pure of all profanation and follow a
rigid cult. It was under his influence that the little book in Leviti-
cus 17–26 called the Holiness Code ("H") was compiled; here
the concept of the exclusive authority of the temple is further accentuated. The fourth of the great Pentateuchal documents, P,
which is dated to about 500 B.C. and shows the influence of Ezra,
uses all antecedent history, beginning with the creation, to enhance the sanctity of rites and institutions connected with the
temple. Ezra's main preoccupation was centralization of authority
in the new temple; he saw the chief danger to its purity in the
habit of intermarriage with devotees of other cults, apparently
widespread, and devoted his best efforts to putting an end to the
practice. That he met with considerable resistance we can see not
only from his own book but also from the book of Ruth, which
is a calculated refutation of Ezra's prohibition; according to that
book David himself would have been illegitimate by Ezra's law.
Among the prophets contemporary with Ezra we find a preoc-

JEWISH
HIGHER
SOVEREIGNTY OF DIVINE LAW

cupation with the abuses which vexed Ezra and support for Ezra's program. Haggai is mainly concerned with the rebuilding of the temple and a purified priesthood; Zechariah is concerned that the high priest should have adequate authority; and Malachi is con-· cerned that the sacrificial cult be worthily maintained.

P was clearly the fundamental law of the Second Common-wealth. The two centuries after Ezra are dim, but at the opening of the hellenistic age we find Judaea a typical hellenistic temple state, with authority, secular as well as religious, in the hands of the high priest. But the teachings of the ancient prophets remained vital. High priest and people alike were subject to the higher sovereignty of the divine law; the high priest was not a sovereign but a minister, and might forfeit his position if he deviated from the law. That is why the Maccabees were eager to find a basis in tradition for their deviations, and why their Pharisee opponents countered them with a different interpretation of tradition. The deviations which the Maccabees desired were in the direction of putting their principality on a footing with other hellenistic prin-cipalities, and this implied adaptation of Greek political theory and practice. It was the mingling of the elements which largely determined subsequent European political theory, and we must therefore look at the patterns which the Greeks had to offer.

We must start with the premise that the political institutions of all Greek peoples, whether Ionian or Dorian, derived from a sin-gle pattern; differences in development are therefore to be at-tributed to conscious design, not, as was once the fashion, to differences in race. In such essentials as religion and language the Greeks were homogeneous, and so they were, until certain in-novations were introduced to meet a specific crisis, in government also. The universal pattern, as far back as it can be traced, was a distribution of powers between king, nobles, and commons. The proportion allotted to each might differ from state to state and from age to age, but even when one element was suppressed, as when the kingship at Athens was replaced by elected magistrates, a vestigial remnant of the older system persisted; ceremonial functions associated with kingship were performed by an official designated "king" for the purpose.

During the seventh and sixth centuries B.C. virtually all the Greek city-states came temporarily under the rule of tyrants; the term denotes not cruel oppression (except in the language of fifth-century Athens) but unconstitutional usurpation of power, which was usually exercised by the tyrant himself, if not by his heir, with marked benevolence. The incidence of tyranny followed a pattern so common that generalizations on the subject were drawn by all theorists from Herodotus to Polybius. Under a weak ruler the nobles aggrandized their power and oppressed the commons. Some leader, usually himself a noble, espoused the cause of the commons and obtained a bodyguard to protect him against the nobles; so armed he seized full power. He himself served the people well, if only to legitimize a dynasty, but his heir was usually haughty and oppressive, and was supplanted by a democracy, which then found it expedient to delegate executive authority to a king, whereupon the cycle could in theory begin anew. A logic equally perspicuous governs the changes in the Athenian constitution associated with the names of Draco and Solon, Cleisthenes and Pericles. Each is perfectly intelligible in terms of the situation it was designed to remedy. Each was promoted or resisted on secular grounds, and none needed to invoke the authority of religion.[11]

For the Spartan reforms associated with the name of Lycurgus religion *was* invoked. It was only after the reforms, which revolutionized all of life, that the term "Spartan" came to denote the utmost in frugality, discipline, and obedience to authority; archaeology and the history of literature show that until the sixth century the Spartans were as luxury-loving and liberal as other Greeks. Xenophon in his *Constitution of the Lacedemonians* praises the Spartan *agoge* in the highest terms for the military virtues it inculcated, and Plutarch in his *Life of Lycurgus* expatiates on the moral advantages of suppressing luxury. But even with the generous construction Plutarch puts upon them we can see from the regulations he cites that Sparta claimed a fuller authority over the lives of its citizens than has ever been claimed by any secular state. Property belonged to the state, and allotments to individuals could not be sold or mortgaged. Children could be reared only if the state approved, and were brought up under state authority. From childhood to old age the Spartan belonged to some military unit and was subject to military authority at all times. His sex life, his food, his amusements, his living quarters were strictly controlled. Sumptuary prescriptions regulated the decorations in his house. He could not accumulate property, nor travel abroad, nor entertain visitors from abroad. The Spartan's whole duty was to serve Sparta; the Spartan woman's to bear sons who would serve Sparta.[12]

The authoritarian administration which regimentation so particularized requires was provided for by manipulating the traditional pattern of king, nobles, and commons. The king could do nothing without the approval of ephors, whom they obeyed, Polybius tells us, "as children obey their parents" (23.11). A vestige of their former position may be seen in their ceremonial refusal to come at the ephors' bidding until they had been called thrice, but their slightest tendency to independent action was punished. On a military campaign the king was accompanied by, and had to do the bidding of, two ephors.

The *gerousia* or council of elders numbered thirty, of which two were the kings. The ordinary members were required to be above sixty years of age (the point of retirement from military service) and to belong to the nobility. The method of election was curious. Each candidate passed before the assembly, which indicated its preference by the volume of its applause; this was gauged by a board of judges shut out of sight. Aristotle (*Politics* 1270b) calls this procedure childish; if the object was to return predetermined candidates while preserving the appearance of free choice, the procedure was far from childish.

The assembly, called Apella in Sparta, included all freeborn Spartiates in good standing, that is, those who had not been disgraced and who paid their contribution to the *syssitia* or common table; their means for doing so were the land allotments worked

by helots. The Apella met in the open air, in the 1
the side of a river. No one could speak out; all tha
was to indicate approval or disapproval of what w
the meeting. Nor was even so limited a function
law provided that "if the people decide crookedly it shall be lawful for the leaders to prorogue the assembly."

About the origin of the ephorate, in which all power was centered, there is great uncertainty. It is quite possible that there were
ephors before the reform, and that they had some lesser, perhaps
religious, function. But whatever their origin, it is evident from
their functions in the Lycurgan system that they were the nerve
center of a completely authoritarian state. This can be seen most
clearly in the circumstance that it was the ephors who were in
charge of the Krypteia, or secret police. It may be that the
Krypteia is a sublimated vestige of a primitive initiation ritual,
and some innocent scholars have compared it to the Boy Scouts;
but we know from Plutarch that the ephors sent young men en-
listed in this service on secret missions which involved terroriza-
tion and assassination of helots. A horrifying account of how the
Krypteia did two thousand selected helots to death is to be read
in Thucydides 4.80. The existence of a secret police charged with
such duties is sufficient indication that a state is totalitarian, and
that authority rests in the group which disposes of the services of
that police.

That the Spartan system was an invention rather than a natural
growth is certain. Even before the modern totalitarianisms opened
our eyes to the implications of the Spartan system Martin Nilsson
had written: [13] "The methodical and purposeful way in which
everything has been made to lead towards one single goal forces
us to see here the intervention of a consciously shaping hand."
The Greeks themselves were no less aware that a system so novel,
so complete, and so consistent must imply an inventor, and common tradition attributed the laws to Lycurgus, who had received
them from Delphi. Herodotus (1.65 f.) reports the words with
which the oracle glorified Lycurgus and then adds: "Some report
besides that the priestess delivered to him the entire system of

ws which are still observed by the Spartans." Diodorus Siculus (7.12) is more positive; he cites two additional lines of the oracle which read: "And you have come asking for a good constitution. Indeed I myself will give you one which no other city on earth will possess." The authority but not the authorship of the laws is ascribed to Delphi by Xenophon, next in time to Herodotus; he says (*Constitution of the Lacedemonians* 8):

But of all the many and beautiful contrivances invented by Lycurgus to kindle a willing obedience to the laws in the hearts of the citizens, none, to my mind, was happier or more excellent than his unwillingness to deliver his code to the people at large until, attended by the most powerful members of the state, he had betaken himself to Delphi and there made inquiry whether it were better for Sparta, and conducive to her interests, to obey the laws which he had framed. And not until the divine answer came, "Better will it be in every way," did he deliver them, laying it down as a last ordinance that to refuse obedience to a code which had the sanction of the Pythian god himself was a thing not illegal only but impious.[14]

Crime has become sin. After Xenophon we have no more hairsplitting; Apollo is recognized as responsible for the Spartan constitution, as a passage at the opening of Plato's *Laws* indicates. The Cretan Cleinias asks, "In Lacedemon I believe they would say that Apollo is their lawgiver; would they not, Megillus?" And the Spartan Megillus answers, "Certainly."

"Concerning Lycurgus the lawgiver," Plutarch says at the opening of his *Life*, "nothing at all can be said which is not disputed, since indeed there are different accounts of his birth, his travels, his death, and above all, of his work as lawmaker and statesman; and there is least agreement among historians as to the times in which the man lived." The only reasonable deduction from the mass of conflicting evidence is that Lycurgus was not the inventor of the Spartan constitution, and that his name (which probably represented an ancient wolf god) was deliberately associated with the new legislation to enhance its credit. If we give Lycurgus up as the author of the constitution that went under his name and hold to the conviction that it was an invention, our sources leave us only with Apollo as the inventor. Apollo *was* the inventor if we understand by Apollo the consistent antidemocratic policy of Delphi, and its particularly intimate connections with Sparta. Delphi was always against Athens and democracy. In the Persian War it Medized and in the Peloponnesian War it Laconized; at the beginning of that war it proclaimed (Thucydides 1.118) that "invited or uninvited" it would take Sparta's part. Later, when Macedonia rose to threaten democracy, Delphi consistently Philipized. Delphi constantly intervened in determining the succession to the kingship at Sparta. Each of the Spartan kings had associated with him two officials called Pythioi who traveled back and forth between Sparta and Delphi and "assisted" the king in administering the oracles. Periodically the ephors would sit gazing at the heavens on a moonless night, and if they observed a shooting star they would suspend the kings from office pending a decision from Delphi.

It was the authority of Delphi, as our sources unanimously testify, that made the Spartans obey their constitution; indeed, it is hard to imagine any force other than religion that could have constrained them to do so. We have come very close to the more authoritarian systems described at the opening of this chapter, except that the executive arm is not the deity himself or his royal agent but an anonymous group of manipulators. And we have gone beyond the ancient Judaean concept in which the people itself was sovereign as the agent of God. On the basis of their previous history we should expect that the easterners would be more susceptible to an authoritarian system claiming a religious sanction than to a polity of the Athenian type, but there were also other factors which favored the Spartan theory. The great philosophic and literary exponent of the Spartan ideal was Plato, in the *Republic* and more frankly in the *Laws*. Plato was an enormous force in the east not merely through education, as has been suggested above, but by the fact that the hellenistic rulers implemented his ideals; the various philosophic justifications for hellenistic kingship all rest ultimately on Platonic doctrine.

Apparently even the Stoics advocated the Spartan system, though they tried to channel it in Stoic directions. After their first flush of revolutionary enthusiasm they realized that only through kingly authority could their reforms come to pass. In Plutarch's *Lives of Agis and Cleomenes* we can see one of them, Sphairos of Borysthenes, guiding and encouraging the Spartan king to restore the ancient equality, which had broken down when a fifth-century ephor named Epitadcus had rescinded the laws which made it impossible to accumulate wealth.[15] The system of land tenure which Cleomenes attempted to restore is set forth in detail in Plutarch's *Life of Lycurgus*, and modern scholars, following the lead of George Grote, have suspected that the entire program was a new Stoic invention, retrojected into the past to give it authority, so that reforms could be represented as restoration of tradition rather than innovation. This, it may be noted, is precisely what the advisers of Josiah and then Ezra had done when they retrojected their innovations to the period of the Exodus, and this is what the Maccabees and their opponents were to do.

It was the Judaean commonwealth which came to terms with the Greek and bequeathed the amalgam to Europe, and we must now turn to the development of political ideology in Judaea.[16] In the early part of the hellenistic period Judaea was, as we have seen, a temple state, under the rule of the high priest; under the ancient monarchy the high priest had not held secular authority. According to tradition the institution called the Great Synod was established by Ezra and continued as the authoritative religious body, performing such functions as fixing the Scriptural canon; but there seems to be no continuity between this body, if it actually existed, and the later Sanhedrin, which was modeled on Greek patterns.

When, in 140 B.C., the Seleucid Demetrius had renounced suzerainty over Judaea the people (how organized we are not told) made Simon "leader and high priest forever, until a true prophet should arise" (I Maccabees 14.41). The provisional character of the designation was due to its revolutionary character: Simon was not of the high priestly family. Simon was only a "leader" (*hegemon*), not a king. Nor did his son John Hyrcanus, who succeeded when independence had been lost and regained and his father had been assassinated at a drunken feast, assume the title of king; his coins bear the legend "John the High Priest and the Commonwealth of the Jews." The title of king was taken by John's sons, Aristobulus (104–103 B.C.) and Alexander Jannaeus (104–76). The assumption of the title was tantamount to a manifesto that Judaea was a secular hellenistic state like any other, and in his ruthlessness and ambition Jannaeus was no different than other petty hellenistic kings. It was no accident that it was under his rule that the pietists became restive, and he used the utmost cruelty to suppress them. This brings us to a consideration of parties and sects in the last century B.C., which are important for political as for religious history; the two, indeed, are inextricably intertwined.

The religious principles of the parties called Sadducee and Pharisee, which represent the two principal tendencies, are functions of disparate conceptions of law and authority. The tendencies are reflected in the literature of the intertestamentary period.[17] According to the more general view prophecy, which embodies the loftiest spiritual teaching of the Old Testament, was followed in natural course by the apocalyptic writings, which in turn gave rise in natural course to the New Testament.[18] The legalism of the scribes and rabbis, in this view, was an incrustation which first choked off and then supplanted the spiritual kernel it was designed to protect. According to the other view the religion of the rabbis was the natural development of the religion of the Old Testament and apocalyptic a morbid growth of certain germs found, or perhaps interpolated, in the late prophets and fostered by a political situation so oppressive as to demand the encouragement and solace of millennary expectations.[19]

Actually the demarcation between the two tendencies is not as definitive as proponents of each have made it. The materials recovered from the deposits near the Dead Sea and the archaeological evidence which Professor Goodenough has plausibly interpreted as indicating a widespread mysticism show that the two

tendencies might have achieved a considerable degree of sym-
biosis before they were forcibly separated.[20] Rabbinic legalism
like New Testament antinomianism may have been purposely
designed to channel developments in certain directions and to
stop its flow in others which might actually represent a more
natural course. In what has been called normative Judaism, that
is, Judaism conceived of as continuing in a uniform and uninterrupted tradition from Moses through the prophets and rabbis
down to the Middle Ages and beyond, deviations from the main
stream, such as the latitudinarianism of at least the diaspora in the
hellenistic and Roman periods, have been regarded as sporadic
offshoots which in no way affected the main stream. That normative Judaism is in fact a consistent and uninterrupted tradition
from the first century A.D. onwards is beyond question; but probability suggests that it was not the dominant form before that
century and that the assumption that it was is based on fictive
retrojection.

Of the Sadducees we know that they were conservative and
aristocratic and loyal to the king, and that they adhered to literal
interpretation of the Bible. The combination is logical; the Bible
was the national constitution and had been officially made so by
the Charter which Antiochus III had granted,[21] and dutiful subjects must adhere to the constitution. The only path for unduti-
ful subjects who yet acknowledged the constitution was to apply
a much freer exegesis, and this is the path the Pharisees took.
Their name (*perushim*) means "separatists," and it has been made
abundantly clear that they comprised the humbler strata of the
community. Even where a rabbinic discussion concerns a matter
apparently purely religious it will be found that the view of the
Pharisees favors the proletariat and that of the Sadducees the
privileged classes.[22] In the eyes of the government the Pharisees
could only be regarded as subversive, and that is why, as Josephus
tells us (*Antiquities* 13.372), Jannaeus took particular pleasure in
crucifying some eight hundred of them in 88 B.C.

From the point of view of political ideology it was the Pharisees, not the Sadducees, who carried forward the theory of the

ancient Israelite polity which, as we have noticed, gave the people a sovereignty independent of king and territory. It was this theory which subsequently enabled the Jews to continue as a polity after king and territory were lost; but before that could happen the Pharisees had to legitimatize their position. Under Queen Salome, who succeeded Alexander Jannaeus in 76 B.C., the Pharisees received recognition. The left moved towards the center, as by a universal law of politics it must, and gradually a new left, Zealot and probably Essene, made itself felt. But the new center prevailed, and so succeeded in consolidating its position, after the fall of the state, that it remained the dominant force permanently and all deviations were sloughed off.

What had given the Pharisees their independent posture in the beginning was their insistence on the right to interpret Scripture, and they were very dextrous in finding Biblical authority for such new regulations as the times required. But the basis of authority was still divine revelation, which was conceived of, at least in the later formulation, as extending through a succession of teachers in the authorized tradition. Even when, at some unfavorable conjuncture, persons of meaner stature held the office their authority was still valid: "Jephthah in his generation is as Samuel in his." The movement from the opposition to the center naturally cost the Pharisees some of their liberty; their new prestige enabled them to give their interpretations authority as rigid as the king's had been. But though they may have lapsed into authoritarianism their theory could still dispense with king and territory, and it was the very rigidity of their authoritarianism which enabled their polity to avoid the extinction which was the lot of peoples who lost king and territory.

Among the Pharisees themselves and among others there were some who were not content with the directions the Pharisees had taken and who turned instead to Messianic expectations. From the point of view of law and authority the Messianic parties too were subversive. Like all revolutionary movements they foresaw the imminent abolition of what had been and the advent of a Kingdom of Heaven, in which intermediaries between divine law and the saved would presumably be rendered unnecessary. When the advent of the new kingdom seemed to be indefinitely postponed there was greater need for the organization of authority to be regularized. The rabbis developed a paragovernmental organization, directed by the heads of their schools, which issued rescripts to and collected assessments from their scattered communicants and disposed of the instrument of excommunication to enforce compliance. It was inevitable that a similar organization be developed in the Church. If the Church learned from its Pharisee opposition and the Pharisees from their Maccabee opposition, as it is altogether probable they did, and if the Maccabees learned from Sparta, as the character of their polity and the letters of Jonathan would suggest, then we might see the influence of Sparta enormously expanded over centuries of European history. It is neither from ancient Athens nor from ancient Israel but from Sparta that a regime which claims control of every detail of the life of individuals or an autocrat who rules by the grace of God derives.

But another channel, fed by increments from the east and perhaps also from Sparta, brought the notion of rule by divine grace to Europe. In the preceding chapter we have seen that the notion of the divine destiny of Rome and of the Romans as an elect responsible to that destiny was made official doctrine in the Augustan principate. We must now look briefly at the antecedents of these ideas and at their implications in the theory of law and authority.[23] Originally Rome too was governed, as we should expect, by king, nobles, and assembly. To this pattern it clung more tenaciously than did the Greeks, for the authority of tradition and precedent, the *mos maiorum*, was always very powerful in Rome; but by altering the balance between these three elements Rome effected more revolutionary changes than did Greece. The sovereign authority of the state was conceived of as an abstract entity called the *imperium*, disobedience to which was treason; the imperium was held by the ruling official or shared among colleagues, and passed from its holder to his successors. When the monarchy gave way to the republic, therefore, the pattern was not essentially changed; instead of being held by one man for life and then passed on to his son, the imperium was held by a pair of consuls for a single year and then passed on to their elected successors. Religious observances which could be discharged only by a king were assigned to a specially appointed official designated *rex sacrificulus* or *rex sacrorum*. Similarly when the republic gave way to the empire, the patterns were retained; the emperor made himself an autocrat merely by simultaneously holding offices which gave him control over the army and treasury and a veto over the acts of lesser officials. The other two elements of the ancient pattern underwent similar revolutionary changes in function while their forms remained superficially constant. The senate was in theory merely a consultative body, not legislative or administrative; but during the great days of the republic it held paramount power, while under the empire it was merely honorific. The popular assemblies too first grew in power and then waned. But the Roman could never speak out in his assembly as the Athenian could in his ecclesia; he could only express approval or disapproval of issues placed before him.

It is a general rule, illustrated by earlier Greek and later European experience, that king and commons support one another against the nobility; and during the republic outstanding leaders of the commons, like the Gracchi or Julius Caesar, were regularly accused by the nobility of aspiring to kingship. With the overthrow of the monarchy (510 B.C.), therefore, and its replacement by aristocratic rule the position of the commons deteriorated. The central theme of Roman political history during the centuries following is the struggle between the orders (whose composition, as we shall see, changed), with the commons steadily striving to acquire larger participation in government. One of their early means for enforcing their will was the strike and the threat to set up a separate polity. In 471 they won a special magistracy, the tribunate of the plebeians, especially designed to protect plebeian interests; the tribunes could impose their *veto* ("I forbid") on any acts detrimental to the interests of their order. The Valerio-Horatian laws of 449 B.C. gave the assemblies greater power, the

Canuleian law (445 B.C.) legitimized marriage between patrician and plebeian, the Licinian-Sextian laws (287 B.C.) opened the consulship itself to plebeians, and eventually it became possible for plebeians to serve as pontiffs and augurs.

Whatever the origin of the distinction between patrician and plebeian may have been, it is clear that the salient differentiation, regularly put forward by the patricians to justify their exclusiveness, was a *religious* distinction. It was this that gave the patricians their monopoly of office-holding; public magistracies involved religious duties for whose performance patrician blood was a prerequisite, and for these duties plebeians were men profane. The effectiveness of religion as a device for securing discipline among the common people was noted by the Greek Polybius, a careful and competent student of Roman institutions, who wrote in the second century B.C. This is what Polybius has to say (6.56.9):

My own opinion at least is that the Romans have adopted this course of propagating religious awe for the sake of the common people. It is a course which perhaps would not have been necessary had it been possible to form a state composed of wise men, but as every multitude is fickle, full of lawless desires, unreasoned passion, and violent anger, the multitude must be held by invisible terrors and such like pageantry. For this reason, I think, not that the ancients acted rashly and at haphazard in introducing among the people notions concerning the gods and beliefs in the terrors of hell, but that the moderns are most rash and foolish in banishing such beliefs.[24]

Romans themselves were as aware of the utility of religion in securing discipline. This passage from Cicero's *Laws* (2.7.15), written perhaps in 45 B.C., shows that religion continued to be a political factor:

So in the very beginning we must persuade our citizens that the gods are the lords and rulers of all things, and that what is done is done by their will and authority; that they are likewise great benefactors of man, observing the character of every individual, what he does, of what wrong he is guilty, and with what intention and with what piety he fulfils his religious duties; and that they take note of the pious and impious. For surely minds which are imbued with such ideas will not fail to form true and useful opinions.[25]

An item in Cicero's personal history provides an interesting footnote. Lucretius wrote his Epicurean classic, *De rerum natura*, as everyone knows, to free mankind of the fear of gods and the fear of death; under the date of 54 B.C., shortly after Lucretius died, Cicero wrote a private letter to his brother Quintus (*Ad Quintum fratrem* 2.9.3) in which he says: "Lucretius' poem has, as you write, many flashes of genius, but also much craftsmanship." It is clear that he read the poem. Ten years later, introducing his *Tusculan Disputations*, Cicero declares that no light had hitherto been shed upon philosophy by any Latin writing. In *Tusculan Disputations* 1.3 he says: "There are said to be many works on this subject [Epicurean philosophy] in Latin carelessly written"—which plainly implies that he had not read them, and in 2.3, referring to Latin works on Epicureanism, he says directly, "These I have not read." The only explanation of Cicero's dissimulation is that to the political class to which he adhered Epicureanism had come to be regarded as a subversive doctrine and its most gifted exponent as dangerous to the established order—because in denying conventional religion he denied the basis of that order's claim to superiority.[26]

Patrician blood continued to command a certain reverence and was always a prerequisite for certain religious functions, as for example for enrollment as a vestal virgin; but when plebeians had intermarried with patricians, had achieved high economic and social position, and had attained entree to the highest offices of state, the distinction between patrician and plebeian became politically meaningless. But now the old distinction was replaced by another which was more meaningful and at least as rigid—that between the office-holding class, called *nobiles*, and the rest of the population, called *populares*. The *nobiles* were an extraordinarily compact group, constituting virtually an oligarchy, and extremely jealous of their prerogatives. A principal reason for Roman reluctance to add provinces in the second century B.C. was that the administration of provinces required officials of a level that would admit them to the nobility and would thus enlarge that exclusive order. The nobles were welded into a tight

group by family relationships, promoted by marriages regularly
contracted for political reasons; family connection was the most
important single factor in a political career. And if we seek for
some word to express what it was that a noble possessed and could
transmit to his family, what it was that the rest of the population
recognized as a legitimate claim upon them, the word is *auctoritas*,
which may be feebly rendered "prestige." In Augustus' account
of his stewardship which we know as the *Res gestae Divi Augusti*
or the *Monumentum Ancyranum* [27] he insisted that his powers did
not exceed those of his colleagues in the various magistracies he
held but that his superiority rested on his greater *auctoritas*. We have
noted the persistent Roman reverence for the tradition of *mos
majorum;* their usage of preserving and exhibiting in their ceremonial rooms the masks of all ancestors who had held curule office
and of these masks being worn by professional bearers at funerals
for members of the family gives some measure of the dignity attached to the office-holding tradition. It is not too much to say
that *auctoritas* too had a religious connotation, as real and as
exigent as "patrician" had once had.

If *mos majorum* conferred such authority on office-holders, it
clothed law with a more definitely religious sanction. Republican
Romans thought democracy of the Athenian type frivolity and
never tired of praising the disciplined responsibility of Roman
citizenship as against the individualistic and politically irresponsible Greeks. Cicero, for example, writes (*Republic* 1.53): "When
equal honor is given to the highest and lowest—for men of both
types must exist in every nation—then this very 'fairness' is most
unfair; but this cannot happen in a state ruled by its upper class."
But Cicero also provides the innate Roman reverence for law with
a philosophic rationale which is more explicitly religious. When
he speaks of the *natural* authority implicit in law, as he repeatedly
does, he is plainly echoing Stoic theory. To the Stoics, it must be
remembered, Zeus and nature are virtually interchangeable terms,
and if the law carries the authority of nature its sanction is in
effect religious. A passage like the following from the *Republic*
(3.22) gives the position:

The law is right reason in agreement with nature; it is of universal application, unchanging and everlasting; it summons to duty by its commands, and averts from wrongdoing by its prohibitions. And it does not lay its commands or prohibitions upon good men in vain, though neither have any effect on the wicked. It is a sin to try to alter this law, nor is it allowable to attempt to repeal any part of it, and it is impossible to abolish it entirely. We cannot be freed of its obligations by senate or people, and we need not look outside ourselves for an expounder or interpreter of it. And there will not be different laws at Rome and at Athens, or different laws now and in the future, but one eternal and unchangeable law will be valid for all nations and all times, and there will be one master and ruler, that is, god, over us all, for he is the author of this law, its promulgator and its enforcing judge.[28]

Law, then, is universally binding, its source is deity, and transgression is sin. All that was left to do was to substitute Rome for the universe and make Augustus the authorized representative of deity, and this, as we have seen in the chapter preceding, is what Augustan propaganda actually did, by showing that the Romans were an elect and Augustus their divinely designated leader, by linking Rome and Augustus as objects of worship, and by making the Roman's highest duty service to the ideal of Rome.

Without provision for pains and penalties the Roman's obligation to revere the ruler might have remained a pious wish, and in fact a frivolous attitude to the emperor was made a capital offense by the device of associating it with the crime of treason. Every state must safeguard itself against treason, and in the early republic anyone "who acted with hostile intent against the state" was said to be guilty of *perduellio*. After the rise of the tribunate the quality which resided in and distinguished the Roman commonwealth was designated *majestas*, and anyone who injured that *majestas* was guilty of the crime of *laesae majestatis*. Cicero specifies (*De inventione* 2.17.53) that anyone "who diminishes the dignity or high estate or power of the Roman people or of those upon whom the Roman people has bestowed power" may be charged with that crime. The Greek historians translate *laesa majestas* by *asebeia*, "impiety." Inevitably the *majestas* of the Roman people came t be embodied in the *majestas* of the emperor, as becomes manifest in a series of laws of the early empire. Not only raising a force against the state, killing a magistrate, supporting public enemies, deserting a post of duty, and the like, but any act of disrespect to the emperor could now be made the basis of a charge of "injured majesty." Tacitus (*Annals* 1.72–74) speaks of a number of such charges involving insulting writings or frivolous treatment of the emperor's statues, and under some emperors carrying a ring or coin bearing the image of the emperor into a latrine or brothel might be considered a capital offense. Even so, it must be remarked, autocratic as the emperor's power in fact was, its rigors were exercised by the forms of law, not by caprice. What kept the subjects of the empire obedient was its efficient military and police power; what the emperor claimed as his justification for exacting obedience, it is no exaggeration to say, was a religious sanction.[29] "The offense called *maiestas*," Ulpian says, "is next to sacrilege"; Professor Nock, citing this passage, speaks of *maiestas* as "almost the secular counterpart of *numen*."[30] It is interesting to observe that in the fourth century the "classicizing" Emperor Julian, called the Apostate, and the orator Libanius sought to revert to the ancient theory that all power is vested in the people, who only delegate it to the king; the king's power does not come from divine authorization.[31] But the theory of the Roman empire was carried forward, virtually without interruption, into the subsequent history of Europe.

That the Roman theory was influenced from without there can be no question, but we may speculate on the volume and direction and quality of this influence. The notion of a deified ruler, itself doubtless influenced by eastern notions, was widespread and ingrained in the eastern part of Rome's empire; it was natural for Rome to continue established systems, and in actual fact Rome's administration was an amelioration in the direction of republicanism. The revolutionary innovation was introducing the system in Rome itself; and at least at its introduction and in ap-
~~nce the authoritarianism of the hellenistic rulers was much
~~finement which made the ruler himself subor-

dinate to a higher authority, so that he held sway not merely as law incarnate but as an executive for universal providence, was a Stoic development; Posidonius' elaboration of this doctrine, as has been suggested above, was the guiding principle which shaped the Augustan regime. In connection with Vergil we have seen that his divinely directed hero and his apocalyptic technique may well have derived from eastern sources, and in the case of Livy that his approach bears a closer resemblance to Old Testament historiography than to his Greek predecessors. One curious note, perhaps more amusing than illuminating, may be mentioned. Tertullian, commenting (*On the Prescription of Heretics* 40) on the religious legislation ascribed to Numa Pompilius by Livy (1.18), says, with some temper: "If we consider the religious enactments of Numa Pompilius . . . is it not obvious that the Devil has imitated the scrupulous observances of the Jewish law?" If Tertullian could have conceived that the legend of Numa took the shape that Livy gives it (the name of Numa had of course long been associated with ritual regulations) much nearer Livy's own time than Numa's, he might have added derision to his anger. Livy himself does record the tradition that Numa received his doctrines from Pythagoras, who was teaching in southern Italy late in the sixth century B.C. This tradition Livy rejects on grounds of chronological and geographical discrepancy, but his real objection is a reluctance to credit foreigners with any share in Roman excellence: "His training was not in foreign studies but in the stern and austere discipline of the ancient Sabines."

But another tradition of Roman indebtedness Livy makes no effort to refute, and that is the relationship with Delphi. The Aeneas legend itself, to be sure, is nowhere specifically connected with Delphi; prophecies concerning his arrival in Italy emanate from Dodona or Delos or are assigned to Apollo under one or another of his cult titles. We know that in the sixth century B.C. Etruscan Caere had a treasury at Delphi and was in touch with the oracle, and the first instance of Delphic prophecy in Roman tradition is connected with an Etruscan, Tarquinius Superbus, the last king of Rome.[32] The story, in Cicero, Livy, and elsewhere, is that Tarquin, disturbed by a portent, sent his sons, accompanied by their cousin, Lucius Junius Brutus, to consult the oracle. Brutus feigned stupidity to secure his own safety, and as a symbol of his true character presented Apollo with a staff of wood in which a rod of gold was enclosed. After the young men had completed their official business they asked the oracle which of them would rule in Rome, and the reply was that he who would first kiss his mother would have the highest power. The Tarquins took this answer literally, but Brutus guessed that "mother" referred to mother earth, and promptly fell down, face to earth, as if by accident. Later he was instrumental in expelling the Tarquins, and in fact became one of the first two consuls elected at Rome. The whole story, even the very existence of this Brutus, has been doubted on cogent grounds; the significant point is that the Roman oligarchy, at the time that it was asserting its authority against opposition from below, found it expedient to claim Delphian sanction for its leadership.

The next recorded consultation of Delphi is in connection with the siege of Veii in 396 B.C., when the oracle foretold that Veii would be taken if the Alban lake would be drained.[33] The lake was drained and Veii taken. Again, there are sufficient reasons to doubt this story, but it is a fact that the Romans made a valuable dedication at Delphi at this time, quite possibly from the tithes of the booty of Veii, in keeping with Camillus' advice that such a measure would prevent the dispersal of the booty among the soldiery. During the Samnite Wars, in the fourth century, Delphi prescribed, as a means to victory, that statues of the bravest and the wisest of the Greeks be erected in a prominent place in Rome.[34] The Romans complied by placing statues of Alcibiades and Pythagoras in the Forum. The choice does seem odd, but we may reflect that Alcibiades typifies aristocratic power and Pythagoras authoritarian religion. After Claudius Marcellus' victory over the Gauls in northern Italy between the First and Second Punic Wars the Romans sent a golden bowl as a thank-offering to Delphi. During the Second Punic War we know of several authentic contacts with Delphi. These generally favored the Romans as against the Carthaginians, prescribed the inauguration of new rituals (as of the Great Mother), and solicited offerings for Delphi. When, after the destruction of Carthage, Rome turned toward the east, Delphi was less friendly. In the later republic and early empire it fell into virtual oblivion, and was resuscitated, largely for antiquarian reasons, by Hadrian.

Spread over a space of centuries, these contacts are only desultory, contrived, by whatever group and for whatever motives, to meet particular situations; they cannot indicate a consistent and continuous policy. But Rome possessed a collection of local prophecies which afforded more consistent and continuous opportunity for "working the oracle" than embassies to foreign sanctuaries would allow. These were the Sibylline Oracles,[35] the manuscripts of which, according to tradition, had been brought by the Sibyl of Cumae to Tarquinius Priscus. Since his time, and throughout the history of pagan Rome, they were in charge of a special commission of "priests," to be consulted only by authority of the senate. The origin of these oracles is surrounded by a cloud of legend; what emerges as fact is that early in its history Rome obtained a set of written prophecies from Greek sources. There is abundant evidence for the use of these oracles in republican times, always to promote a particular policy. When the governing group had decided to adopt some special measure the oracles were made to provide a forecast that this was the only solution for a national emergency. It is obvious that the specific emergencies could not have been foreseen centuries in advance, and obvious, therefore, that manipulation of oracles was a conscious device for giving authority to measures which might otherwise meet with resistance. The practice is exactly analogous to Sparta's; whether or not Sparta's example or Plato's literary dissemination of it was an appreciable factor, the perceptible effects upon the Roman polity are exactly analogous to the effects of Greek influence upon the Maccabean polity. It was from hellenistic precedents that the Roman emperors adapted their authoritarianism and the religious sanction to justify it. In Rome before the hellenistic theory was adopted, and in Greece before that theory was developed, sovereignty resided in the people and the ruler was in essence its executive agent.

Not only in areas commonly designated cultural, then, but even in the political organization and practices which were its particular pride Rome learned from the east. It was Rome and the Church which gave Europe the configuration of its culture, in the wider sense of the word, and shaped the lives of all Europeans. Both Rome and the Church are products of hellenistic fusion.

NOTES

THE references below are intended not so much as documentation but rather to indicate where fuller or more specialist treatment may be found. Where possible standard works which are themselves fully documented are cited. A few titles which are referred to frequently are abbreviated as follows:

Baron: Salo W. Baron, A Social and Religious History of the Jews (New York, 1952 ff.)

CAH: The Cambridge Ancient History (Cambridge, 1923 ff.)

LCL: Loeb Classical Library (texts and translations of Greek and Latin authors, published by Harvard University Press)

Pauly-Wissowa: Paulys Realencyclopädie der classischen Altertumswissenschaft, edited by Wissowa, Kroll, et al.

Pfeiffer: R. H. Pfeiffer, Introduction to the Old Testament (New York, 1949)

Rostovtzeff, Hellenistic World: M. Rostovtzeff, The Social and Economic History of the Hellenistic World, 3 vols. (Oxford, 1941)

TAPA: Transactions and Proceedings of the American Philological Association

I: GENESIS AND DIFFUSION

1. A characteristically aristocratic view of the Greeks is that of W. Jaeger, *Paideia*, trans. G. Highet, 3 vols. (New York, 1939–44). C. M. Bowra's exquisite *The Greek Experience* (Cleveland, 1958) stops at 404 B.C.

2. E. R. Curtius, *European Literature and the Latin Middle Ages*, trans. W. R. Trask (New York, 1953), pp. 7 ff., shows how *coalescence* rather than *survival* characterizes the Romanization of European literature.

3. The point is well made by G. Highet, *The Classical Tradition* (Oxford, 1949), p. 127.

4. This is shown in a perceptive study of the different conceptions of time by Tom F. Driver, *The Sense of History in Greek and Shakespearean Dramatic Form* (Columbia University dissertation, microfilm, 1957).

5. G. Bagnani, "Winckelmann and the Second Renaissance," *American Journal of Archaeology* 59 (1955), 107–18; cf. H. C. Hatfield, *Winckelmann and His German Critics* (New York, 1943). Winckelmann's dates are 1717–68.

6. Ruth Benedict, *Patterns of Culture* (New York, 1934), pp. 23 f.

7. W. F. Albright, *From the Stone Age to Christianity* (New York, Anchor, 1957), pp. 337 f.

8. C. F. A. Schaeffer, *Ugaritica*, 2 vols. (Paris, 1939–46), I, 22 f., and Chap. 2.

9. H. G. Gueterbock, *Kumarbi: Mythen von Churritischen Kronos* (Zurich and New York, 1946), and in *American Journal of Archaeology* 52 (1948), 123–34. The Kumarbi material is trans. by A. Goetze in J. B. Pritchard, *Ancient Near Eastern Texts Relating to the Old Testament* (Princeton, 1950), p. 120. An ex-

cellent summary of the whole matter is A. Lesky, "Griechischer Mythos und Vorderer Orient," *Saeculum* 6 (1955), 35–52.

10. M. P. Nilsson, *Geschichte der griechischen Religion* (Munich, 1941), I, 527 f.

11. See C. H. Gordon, "Homer and the Bible: The Origin and Character of East Mediterranean Literature," *Hebrew Union College Annual* 26 (1953), 43–108; cf. F. Dirlmeier, "Homerisches Epos und Orient," *Rheinisches Museum* 98 (1955), 22 f. Luigia A. Stella, *Il poema d'Ulisse* (Florence, 1955), makes much of oriental matter in the *Odyssey*, as against e.g. Rhys Carpenter, *Folk Tale, Fiction, and Saga in the Homeric Epics* (Berkeley, 1946), who favors northern influences. On the similarity of literary techniques and of the concept of the epic hero, see C. M. Bowra, *Heroic Poetry* (London, 1952). Most recently Gordon has shown that Minoan Linear A, used early in the second millennium B.C., is Semitic; see his "Minoan Linear A," *Journal of Near Eastern Studies* 17 (1958), 245–55.

12. On New Testament parallels see R. Garbe, *Indien und das Christentum* (Tübingen, 1914); W. N. Brown, *The Indian and Christian Miracles of Walking on the Water* (Chicago, 1928). On Old Testament, W. Kirfel, "Indische Parallelen zum Alten Testament," *Saeculum* 7 (1956), 369–84.

13. See Gertrude R. Levy, *The Sword from the Rock* (London, 1953).

14. The "Epicurean" parallels are cited in Chap. 11, below. For relations of Proverbs with Amenemope see Pfeiffer, p. 648; with Hesiod, F. Dornseiff, "Hesiods Werke und Tage und das alte Morgenland," *Philologus* 89 (1934), 397–415, and also the Introduction to A. W. Mair's translation (Oxford, 1908). F. M. Cornford, *Principium Sapientiae* (Cambridge, 1952), maintains that Hesiod's cosmogony derives from oriental creation myths which originated in ritual hymns celebrating the magical power of kingship; see also H. Hein, *Hesiods Theogonia als phoenikische Kosmologie* (1956).

15. There is a sane discussion of Orphism in W. K. C. Guthrie, *The Greeks and Their Gods* (Boston, 1950); see also G. Thomson, *Studies in Ancient Greek Society: The Prehistoric Aegean* (London, 1954). Cf. M. P. Nilsson, "Early Orphism and Kindred Religious Movements," *Harvard Theological Review* 28 (1935), 184: "There is plenty of evidence for the fact that mystic, ascetic, and cathartic religious ideas were widespread in the archaic age and appealed strongly to the people." The most enthusiastic champion of the historicity and antiquity of Orpheus is R. Böhme, *Orpheus: Das Alter des Kitharoden* (Berlin, 1953). As an epigraph Böhme has: "Mallarmé: 'La Poésie c'est entièrement detournée de sa voie depuis la grande déviation homérique!' 'Avant Homère quoi?' 'Orphée.'"

16. See Albright, *Stone Age to Christianity*, pp. 176 f., for documentation. Breasted, *Development of Religious Thought in Ancient Egypt* (1912), p. 212, declares that messianism appears in Egypt "nearly a thousand years before its appearance among the Hebrews."

17. For Greek penetration of the east before the hellenistic age see Rostovtzeff, *Hellenistic World*, I, 74 ff.; Albright, *Stone Age to Christianity*, pp. 337 f. For Greeks in Egypt through the whole of antiquity see S. Davis, *Race Relations in Ancient Egypt* (London, 1951), esp. pp. 18 ff.

18. See O. Sellers, *The Citadel of Beth Zur* (Philadelphia, 1933), p. 10; cf. p. 41: "Culturally, from the early part of the fifth century Palestine was dominated by Greece." For other early Hebrew-Greek connections see Baron, I, 184 f., I, 376 f.

19. Baron, I, 130 f. with notes.

II: EXCLUSIVENESS AND INTEGRATION

1. Jüthner, *Hellenen und Barbaren* (Leipzig, 1923), provides documentation.
2. M. P. Nilsson, *Cults, Myths, Oracles and Politics in Ancient Greece* (Lund, 1951), pp. 96–98.
3. Oxyrhynchus Papyri XI, No. 1364; most conveniently in Diels-Kranz, *Die Fragmente der Vorsokratiker*, 7th ed. (Berlin, 1954), II, 346 ff., No. 87.
4. F. Heinimann, *Nomos und Physis* (Basel, 1945), pp. 13 ff.
5. Material collected in F. Weber, *Platons Stellung zu den Barbaren* (Munich, 1904).
6. Recovered by J. Bernays out of Porphyry; see his *Theophrastos Schrift über die Frömmigkeit* (Berlin, 1866), p. 97.
7. See D. R. Dudley, *A History of Cynicism* (London, 1937), pp. 34 f.
8. See M. Mühl, *Die antike Menscheitsidee* (Leipzig, 1928); M. Hadas, "From Nationalism to Cosmopolitanism," *Journal of the History of Ideas* 4 (1943), 105–11.
9. W. W. Tarn, *Hellenistic Civilisations*, 3d ed. (London, 1952), p. 79.
10. See N. W. DeWitt, *Epicurus and His Philosophy* (Minneapolis, 1954), pp. 3 ff., 328 ff.
11. IV Maccabees 8.16 ff., 27 f.; Wisdom 2.10.   12. CAH, IV, 89.
13. See W. W. Tarn, *The Greeks in Bactria and India*, 2d ed. (Cambridge, 1951), pp. 37, 376.
14. For Roman attitudes toward foreigners in the early empire see G. Walser, *Rom, das Reich und die fremden Völker in der Geschichtsschreibung der frühen Kaiserzeit* (Baden-Baden, 1951).

III: ALEXANDER AND THE *OIKOUMENE*; THE SUCCESSORS

1. The best book on Alexander is W. W. Tarn, *Alexander the Great*, 2 vols. (Cambridge, 1948); Vol. I, which contains the narrative, is available in paperback (Boston, Beacon, 1956). Most relevant to the subject of the present work is P. Cloché, *Alexandre le Grand et les essais de fusion entre l'Occident gréco-macédonien et l'Orient* (Neuchâtel, ?1954). The standard histories of the period are Rostovtzeff, *Hellenistic World*, and CAH, Vols. VI and VII. An excellent short account is Tarn's *Hellenistic Civilisation*, 3d ed. (London, 1952).
2. Arrian *Anabasis of Alexander* 7.11 and Tarn's comments, *Alexander the Great*, I, 115, 147.
3. See Introduction of Margarete Bieber, *The Sculpture of the Hellenistic Age* (New York, 1955).
4. For an appreciation see, besides the standard histories of Greek literature, A. Körte, *Hellenistic Poetry*, trans. Hammer and Hadas (New York, 1929).
5. For the status of Egypt and Syria see Rostovtzeff in CAH, Vol. VII, Chaps. 4 and 5.
6. CAH, VII, 153.
7. On the rationale of hellenistic kingship see Rostovtzeff, *Hellenistic World*, I, 268 ff., with bibliography at III, 1379 ff., and especially E. R. Goodenough, "The Political Philosophy of Hellenistic Kingship," *Yale Classical Studies* 1 (1928), 55–104. Three treatises *Peri basileias* are studied in L. Delatte, *Les Traites de la royauté d'Ecphante, Diotogène et Sthenidas* (Paris, 1942), and dated to the first century; but this does not prove that their ideas are that late.
8. See Tarn, *Hellenistic Civilisation*, pp. 138 f.; T. R. S. Broughton in *Studies in*

Roman Economic and Social History in Honor of A. C. Johnson (Princeton, 1951), pp. 236–51.

9. For a discussion and listing see V. Tcherikover, *Die hellenistische Städtegründungen vom Alexander dem Grossen bis auf die Römerzeit (Philologus, Suppl.,* Vol. XIX, 1926); A. H. M. Jones, *The Greek City from Alexander to Justinian* (Oxford, 1940), pp. 1–50.

10. The external uniformity of the hellenistic world is stressed and illustrated in Rostovtzeff, *Hellenistic World,* II, 1032 ff., III, 1582 ff.

IV: BARBARIAN RECEPTIVITY

1. Trans. F. C. Babbitt, LCL.

2. A. H. M. Jones, *The Greek City from Alexander to Justinian* (Oxford, 1940), p. 9.

3. Jones, *op. cit.,* p. 7.   4. Jones, *op. cit.,* pp. 47 ff.

5. M. P. Nilsson, *Cults, Myths, Oracles and Politics in Ancient Greece* (Lund, 1951), pp. 96 ff.

6. Jones, *op. cit.,* pp. 48 ff.   7. See Chap. 5, below.

8. See Chap. 8, below.   9. See Chaps. 11 and 12, below.

10. See below, p. 92.

11. Baron, I, 167 ff., after examining the evidence concludes (p. 171) that "Diaspora Jewry far outnumbered that of Palestine even before the destruction of the Second Temple." According to his calculations "every fifth 'Hellenistic' inhabitant of the Eastern Mediterranean was a Jew."

12. See below, p. 49; cf. M. Smith, "The Image of God: Notes on the Hellenization of Judaism," *Bulletin of the John Rylands Library* 40 (1958), 473–512.

13. See the publications of H. Schwabe and others in the *Bulletin* and the *Journal of the Jewish Palestine Exploration Society,* from 1942 onwards.

14. See E. R. Goodenough, *Jewish Symbols in the Greco-Roman Period* (New York, 1953), I, 178 ff. On the synagogues in general see E. L. Sukenik, *Ancient Synagogues in Palestine and Greece* (London, 1934).

15. Jones, *The Greek City,* p. 36.

16. Cf. F. Preisigke, *Namenbuch* (Heidelberg, 1922); W. Otto, *Kulturgeschichte des Altertums* (Munich, 1925), pp. 98 ff.

17. Otto, *op. cit.,* p. 100, citing B. Clay, *Records in the Library of J. P. Morgan,* II, 6.

18. Baron, I, 373, n. 12, provides bibliography.

19. See Rostovtzeff, *Hellenistic World,* I, 523, III, 1442.

20. Jones, *The Greek City,* p. 36.

21. See V. Tcherikover, *Corpus papyrorum Judaicarum* (Harvard, 1957), pp. 28 f.

22. H. J. Leon, "The Names of Jews in Ancient Rome," TAPA 59 (1942), 205 ff.

23. See Baron, I, 167 ff.

24. Accessible in Hunt and Edgar, *Non-Literary Papyri* (LCL), I, 212 ff., or, trans. alone, in M. Hadas, *A History of Rome* (New York, Anchor, 1956), pp. 107 f.

25. See G. LaPiana, *Foreign Groups at Rome during the First Centuries of the Empire* (reprinted from *Harvard Theological Review* 20; Cambridge, Mass., 1927), pp. 341 ff.

26. See J. C. Dancy, *A Commentary on 1 Maccabees* (Oxford, 1954), pp. 47, 78–82.

27. See *Jewish Encyclopedia* s.v. "Costume," IV, 294 f.

28. See Chap. 6, below. How essential the gymnasium was to a community is indicated by a remark of Pausanias (10.4.1) on Panopeus: "This city—that is, if one can call a place a city when it has no government building, no gymnasium, no theater, no public water supply . . ."

29. For the distribution of Greek theaters see M. Bieber, *The History of the Greek and Roman Theater* (Princeton, 1939), Index s.v. "Theater."

30. For evidence on the extension of Greek tragedy see A. E. Haigh, *The Tragic Drama of the Greeks* (Oxford, 1896), pp. 437 ff. For appreciations of the theater by Jews, especially Philo, see E. Schürer, *Geschichte des jüdischen Volkes im Zeitalter Jesu Christi*, II, 4th ed. (Leipzig, 1907), 45 f.

31. The inscription upon which this is based is translated and discussed in A. Deissmann, *Light from the Ancient East* (London, 1927), p. 451.

32. See below, pp. 130 f.   33. See Chap. 14, below.

34. See E. Weigand, "Baalbek und Rom: Die römische Reichskunst in ihrer Entwicklung und Differenzierung," *Jahrb. d. Archäol. Inst.* 29 (1914), 37 ff., and "Die Orient- oder Rom- Frage in der frühchristlichen Kunst," *Zeitsch. f. neutestamentl. Wissensch.* 22 (1923), 233 ff. The native element is emphasized by P. Collart in *Festgabe für A. von Salis* (Basel, 1951).

35. See Goodenough, *Jewish Symbols*, I, 178 ff.

36. See Baron, II, 8 f.; II, 155; and notes.

37. The basic work is L. Mitteis, *Reichsrecht und Volksrecht in den östlichen Provinzen des römischen Kaiserreichs* (Leipzig, 1891). For the expansion of Greek law see F. Pringheim, "Ausbreitung und Einfluss des griechischen Rechts," *Sitzber. Heidelberger Akademie der Wissensch., Philosoph.-Hist. Klasse*, 1952, p. 1. On the mixture of systems in Egypt see Z. Wenger, "Nationales, griechisches und römisches Recht in Aegypten," *Atti del IV Congresso Internazionale di Papirologia, Firenze 1935* (1936), pp. 159–81.

38. See E. Bickerman, *Der Gott der Makkabäer* (Berlin, 1937), and his *The Maccabees*, trans. M. Hadas (New York, 1947), pp. 80 f.

39. See J. Juster, *Les Juifs dans l'empire romain* (Paris, 1914), II, 88; Baron, II, 415. B. Cohen mentions some interesting parallels in the law of possession in *Proceedings of the American Academy for Jewish Research* 6 (1935), 123–38.

40. See Rostovtzeff, *Hellenistic World*, I, 472 ff.

41. Concise accounts of the Maccabean insurrection may be found in R. H. Pfeiffer, *History of New Testament Times with an Introduction to the Apocrypha* (New York, 1949), pp. 8 ff., or in the introduction to Dancy, *Commentary on 1 Maccabees*. The standard work on the intertestamentary period remains E. Schürer, *Geschichte des jüdischen Volkes im Zeitalter Jesu Christi*, 3d and 4th eds., 4 vols. (Leipzig, 1901–11).

V: LANGUAGE AND ETHOS

1. On the *koine* and on the history of Greek and its diffusion see Karl Brugmann-Eduard Schwyzer, *Griechische Grammatik* (Munich, 1953), pp. 116 ff.

2. See e.g. E. S. Forster, *A Short History of Modern Greece* (London, 1941), p. 214.

3. F. X. Wutz, *Die Transkriptionem von der Septuaginta bis zu Hieronymus* (Beiträge zur Wissenschaft vom A. T., Stuttgart, 1925-33).

4. For this version see D. C. Hesseling, *Le Cinq Livres de la loi* (Leiden, 1897).

5. This is the consensus of all modern students of Septuagint Greek; for a concise bibliography see Pfeiffer, p. 104.

6. See Chap. 18, below.

7. They are numerous enough to justify a special lexicon: S. Krauss, *Griechische und lateinische Lehnwörter in Talmud, Midrasch, und Targum*, 2 vols. (Berlin, 1898-99). This work is susceptible to serious criticism, as by G. Zuntz, "Greek Words in the Talmud," *Journal of Semitic Studies* 1 (1956), 129-40, but is still useful.

8. See S. Lieberman, *Greek in Jewish Palestine* (New York, 1942), pp. 144 ff.; Baron, II, 141 ff.

9. Eusebius, *History of the Martyrs in Palestine* (Syriac version), ed. W. Cureton, pp. 3 f.—cited in Baron, II, 385.

10. See Lieberman, *op. cit.*, pp. 47 f.

11. G. Kittel, *Theologisches Wörterbuch zum Neuen Testament* (Stuttgart, 1933 ff.; Vol. V, to letter *pi*, 1954) deals specifically with the new connotations of old words. Cf. M. Smith, "The Image of God: Notes on the Hellenization of Judaism," *Bulletin of the John Rylands Library* 40 (1958), 473-512.

12. This view is favored by F. J. E. Raby, *Christian Latin Poetry* (Oxford, 1927), p. 21.

13. W. Beare, *Latin Verse and European Song* (London, 1957), pp. 212 f.

14. We are not here concerned with philosophic concepts, for which see e.g. J. F. Callahan, *Four Views of Time in Ancient Philosophy* (Harvard, 1948), or R. B. Onians, *The Origins of European Thought* . . . (Cambridge, 1951), but with the notion of time as reflected in literature. B. A. van Groningen, *In the Grip of the Past* (Leiden, 1953), deals with the subject and says many useful things, but his central position, as indicated in his title, is in the judgment of the present writer wholly mistaken.

15. For acute appreciations of the ethos of Hebrew see S. Smith in CAH, I, 95 ff.; Pfeiffer, pp. 18 ff.

16. See especially Thorleif Boman, *Das hebräische Denken im Vergleich mit dem griechischen*, 2d ed. (Göttingen, 1954).

17. E. Auerbach, *Mimesis* (New York, Anchor, 1956), pp. 9 ff.

18. See M. Hadas, *Ancilla to Classical Reading* (New York, 1954), pp. 42 ff.

19. See below, p. 121.

20. On the sense of the aorist see J. Humbert, *Syntaxe grècque* (Paris, 1945), pp. 124 f.

21. See Hadas, *Ancilla*, pp. 142 f.

22. See T. F. Driver, *The Sense of History in Greek and Shakespearean Dramatic Form* (Columbia University dissertation, microfilm, 1957).

23. See Chap. 20, below.

VI: EDUCATION: GENTLEMEN, SCRIBES, SAINTS

1. See *Foreign Language Press in New York* (W.P.A. Writers' Project, 1941).

2. The basic work is H. I. Marrou, *A History of Education in Antiquity*, trans. G. Lamb (New York, 1956).

3. See W. Jaeger, *Paideia, The Ideals of Greek Culture*, trans. G. Highet (New York, 1939), pp. 1–54.

4. Trans. B. Jowett.

5. Trans. B. Jowett, in R. McKeon, *The Basic Works of Aristotle* (New York, 1941), pp. 1306 f.

6. Marrou, *History of Education in Antiquity*, p. 115.

7. See O. W. Reinmuth, "Genesis of the Athenian Ephebia," TAPA 83 (1952), 34–50. Reinmuth demonstrates that the ephebate did not start, as had been maintained, in the fourth century.

8. The point is made in M. P. Nilsson, *Die hellenistische Schule* (Munich, 1955), pp. 30 ff.

9. Nilsson, *op. cit.*, pp. 80 f. His Foreword (page v) speaks of secondary education as one of the great achievements of the Greeks.

10. Trans. K. von Fritz and E. Kapp, *Aristotle's Constitution of Athens* (New York, 1950), pp. 114 f.

11. On the educational enterprise of the Epicureans and its effects see N. W. DeWitt, *Epicurus and His Philosophy* (Minneapolis, 1954), *passim*.

12. Chap. 14, below.

13. On the place and function of the Egyptian scribe see CAH, II, 224 f.; of the Assyrian, CAH, III, 103. For a brief treatment of scribal education in the ancient Near East generally see Marrou, *History of Education in Antiquity*, pp. xiv ff., 355 f.

14. On education among the Jews see G. F. Moore, *Judaism* (Harvard, 1927), I, 308–22.

15. See M. Hadas, *Ancilla to Classical Reading* (New York, 1954), pp. 34 ff.

16. On Sappho's connection with Orphism see J. Carcopino, *De Pythagore aux Apôtres* (Paris, 1956), pp. 24–35. The Leucadian Leap which is associated with Sappho became a regular Pythagorean symbol: see Carcopino, pp. 36–81.

17. On the notion of immortality conferred by learning see H. Marrou, *MOYCIKOC ANHP* (Grenoble, 1938).

VII: PLATO THE HELLENIZER

1. Much of what follows is an adaptation of my "Plato in Hellenistic Fusion," *Journal of the History of Ideas* 19 (1958), 3–13.

2. See R. A. Pack, *The Greek and Latin Literary Texts from Greco-Roman Egypt* (Ann Arbor, 1952).

3. The expression is that of E. Rohde, "Die Religion der Griechen," in his *Kleine Schriften* (Leipzig, 1901), II, 338, but the view is repeated in more modern books. W. Jaeger, *Aristoteles* (1922) speaks of the Academy as a *Brennpunkt orientalisierender Strömungen*.

4. With admirable thoroughness and erudition, e.g., by Jula Kerschensteiner, *Platon und der Orient* (Stuttgart, 1945). Such high authorities on religious beliefs as Cumont and Nilsson both deprecated the assumption of oriental influence in Plato, and so, among others, does E. Blochet in a series of papers in *Museon* (47–49, 1934–36). At 47, 143, Blochet writes: "Les théories les plus abstruses de Platon s'expliquent sans la moindre difficulté par l'évolution de la pensée hellénique sur le terrain grec . . . sans qu'il soit besoin d'y chercher la moindre influence

de l'Orient." Plato's sojourn in Egypt is still maintained by e.g. R. Godel, "Platon à Héliopolis d'Egypte," *Bulletin de l'Association G. Budé*, 1956, pp. 69–118.

5. *Judaism* (Harvard, 1927), II, 394 f.

6. Aristobulus in Eusebius *Praeparatio evangelica* 13.12 and Eupolemus in *ibid.* 9.26 (= Clement *Stromata* 1.153). Numenius of Apamea (Frg. 10, from Clement *Stromata* 1.22) said, "What is Plato but Moses speaking Attic?" and on the basis of this remark Theodoretus declared that "Plato filched from Moses' theology." Musaeus is equated with Moses in Artapanus (Eusebius *Praep. ev.* 9.27). For these authors see Chap. 8, below.

7. See E. Bickerman, *The Maccabees* (New York, 1947), pp. 80 f.

8. See below, p. 92.   9. See below, pp. 84 f.   10. See below, p. 93.

11. *E Platôn philônizei ê Philôn platônizei:* Jerome *De viribus illustribus* 11; Suidas s.vv. *Abraam* and *Philon;* Photius *Bibliotheca* 105.

12. Cf. H. A. Wolfson, *Philo* (Cambridge, Mass., 1947), I, 112 f.: "Philo's treatment of Plato may therefore perhaps be considered as a criticism of the common understanding of Plato, or of Plato in its original version, but at the same time also as an adoption of Platonism in its essential principles and a revision thereof and an adaptation thereof to certain essential teachings of Scripture."

13. *De opificio mundi* 6.25. Philo follows the Alexandrian Jewish tradition of deriving Plato from Moses.

14. H. A. Wolfson, *The Philosophy of the Church Fathers* (Cambridge, Mass., 1956), esp. pp. 7 ff.

15. The latest edition, with full introduction, is J. Reider, *The Book of Wisdom* (New York, 1957). The problems of the genesis and provenience of the book are best dealt with in F. Focke, *Die Entstehung der Weisheit Salomos* (Göttingen, 1913). The Greek material is analyzed in I. Heinemann, *Poseidonios' metaphysische Schriften* (Breslau, 1921–28), I, 136 ff.

16. As presented e.g. in A. Dietrich, Nekyia: *Beiträge zur Erklärung der neuentdeckten Petrusapokalypse*, 2d ed. (Leipzig, 1913).

17. See G. H. McCurdy, "Platonic Orphism in the Testament of Abraham," *Journal of Biblical Literature* 61 (1942), 213 ff.

18. See M. Hadas, *The Third and Fourth Books of the Maccabees* (New York, 1953). Connections with Platonism are discussed at pp. 115 ff. See also Heinemann, *op. cit.*, pp. 154 ff.

19. See above, p. 49; cf. M. Smith, "The Image of God: Notes on the Hellenization of Judaism," *Bulletin of the John Rylands Library* 40 (1958), 473–512.

20. E. R. Dodds, *The Greeks and the Irrational* (Berkeley, 1951), p. 219.

VIII: BARBARIAN APOLOGETICS

1. Trans. C. B. Gulick, LCL.

2. Trans. M. Hadas, *Heliodorus: An Ethiopian Romance* (Ann Arbor, 1957), p. 79.

3. Trans. H. St. J. Thackeray, LCL.

4. The most illuminating study is R. Merkelbach, *Die Quellen der griechischen Alexanderromans* (Munich, 1954).

5. B. E. Perry, *Aesopica* (Urbana, 1955), I, 4 ff. The Life in the longer version is called "G."

6. P. 34.

7. Trans. S. Zeitlin with Introduction and commentary by S. Tedesche, *The First Book of Maccabees* (New York, 1950).

8. The question of genuineness has provoked a prodigious literature, to which F. M. Abel, *Les Livres des Maccabées* (Paris, 1949), p. 232, provides a key; see also Baron, I, 185, 377.

9. See A. H. M. Jones, *The Greek City from Alexander to Justinian* (Oxford, 1940), p. 50.

10. For hellenistic canons of veracity for narrative prose see Chap. 10, below.

11. For Hecataeus see Pauly-Wissowa, VII, 2750–69 (Jacoby); for Manetho, Pauly-Wissowa, XIV, 1060–1101 (Laqueur).

12. From Diodorus Siculus 40.3.

13. See Heinemann's excellent study of ancient antisemitism in Pauly-Wissowa Suppl., V, 3–43, esp. p. 23.

14. See Chap. 18, below.   15. See Chap. 14, below.

16. See Chap. 10, below.

17. See introductions to M. Hadas, *Three Greek Romances* (New York, Anchor, 1953) and *Heliodorus: An Ethiopian Romance* (Ann Arbor, 1957).

18. Newest edition: M. Hadas, *Aristeas to Philocrates* (New York, 1950).

19. For Alexander Polyhistor see Pauly-Wissowa, I, 1449 ff. (Schwartz).

20. The classic study of these fragments remains J. Freudenthal, *Hellenistische Studien: Alexander Polyhistor und die von ihm erhaltenen Reste jüdischer und samaritanischer Geschichtswerke* (Breslau, 1875). Far the best editions are those in F. Jacoby, *Die Fragmente der griechischen Historiker* III c (1958); that of W. N. Stearns, *Fragments from Graeco-Jewish Writers* (Chicago, 1908) is wholly unsatisfactory. The standard treatments are E. Schürer, *Geschichte des jüdischen Volkes im Zeitalter Jesu Christi*, Vol. III, 4th ed. (Leipzig, 1909), and Otto Stählin in Christ-Schmid, *Geschichte der griechischen Literatur*, 6th ed., II, 1 (Munich, 1920), 536–656.

21. On Demetrius see Schürer, *op. cit.*, pp. 472 ff.; Stählin, *op. cit.*, pp. 588 f.; Schwartz in Pauly-Wissowa, IV, 2813.

22. On Eupolemus see Schürer, *op. cit.*, pp. 351–54; Stählin, *op. cit.*, pp. 589 f.; Jacoby in Pauly-Wissowa, VI, 1227 ff.; P. Wendland, *Die hellenistische-römische Kultur in ihren Beziehungen zu Judentum und Christentum* (Tübingen, 1912), pp. 198 ff.

23. Trans. in E. Barker, *From Alexander to Constantine* (Oxford, 1956), pp. 97 ff.; text in Dittenberger, *Orientis graeci inscriptiones selectae*, 2 vols. (Leipzig, 1903–5), I, 140–66 (No. 90).

24. On Artapanus see Schürer, *op. cit.*, 477–80; Wendland, *op. cit.*, pp. 199 f.; Schwartz in Pauly-Wissowa, II, 1306, and especially Heinemann (s.v. "Moses") in Pauly-Wissowa, XVI, 365 ff.

25. See M. Braun, *History and Romance in Graeco-Oriental Literature* (Oxford, 1938), pp. 26 ff. I. Lévy, *La Légende de Pythagore de Grèce en Palestine* (Paris, 1927), suggests that this romance was a vehicle for Pythagorean doctrine, which thus made its way into subsequent Jewish and Christian thought.

26. See R. Merkelbach, *Die Quellen des griechischen Alexanderromans* (Munich, 1954), pp. 74 ff.

27. On the Elder Philo and Theodotus see Schürer, *op. cit.*, pp. 497 ff.; Stählin, *op. cit.*, pp. 606 ff.; J. Gutmann in *Eshkolot* (Jerusalem, 1954), pp. 49–72.

28. Text, commentary, and discussion in J. Wieneke, *Ezechielis Iudaei exagoge* (Monasterii Westfalorum, 1931). See also Schürer, *op. cit.*, pp. 500 ff.; Stählin, *op. cit.*, pp. 607 f.; Dietrich in Pauly-Wissowa, VI, 1701 f.

29. On Aristobulus see Stählin, *op. cit.*, pp. 603 ff.; Gercke in Pauly-Wissowa, II, 918 ff.; P. Wendland in *Jewish Encyclopedia*, II, 97.

30. H. A. Wolfson, *Philo* (Cambridge, Mass., 1947), I, 95, rejects the suggestion that Aristobulus' "Philonic" passages derive from Philo. C. Siegfried, *Philo von Alexandria als Ausleger des Alten Testaments* (Jena, 1875), pp. 24 ff., finds it perfectly credible that Aristobulus (and others) could use allegorical interpretation of the Stoic pattern in the second century B.C.

31. On the significance of these see Chap. 18, below.

IX: EXOTICS IN THE MAIN STREAM

1. See Chap. 8, Barbarian Apologetics.

2. The index of F. Susemihl, *Geschichte der griechischen Literatur in der Alexandrinerzeit* (Leipzig, 1891–92), or of the second part of Christ-Schmid-Stählin, *Geschichte der griechischen Literatur* (Munich, 1920–24) shows how numerous such persons were.

3. See M. Pohlenz, *Die Stoa*, 2 vols. (Göttingen, 1948), and his *Stoa und Stoiker* (Zurich, 1950); cf. J. Bidez, *La Cité du Monde et la Cité du Soleil chez les Stoiciens* (Paris, 1932).

4. The outstanding authority on Posidonius is K. Reinhardt; his *Poseidonios* (Heidelberg, 1921) is brought up to date in his very full article in Pauly-Wissowa, XXII (1953), 558–826.

5. See I. Heinemann, *Poseidonios' metaphysische Schriften*, 2 vols. (Breslau, 1921, 1928), I, 1–10 ff.

6. See Heinemann, *op. cit.*, I, 136–58; M. Mühl, "Zu Posidonius und Philo," *Wiener Studien* 60 (1942), 28 ff.

7. Cf. J. Kaerst, *Studien zur Entwickelung der Monarchie in Altertum* (Munich and Leipzig, 1898), pp. 65 f.

8. See Pohlenz, *Stoa und Stoiker*, pp. 266 f., 341 f.   9. See Chap. 18, below.

10. The history of Gadara, with documentation, may be found in E. Schürer, *Geschichte des jüdischen Volkes in Zeitalter Jesu Christi*, II, 4th ed. (Leipzig, 1907), 157–61.

11. On Menippus see A. and M. Croiset, *Histoire de la littérature grecque*, V (Paris, 1928), 48; Christ-Schmid-Stählin, *Geschichte der griechischen Literatur*, I, 86; Helm in Pauly-Wissowa, XVI, 888.

12. P. Wendland, *Die hellenistisch-römische Kultur in ihren Beziehungen zu Judentum und Christentum*, 3d ed. (Tübingen, 1912), 75–81.

13. On Varro's Menippean Satires see Schanz-Hosius, *Geschichte der römischen Literatur*, I, 4th ed. (Munich, 1927), 555–78; K. Mras, *Neue Jahrbucher für das klassische Altertum* 33 (1914), 390–420.

14. O. Weinreich in *Hermes* 51 (1916), 413 f.

15. R. Helm, *Lucian und Menipp* (Leipzig, 1906).

16. Hariri's *maqamat* are available in translation: T. Chenery, *The Assemblies of Al Hariri* (London, 1867); see the introduction to this book and also to M. Hadas, *Zabara's Book of Delight* (New York, 1932).

17. For Meleager see Christ-Schmid-Stahlin, *Geschichte der griechischen Literatur,* pp. 326 f.; Geffcken in Pauly-Wissowa, XVI, 481 ff.

18. *Ancient Greek Literature* (New York, 1897), p. 394.

19. J. W. Mackail, *Select Epigrams from the Greek Anthology* (London, 1906), pp. 35 f.

20. F. A. Wright, *The Poets of the Greek Anthology* (London, n.d.), p. 123.

21. On Philodemus see Pauly-Wissowa, XIX, 2444–82, where adequate bibliography is given.

22. The *In Pisonem* passage is 68–72. Cicero's obligations to Philodemus are indicated in Schanz-Hosius, *Geschichte der römischen Literatur,* pp. 506, 511, and in the commentaries. For the influence on Horace see the Kiessling-Heinze commentary on *Ars poetica* 130, 319, 357, 449.

23. See Schanz-Hosius, *op. cit.,* pp. 274, 402.

24. A. Körte, "Augusteer bei Philodem," *Rheinisches Museum* 45 (1890), 172–77.

X: HISTORIOGRAPHY

1. See Chap. 6, above.

2. Trans. M. Hadas, *Plutarch: On Love, the Family, and the Good Life* (New York, Mentor, 1957), pp. 180 f.

3. B. A. van Groningen, *In the Grip of the Past* (Leiden, 1953), maintains that the view of the past here described as an innovation had always obtained, but he strains the evidence and tends to disregard its dating.

4. Admirably dealt with in B. L. Ullman, "History and Tragedy," TAPA 73 (1942), 25–53.

5. See Gisela Schmitz-Kahlmann, "Das Beispiel der Geschichte im politischen Denken des Isokrates," *Philologus, Suppl.,* Vol. 31, No. 4 (1939). Cf. E. Mikkola, *Isokrates, seine Anschauungen im Lichte seiner Schriften* (Helsinki, 1954).

6. Examples in M. P. Nilsson, *Cults, Myths, Oracles, and Politics in Ancient Greece* (Lund, 1951), pp. 49 ff.

7. For brief accounts of the historians mentioned here and in the paragraphs following see M. Hadas, *History of Greek Literature* (New York, 1950), pp. 129, 193 ff.

8. *Hellenistic Civilisation,* 3d ed. (London, 1952), p. 250.

9. The several elements are analyzed by R. Merkelbach, *Die Quellen der griechischen Alexanderromans* (Munich, 1954); cf. P. Treves, "Il problema storiografico del romanzo di Alessandro," *Rivista di filologia e d'istruzione classica* 33 (1955), 250–75.

10. See e.g. A. Abel, *Le Roman d'Alexandre légendaire medieval* (Brussels, 1955).

11. See F. Jacoby, *Atthis: The Local Chronicles of Ancient Athens* (Oxford, 1949).

12. See F. Leo, *Griechisch-römische Biographie* (Berlin, 1901); his distinction between peripatetic and Alexandrian types is untenable. Also: D. R. Stuart, *Epochs of Greek and Roman Biography* (Berkeley, 1928).

13. See P. Scheller, *De hellenistica historiae conscribendae arte* (Leipzig, 1911), pp. 79 ff. This is the best characterization of hellenistic historiography. See also F. W. Walbank in *Bulletin of the Institute of Classical Studies of the University of London,* 1955, pp. 4–14.

14. Trans. W. R. Paton, LCL.

15. In Sextus Empiricus *In grammaticos* 655, 25b.

16. See M. Hadas, *Ancilla to Classical Reading* (New York, 1954), pp. 43 ff.

17. See Introductions to M. Hadas, *Three Greek Romances* (New York, Anchor, 1953), and *Heliodorus: An Ethiopian Romance* (Ann Arbor, 1957).

18. See M. Hadas, *Aristeas to Philocrates* (New York, 1951), pp. 78 ff.

19. See Chap. 12, below.   20. See Chap. 19, below.

21. This is proved from a thorough analysis of the Joseph story in *Antiquities* 2.39–59 by M. Braun, *Griechischer Roman und hellenistische Geschichtsschreibung*, "Frankfurter Studien zur Religion und Kultur der Antike," No. 6 (Frankfurt am Main, 1934), pp. 23–117.

22. See H. St. J. Thackeray, *Josephus the Man and the Historian* (New York, 1929).

23. See *The Idea of History in the Ancient Near East*, ed. R. C. Dentan, "American Oriental Series," No. 38 (New Haven, 1955), which contains papers, with bibliographies, by R. H. Bainton, Ludlow Bull, Millar Burrows, G. G. Cameron, Erich Dinkler, Julian Obermann, Paul Schubert, E. A. Speiser, C. B. Welles. For a convenient selection of texts see J. B. Pritchard, *Ancient Near Eastern Texts Relating to the Old Testament* (Princeton, 1950), pp. 227–322.

24. R. G. Collingwood, *The Idea of History* (Oxford, 1946), p. 12.

25. *The Idea of History in the Ancient Near East*, ed. Dentan, pp. 32 f.

26. See the excellent survey of E. A. Speiser in *ibid.*, pp. 35–76.

27. See D. D. Luckenbill, *Ancient Records of Assyria and Babylonia* (Chicago, 1926).

28. See S. Smith in CAH, III, 111 f.   29. CAH, III, 237.

30. Appreciations are to be found in all modern introductions to the Old Testament; Pfeiffer, pp. 171 ff., is excellent. Pfeiffer and W. G. Pollard, *The Hebrew Iliad* (New York, 1957) presents a fresh translation of J separated from its additions and an enthusiastic introduction. For useful bibliography of recent work on ancient Jewish historiography see O. Eissfeldt, *Geschichtsschreibung im Alten Testament: Ein kritischer Bericht über die neueste Literatur dazu* (Berlin, 1948).

31. Quoted by Baron, I, 100, from E. Meyer's *Die kulturelle, literarische und religiöse Entwicklung des israelitischen Volkes in der älteren Königszeit*, p. 4.

32. See Pfeiffer, pp. 782–812; O. Eissfeldt, *Einleitung in das alte Testament*, 2d ed. (Tübingen, 1956), pp. 654–69.

33. Pfeiffer, p. 806.

34. Eissfeldt would put the body of the book earlier but agrees it may have been added to and worked over as late as 200.

35. Newest edition: S. Zeitlin and S. Tedesche, *The First Book of Maccabees* (New York, 1950); the quotation below is from this edition.

36. Newest edition: S. Zeitlin and S. Tedesche, *The Second Book of Maccabees* (New York, 1952); the quotation below is from this edition.

37. Newest edition: M. Hadas, *The Third and Fourth Books of the Maccabees* (New York, 1953).

38. See M. Hadas, "III Maccabees and the Tradition of Patriotic Romance," *Chronique d'Egypte* 47 (1949), 97 ff.

XI: DRAMA AND DIATRIBE

1. See Chap. 6, above.

2. See M. Hadas, *The Third and Fourth Books of the Maccabees* (New York, 1953), 100 f. and Index s.v. "Tragic imagery."

3. P. 99.   4. See above, p. 95.

5. For summary and comment see T. H. Gaster, *Thespis* (New York, 1950), pp. 62 f.

6. See Chap. 12, below.

7. *Jewish Encyclopedia* s.v. "Shemoneh Esreh," XI, 270–83.

8. Pointed out by Y. F. Baer, *Israel among the Nations* (in Hebrew: Jerusalem, 1955), pp. 31–35.

9. Trans. H. W. Smyth, LCL.   10. Gaster, *Thespis*.

11. Pfeiffer, pp. 660 ff., gives an excellent summary of critical opinion on Job.

12. Trans. M. Friedlaender, *Guide to the Perplexed* (London, 1925), pp. 296 f.

13. *Praelectiones de sacra poesi Hebraeorum* (Oxford, 1753); see Pfeiffer, p. 683.

14. New York, 1918. It should be mentioned that the book has a laudatory preface by the eminent George Foot Moore.

15. See M. Hadas and J. H. McLean, *The Plays of Euripides* (New York, 1936), Introduction. Such an interpretation of the Euripidean gods out of the machine was first suggested by A. W. Verrall, and is the basis of the interpretations of Euripides in e.g. G. Norwood, *Greek Tragedy* (Boston, 1920).

16. *The Messages of the Poets* (Vol. VII of *The Messages of the Bible*: New York, 1909), pp. 76 f. From Kuhl's notice of Gans, *De invloed van Aeschylus' Prometheus op het Boek Job* in *Theologische Rundschau* 34 (1952), 240, it appears that the same view is held in that book, which is not accessible to me.

17. Pp. 678 f.

18. This view was propounded by W. Schmid, *Untersuchungen zum gefesselten Prometheus*, "Tübinger Beiträge z. Altert.," No. 9 (Stuttgart, 1929), repeated by him in W. Schmid and O. Stählin, in *Geschichte der griechischen Literatur* I, iii, 1 (Munich, 1940), pp. 281–308. Schmid's view is supported in F. Heinimann, *Nomos und Physis* (Basel, 1945), pp. 44, 92. For strongly put arguments against, see M. Pohlenz, *Die griechische Tragödie* (Göttingen, 1954), II, 42 ff.

19. See Norwood, *Greek Tragedy*, p. 37.

20. Pfeiffer, p. 703.

21. On the relationship of Ecclesiastes to Greek teaching see H. Ranston, *Ecclesiastes and the Early Greek Wisdom Literature* (London, 1925); H. W. Hertzberg's commentary (Leipzig, 1932), pp. 47 ff.; Pfeiffer, pp. 724 ff.

22. Trans. E. A. Speiser in J. B. Pritchard, *Ancient Near Eastern Texts Relating to the Old Testament* (Princeton, 1950), p. 90.

23. Trans. J. A. Wilson in Pritchard, *op. cit.*, p. 467.

24. Pfeiffer, p. 730.   25. Edition of C. Siegfried (1898).

26. *Die hellenistische-römische Kultur* (Tübingen, 1912), p. 356; "Endlich bietet die Diatribe mit ihrer lebhaften Durchsetzung der Rede durch Einwürfe und Fragen, durch Anrede des Gegners, mit ihrer Vorliebe für kurze parataktische Glieder, durch die besonders die Bedingung, statt untergeordnet zu werden, der Folge syntaktisch beigeordnet wird, für manche paränetische Partien der pauli-

nischen Briefe auffallende Parallelen." The relationship of the Epistles to the diatribe is fully treated in R. Bultmann, *Der Stil der paulinischen Predigt und die kynisch-stoische Diatribe*, "Forschungen zur Rel. und Lit. der A. und N.T.," No. 13 (Göttingen, 1910).

27. *Das Buch der Predigers oder Koheleth* (Bonn, 1925), esp. p. 11.

28. See A. Oltramare, *Les Origines de la Diatribe romaine* (Geneva, 1926).

29. See R. Helm in Pauly-Wissowa, XII (1924), 23; Wendland, *Die hellenistische-römische Kultur in ihren Beziehungen zu Judentum und Christentum* (Tübingen, 1912), pp. 91 f.

30. E. Norden, *Agnostos Theos: Untersuchungen zur Formen-Geschichte religiöser Rede* (Leipzig, 1913, and reprints). This close-packed and usefully documented book should be consulted by those interested. More recent studies are B. Gaertner, *The Areopagus Speech and Natural Revelation* (Uppsala, 1955), and H. Hommel, "Neue Forschungen zur Areopagrede, Acta 17," *Zeitschrift für die Neutestamentliche Wissenschaft* 46 (1955), 145–78.

31. "Poimandres" is the first, and oldest and best, of the eighteen treatises in the *Hermetica* or *Hermes Trismegistos*, of which text and French translation are now available by Nock and Festugière in the Budé series. A detailed study, with text appended, germane to the present context is R. Reitzenstein, *Poimandres: Studien zur griechisch-ägyptischen und frühchristlichen Literatur* (Leipzig, 1904). *Poimandres* ("shepherd of men") has close affinities with the Christian *Shepherd of Hermas*.

32. Fragments of the *Kerygma Petri* are found in Clement. For this and other relevant pieces (Barnabas, the Clementines) see Norden, *Agnostos Theos*, pp. 4 ff.

33. The date and the probability of Jewish authorship have been established by J. Bernays, *Die heraklitischen Briefe: Ein Beitrag zur philosophischen und religionsgeschichtlichen Literatur* (Berlin, 1869); cf. Norden, *Agnostos Theos*, p. 31.

34. *Agnostos Theos*, pp. 47 ff.

XII: LOVE, TRIANGULAR AND PURE

1. See R. Briffault, *The Mothers*, 3 vols. (New York, 1927). Relevant matter on the Greeks may be found at I, 398–414; on succession to rule through connection with a woman at III, 43–45. Cf. *also Reallexikon der Vorgeschichte*, s.vv. "Fraueneinfluss," IV, 92–104, and "Mutterrecht," VIII, 360–80.

2. H. R. Hall, CAH, I, 279.   3. II Samuel 16.21.

4. George Thomson, *Studies in Ancient Greek Society: The Prehistoric Aegean* (New York, 1949), is the most stalwart (but by no means the only) advocate of the theory that matriarchy prevailed in Greece in the second millennium B.C. and that traces of the system have survived in Homer. There are strong opponents of the view also.

5. This illustration is drawn from J. A. K. Thomson, *Studies in the Odyssey* (Oxford, 1914), p. 168.

6. Nicolaus of Damascus 49 (*Fragmente der griechischen Historiker* 90 F 47) gives a fuller account of Gyges' family connections but says nothing to invalidate Herodotus' story or its interpretations. For the newly discovered fragments of a Greek tragedy on the subject of Gyges and Candaules' wife see note 23, below.

7. This is the consensus of scholarship; see e.g. Wilamowitz' introduction to his

edition (Berlin, 1891); L. Meridier, *Hippolyte d'Euripide* (Paris, n.d.); and Pauly-Wissowa, s.vv. "Hippolytos," VIII, 1868 ff., and "Phaedra," XIX, 1543–52.

8. The Potiphar, Stepmother, and Chaste Youth motifs are recognized in various treatments of the play, e.g., Christ-Schmid-Stählin, *Geschichte der griechischen Literatur* I, iii, 1 (Munich, 1940), 377–90.

9. For these personages see s.vv. in W. H. Roscher, *Ausführliches Lexikon der griechische und römische Mythologie,* and cf. Stith Thompson, *Motif-Index of Folk-Literature,* S31 and 31.1.

10. So e.g. Wilamowitz in his edition and Leo's introduction to his text of Seneca. Cf. H. F. Wolf, *Untersuchungen zu Senecas dramatischen Technik* (Leipzig, 1933), pp. 24–47.

11. M. Braun, *History and Romance in Graeco-Oriental Literature* (Oxford, 1938), pp. 44–93.

12. So R. H. Charles, still the standard authority on the subject; new evidence for a very early dating is adduced by E. Bickerman, "The Date of the Testaments of the Twelve Patriarchs," *Journal of Biblical Literature* 69 (1950), 245–60. Charles' translation is reprinted from his full text edition (London, 1908) in his *Apocrypha and Pseudepigrapha of the Old Testament* (Oxford, 1913), II, 282–367; there is a convenient S.P.C.K. reprint with introduction by W. O. E. Oesterley (London, 1917).

13. So M. DeJonge, *The Testaments of the Twelve Patriarchs* (Assen, 1953).

14. So, with due consideration of DeJonge's work, O. Eissfeldt, *Einleitung in das Alte Testament,* 2d ed. (Tübingen, 1956), 780–86.

15. So Braun, *History and Romance,* pp. 93 f. There seems to have existed an analogous Moses Romance, with erotic content, from which authors like Artapanus, Philo, and Josephus drew (see Heinemann in Pauly-Wissowa, XVI, 365 ff.), and an Alexander Romance which was one of the sources of Pseudo-Callisthenes: see R. Merkelbach, *Die Quellen des griechischen Alexanderromans* (Munich, 1954).

16. M. Braun, *Griechischer Roman und hellenistische Geschichtsschreibung,* "Frankfurter Studien zur Religion und Kultur der Antike," No. 6 (Frankfurt am Main, 1934), pp. 23–117.

17. The motif occurs at least once in each of the Greek Romances; K. Kerényi, *Die griechisch-orientalische Romanliteratur in religionsgeschichtlicher Beleuchtung* (Tübingen, 1927), holds that all derive from an Isiac aretalogy.

18. Below, Chap. 13.

19. See introduction to M. Hadas, *Three Greek Romances* (New York, Anchor, 1953).

20. Plutarch *Demetrius* 38; Lucian *De dea syria* 17–18; Appian *Syr.* 59–61; Valerius Maximus 5.7, ext. 1.

21. See Chap. 9, above.

22. *De fabellis antiquis earumque ad Christianos propagatione* (Göttingen, 1911), pp. 11 f. A good chapter on "Greek and Early Christian Novels" is to be found in T. R. Glover, *Life and Letters in the Fourth Century* (Cambridge, 1901), pp. 357–86. A probable case of Christian use of and interpolation in Achilles Tatius' romance is pointed out in Q. Cataudella, "Giovanni Crisostomo 'imitatore' di Aristofane," *Athenaeum* 18 (1940), 236–43.

23. The fragments were first published by E. Lobel, "A Greek Historical Drama," *Proceedings of the British Academy* 35. Fifth-century dating is also maintained by D. L. Page, *A New Chapter in the History of Greek Tragedy* (Cam-

bridge, 1951). A hellenistic date is argued for by K. Latte, in *Eranos* 48 (1950), 136 ff.; A. Lesky, in *Anzeiger für die Altertumswissenschaft* 3 (1950), 248; 5 (1952), 152 f., and *Hermes* 81 (1953), 1 ff. The papyrus itself is of the third century.

24. M. Rozelaar, "Shir ha-Shirim al Reka ha-Shirah ha-Erotit ha-Yavanit ha-Hellenistit," *Eshkolot* (Jerusalem, 1954), pp. 33–48. The paragraphs which follow are adapted from this work, with Dr. Rozelaar's generous permission, because his own publication is not easily accessible to many readers.

25. See e.g. M. Bieber, *Hellenistic Sculpture* (New York, 1954), Figs. 611–20.

26. Trans. H. T. Riley (Bohn).

27. Trans. W. R. Paton, LCL; and so the citations from the *Palatine Anthology* which follow.

28. E. Mireaux, *La Reine Bérénice* (Paris, 1951).

29. Trans. F. C. Grant, *Hellenistic Religions* (New York, 1953), pp. 9 f. The text of the so-called Chronicle of Lindus is most easily accessible in Lietzmann's *Kleine Texte*, No. 131.

30. Trans. M. Hadas, *Plutarch on Love, the Family, and the Good Life* (New York, Mentor, 1957), p. 13.

XIII: ARETALOGIES AND MARTYRDOMS

1. See Pauly-Wissowa, II (1895), 670 ff., and especially Suppl. 6 (1935), 13–15. Cf. A. Kiefer, *Aretalogische Studien* (Freiburg i. Br., 1929), and R. Reitzenstein, *Hellenistische Wundererzählungen* (Leipzig, 1906).

2. Cf. *inter al.* Isaiah 42.12, 43.21, 63.7, Habakkuk 3.3; also I Peter 2.9. In an expression like *tas aretas theou kerussein* the Hebrew original for *aretas* actually means "wonders."

3. See N. W. DeWitt, *Epicurus and his Philosophy* (Minneapolis, 1954), pp. 328 ff., and his *St. Paul and Epicurus* (Minneapolis, 1954), pp. 3 ff.

4. Reitzenstein, *Hellenistische Wundererzählungen*, pp. 4 ff., cites a number, of which the closest and most interesting is from Jerome on Hilarion, 39.

5. On Iambulus' and other utopian writings see D. Winston, *Iambulus: A Study of Greek Utopianism* (Columbia University dissertation, microfilm, 1956).

6. Cf. e.g. O. Eissfeldt, *Einleitung in das Alte Testament*, 2d ed. (Tübingen, 1956), 493 f.

7. Translated, with Apollonius' letters and Eusebius' treatise, in F. C. Conybeare's LCL ed.

8. See Reitzenstein, *Hellenistische Wundererzählungen*, pp. 53 ff. For the literary reworking of original accounts, cf. the opening of Luke: "Inasmuch as many have undertaken to compile a narrative . . . it seemed good to me also . . . to write an orderly account. . . ."

9. On heroes and heroization see E. Rohde, *Psyche* (English trans., London, 1925), pp. 115 ff.

10. See A. Ronconi, "Exitus illustrium virorum," *Studi italiani di filologia classica* 17 (1940), 332. Ronconi shows how the tradition established by the death of Socrates was carried on by the Stoics and then taken up by the pagan and Christian martyrdoms. Tacitus used the device to glorify the opposition to the Caesars.

11. On Calanus see Pauly-Wissowa, X (1919), 1544 f. His story is told or referred to in Arrian 7.2 f., Strabo 15.715 ff., Diodorus 17.107, Plutarch's *Alexander* 65, 69 f., Athenaeus 10.437a, Aelian 2.41, Lucian's *Peregrinus* 25, Philo, *Quod omnis*

probus liber 14. This last is quoted below in F. H. Colson's translation in Vol. IX of the LCL edition of Philo.

12. See M. Hadas, *The Third and Fourth Books of the Maccabees* (New York, 1953), pp. 116 ff., 125 ff.

13. Trans. in *Ante-Nicene Christian Library*, ed. A. Roberts and J. Donaldson, I (Edinburgh, 1870), 84.

14. See H. Thurston in *Encyclopedia of Religion and Ethics* (New York, 1921), XI, 55; cf. H. W. Surkau, *Martyrien in jüdischer und frühchristlicher Zeit* (Göttingen, 1938).

15. See H. A. Musurillo, *The Acts of the Pagan Martyrs: Acta Alexandrinorum* (Oxford, 1954).

16. *Op. cit.*, p. 275.   17. Cited by Musurillo, *op. cit.*, 238.

18. On Hermippus see Pauly-Wissowa, VIII (1912), 845–52; cf. R. Hope, *The Book of Diogenes Laertius* (New York, 1930), pp. 163 ff.

19. Statistics are supplied by Musurillo, *op. cit.*, 239 ff.

20. See Reitzenstein, *Hellenistische Wundererzählungen*, pp. 37 ff. At p. 55 he says, with some justification: "Ich glaube schon jetzt sagen zu dürfen, dass Propheten- und Philosophen Aretalogien das literarische Vorbild für die christlichen Apostelakten gegeben haben."

21. K. Kerenyi, *Die griechisch-orientalische Roman literatur in religionsgeschichtlicher Beleuchtung* (Tübingen, 1927).

XIV: CULT AND MYSTERY

1. The standard work on the subject is M. P. Nilsson's monumental *Geschichte der griechischen Religion,* 2 vols. (Munich, 1941, 1950). A convenient and sane English book is W. K. C. Guthrie, *The Greeks and Their Gods* (Boston, 1950).

2. W. Otto, *The Homeric Gods,* trans. M. Hadas (New York, 1954). Otto gives an elaborate contrast of the nature and operation of the chthonic and Olympian gods and makes Homer one of the world's great religious reformers.

3. J. Burckhardt, *Griechische Kulturgeschichte* (Berlin, 1930), II, 198 ff., gives a picturesque and still valuable description of the manifestations of religious life in the Greek landscape.

4. So e.g. C. Schneider, "Die griechische Grundlagen der hellenistische Religionsgeschichte," *Archiv für Religionswissenschaft* 36 (1939), 300–347.

5. Trans. R. C. Jebb, *The Characters of Theophrastus* (London, 1909), pp. 139 ff.; cf. H. Bolkestein, *Theophrastos' Charakter der Deisidaimonia als Religionsgeschichtliche Urkunde*, "Religionsgeschichtliche Versuche und Vorarbeiten," XXI, 2 (Giessen, 1929).

6. A number are given in F. C. Grant, *Hellenistic Religions: The Age of Syncretism* (New York, 1953), which is a convenient collection of texts. Other striking passages are cited in A. D. Nock, "Early Gentile Christianity," in *Essays on the Trinity and the Incarnation,* ed. A. E. J. Rawlinson (London, 1928), p. 70. For rules of ritual purity see Nilsson *Geschichte der griechischen Religion,* I, 80–100 and T. Wächter, *Reinheitsvorschriften, im Griechische Kult,* "Religionsgeschichtliche Versuche und Vorarbeiten," IX, 1 (Giessen, 1910).

7. Grant, *op. cit.*, p. 26; cf. Nilsson, *op. cit.*, I, 82.

8. Grant, *op. cit.*, pp. 26 f.; text in Dittenberger, *Sylloge inscriptionum Graecarum,* 3d ed., No. 999.

9. Grant, *op. cit.*, pp. 27 f.

10. See A. D. Nock, *Conversion* (Oxford, 1933), pp. 48, 280. S. Dow, "The Egyptian Cults in Athens," *Harvard Theological Review* 30 (1937), 183–232, shows that such cults made their first appearance early in the fourth century and became reasonably respectable in the third, but never rose much above a "metic" status.

11. For a full treatment of this subject see G. LaPiana, *Foreign Groups at Rome during the First Centuries of the Empire*, reprinted from *Harvard Theological Review* 20 (1927).

12. From N. A. Nikam and Richard McKeon, *The Edicts of Asoka* (Chicago, 1958), p. 29.

13. Grant, *Hellenistic Religions*, pp. 28 ff.; cf. Nock, *Conversion*, pp. 216 f.

14. Convenient collections of the literary, epigraphical, and papyrological materials are listed in the succinct summary under "Sarapis" in the *Oxford Classical Dictionary;* add P. Jouguet, "Les Premiers Ptolemée et l'Hellenisation de Sarapis," in *Hommages Bidez-Cumont* (Brussels, 1950), pp. 159 ff.

15. From Nock, *Conversion*, pp. 51 f.; cf. P. Roussel, *Les Cultes égyptiens à Délos* (Paris, 1915–16), pp. 71 ff.

16. Particularly by Roussel, *op. cit.*

17. *Isis and Osiris* 67, 377 f., trans. F. C. Babbitt, LCL.

18. A good guide to the abundant literature on the mysteries is Nilsson, *Geschichte der griechischen Religion*, I, 440 ff., 619 ff. The most enlightening single treatment is A. D. Nock, "Hellenistic Mysteries and Christian Sacraments," *Mnemosyne* 5 (1952), 177–213. *The Mysteries: Papers from the Eranos Yearbooks* (New York, 1956) has a series of studies of widely dispersed areas. For connections with Christianity see S. Angus, *The Mystery Religions and Christianity*, 2d ed. (New York, 1928).

19. In "Early Gentile Christianity," *Essays on the Trinity and the Incarnation*, ed. Rawlinson, p. 57.

20. For the religious background of Pythagoreanism see W. K. C. Guthrie, *Orpheus and Greek Religion* (London, 1935); there are illuminating remarks in E. R. Dodds, *The Greeks and the Irrational* (Berkeley, 1951): see index s.v.

21. For a good general account of Neopythagoreanism see R. Festugière in *Revue des études grecques* 50 (1937), 470 ff.

22. Paris, 1927 ("Bibliothèque de l'Ecole des hautes études," No. 250). The connection between the Essence and the Pythagoreans is supported by F. Cumont, "Esséniens et Pythagoriciens d'après un passage de Josèphe," *Comptes rendues de l'Académie des inscriptions et des belles lettres*, 1930, pp. 99–112.

23. Jérôme Carcopino, *De Pythagore aux Apôtres* (Paris, 1956).

24. Conveniently accessible in T. H. Gaster, *The Dead Sea Scriptures* (New York, Anchor, 1956), pp. 33 ff.

25. A. Dupont-Sommer, *The Jewish Sect of Qumran and the Essenes* (New York, 1955), Index s.v. "Pythagoras." The entire problem is reviewed in G. Molin, "Qumran-Apokalyptik-Essenismus," *Saeculum* 6 (1955), 244–81, where the connections with Pythagoreanism are belittled.

26. Gaster, *Dead Sea Scriptures*, pp. 21 ff., presents such a list.

27. Carcopino, *De Pythagore aux Apôtres*, pp. 80 f.

28. The Greek survivals in the Greek Orthodox Church are enumerated, with some sectarian animus, by A. Harnack, *What is Christianity?* (reprinted New York, 1957), p. 241: "I do not expect to be contradicted if I answer that this official ecclesiasticism with its priests and its cult, with all its vessels, saints, vest-

ments, pictures, and amulets, with its ordinances of fasting and its festivals, has absolutely nothing to do with the religion of Christ. It is the religion of the ancient world, tacked on to certain conceptions in the Gospels, or, rather, it is the ancient religion with the Gospel absorbed into it."

XV: PRAYER AND CONFESSION

1. Condescending patronage characterizes such books as Bullfinch's *Age of Fable* (and its numerous analogues in Europe) from which generations have acquired their knowledge of the Greek gods. But it is implicit in such scholarly and useful and essentially sympathetic books as S. Angus, *The Religious Quest of the Graeco-Roman World* (New York, 1929) and A. Deissmann, *Light from the Ancient East* (London, 1927).

2. W. F. Otto, *The Homeric Gods: The Spiritual Significance of Greek Religion,* trans. M. Hadas (New York, 1954), p. 6.

3. Trans. R. Lattimore. For an analysis of this and Greek prayer generally see K. von Fritz, "Greek Prayer," *Review of Religion* 9 (1945), 3 ff.

4. Trans. B. Jowett.

5. Trans. P. E. Matheson, *Epictetus, the Discourses and Manual* (Oxford, 1916).

6. Frg. 537 von Arnim (from Stobaeus), trans. Walter Pater, abridged by E. Bevan, *Later Greek Religion* (London, 1927), pp. 14 f.

7. See R. H. Pfeiffer, *History of New Testament Times with an Introduction to the Apocrypha* (New York, 1949), p. 376.

8. See C. C. Torrey, *The Apocryphal Literature* (New Haven, 1945), pp. 82 ff. On the prayers in Tobit see Pfeiffer, pp. 278, 281 ff.

9. Cf. especially Xenophon of Ephesus 4.3, trans. M. Hadas, *Three Greek Romances* (New York, Anchor, 1953), p. 147.

10. For a concise history of the conceptions of prayer from the New Testament through Origen see E. G. Jay, *Origen's Treatise on Prayer* (London, 1954), pp. 1–75.

11. For discussion and documentation see R. B. Tollinton, *Clement of Alexandria, A Study in Christian Liberalism* (London, 1914), II, 92 ff.

12. Jay, *op. cit.*, p. 61.

13. See G. F. Moore, *Judaism* (Cambridge, Mass., 1927), II, 212 ff. The translations cited are Moore's.

14. Trans. Alice Zimmern, *Porphyry to Marcella* (London, 1896).

15. Trans. Bevan, *Later Greek Religion,* p. 227.

16. Trans. Angus, *Religious Quest,* p. 9.

17. The fullest work is R. Pettazzoni, *Confessione dei peccati,* 3 vols. (Bologna, 1929–36). Pettazzoni's "Confession of Sin and the Classics," *Harvard Theological Review* 30 (1937), 1–14, presents a complete list of examples of which those cited below are specimens.

18. E. Norden, *Aeneis VI,* 2d ed. (Leipzig, 1916), p. 276.

XVI: BLESSED LANDSCAPES AND HAVENS

1. Cf. *Ethics of the Fathers* 3: "One who interrupts his study to exclaim, 'How handsome this tree, how handsome this field!' it is accounted to him as a mortal sin."

2. Trans. Samuel Butler.

3. Trans. H. G. Evelyn-White, LCL.

4. Trans. J. E. Sandys, LCL.

5. Trans. H. R. Fairclough, LCL.

6. See Chap. 6.

7. "The Sapphic Ostracon," TAPA 73 (1942), 308-18; the paragraph following owes much to this paper. Text and translation are also given in D. L. Page, *Greek Literary Papyri*, I, 374-79 (LCL).

8. Trans. H. W. and F. G. Fowler, *The Works of Lucian* (Oxford, 1905), II, 156 ff.

9. Trans. M. Hadas, *Three Greek Romances* (New York, Anchor, 1953), p. 38.

10. Trans. H. St. J. Thackeray, LCL.

11. The classic work remains A. Dieterich, *Nekyia: Beiträge zur Erklärung der neuentdeckten Petrusapokalypse*, 2d ed. (Leipzig, 1913). See also E. Rhode, *Psyche*, 8th ed. (Tübingen, 1921), I, 68 ff., II, 214 ff., III, 369 ff.; E. Norden, *Aeneis VI*, 2d ed. (Leipzig, 1916), pp. 18 ff., 295 ff. For translation and commentary see M. R. James, *The Apocryphal New Testament* (Oxford, 1924), pp. 505 ff. Further bibliography may be found in Turyn's "The Sapphic Ostrakon," TAPA 73 (1942), 308-18.

12. These matters are discussed in Dieterich, *Nekyia*, and the various works cited in the note preceding. Turyn (pp. 314 f.) mentions as interesting examples the Passio SS. Perpetuae et Felicitatis 11.5 and the History of Barlaam and Josaphath 280, ed. Boissonade.

13. See E. R. Curtius, *European Literature and the Latin Middle Ages* (New York, 1953), pp. 183 ff.

14. Trans. J. M. Mitchell, *Petronius: The Satyricon* (London, n.d.), p. 223.

15. Trans. M. Rosenblum, *Luxorius* (New York, 1961), No. 46.

16. Trans. Jack Lindsay, *Song of a Falling World* (London, 1948), pp. 61 f.

17. See Curtius 197; the Libanius passage is quoted from Curtius.

18. Relevant passages are collected and discussed in C. Bonner, "Desired Haven," *Harvard Theological Review* 34 (1941), 49-67. Professor Bonner does not speak of influence but thinks of the parallels as showing "that there is no difference in kind between the emotion experienced by the earnest Christian and that of the pagan who followed one of the higher forms of the older religion" (p. 66). He cites very aptly the parallel between *Suppliants* 190, "Stronger than a castle is an altar; 'tis a shield invulnerable," and Luther's "Ein' feste Burg ist unser Gott, ein gutes Wehr und Waffen," of which G. Méautis had remarked, "Etrange rapprochement, preuve singulière de l'identité du sentiment religieux à travers des siècles." *Eschyle et la Trilogie* (Paris, 1936), p. 52.

XVII: ART

1. For an appreciation of the Originality of hellenistic art, especially sculpture, see Margarete Bieber, *The Sculpture of the Hellenistic Age* (New York, 1955), pp. 3-6.

2. See H. R. Hall in CAH, III, 325.

3. P. Cloché, *Alexandre le Grand et les essais de fusion entre l'Occident gréco-macédonien et l'Orient* (Neuchâtel, ?1954), pp. 256-72, deals with fusion in art.

4. *Kulturgeschichte des Altertums* (Munich, 1925), pp. 125 ff.

5. "Die Schicksale des Hellenismus in der bildenden Kunst," *Neue Jahrbücher für Klassische Altertum* 15 (1905), 19 ff., and repeated in other writings.

6. On the Alexander Sarcophagus see Bieber, *Sculpture*, pp. 72 ff.

7. On hellenistic wall decoration see Mary H. Swindler, *Ancient Painting* (New Haven, 1929), pp. 303 ff. The origins of wall divisions and the modes of decorating them are analyzed in M. Rostovtzeff, "Ancient Decorative Wall Painting," *Journal of Hellenic Studies* 39 (1919), 144–63.

8. The fullest publication, richly illustrated, is J. P. Peters and H. Thiersch, *Painted Tombs in the Necropolis at Marissa* (London, 1905); see also Swindler, *Ancient Paintings*, pp. 349 ff. and Figs. 556–59. The paintings are described and discussed, mainly for their religious significance, in E. R. Goodenough, *Jewish Symbols in the Greco-Roman Period* (New York, 1953), I, 65 ff. and Figs. 6 ff.

9. This scene is reproduced and discussed in Rostovtzeff, *Hellenistic World*, II, 520.

10. H. C. Butler, *Syria: Architecture, Section A* (Leyden, 1919), Pl. 1, pp. 1–25. Butler dates the monument to the period of Ptolemy Philadelphus (285–247 B.C.).

11. Peters and Thiersch, *Painted Tombs*, p. 92.

12. These have been known since the early nineteenth century. The fullest publication is M. Rostovtzeff, *Decorative Painting in the South of Russia* (St. Petersburg, 1914), which has 600 pages of text and 112 plates; see his article cited in note 7 above and also his *Skythen und der Bosporus* (Berlin, 1931), pp. 227 ff. See also E. H. Minns, *Scythians and Greeks* (Cambridge, 1913), pp. 316 ff.

13. The standard work has been Alfred Foucher, *L'Art gréco-bouddhique du Gandhâra* (Paris, 1905–51); see also his *The Beginnings of Buddhist Art*, trans. L. A. and F. W. Thomas (London, 1917). I. Lyons and H. Ingholt, *Gandhâra Art in Pakistan* (New York, 1957), provides a rich collection of photographs. There is a very perceptive appreciation, with demonstration of Greek influence, in G. Highet, *The Migration of Ideas* (New York, 1954), pp. 33 ff. A most useful tool is H. Deydier, *Contribution a l'étude de l'art du Gandhâra* (Paris, 1950), which lists and summarizes work done on the subject since 1922. For the historical background see W. W. Tarn, *The Greeks in Bactria and India*, 2d ed. (Cambridge, 1951).

14. Foucher, *L'Art gréco-bouddhique*, II, 467.

15. See H. Ingholt's commentary in the catalogue of the Yale University Art Gallery exhibition, *Palmyrene and Gandharan Sculpture* (New Haven, 1954).

16. B. Rowland, "Gandhara and Early Christian Art," *American Journal of Archaeology* 49 (1945), 445–48.

17. For discussion and documentation of the matter in this and the following paragraph see H. H. Dubs, "A Roman Influence upon Chinese Painting," *Classical Philology* 38 (1943), 13 ff. Professor Dubs kindly acknowledges his indebtedness to the present writer for the suggestion that Roman influence was involved; the suggestion was originally given to Professor Duyvendak. See also Dubs' paper in *American Journal of Philology* 62 (1941), 322 ff., and now his *A Roman City in Ancient China* (London, 1957), which enlarges on these papers.

18. See Ingholt in Yale University Art Gallery catalogue, *Palmyrene and Gandharan Sculpture*.

19. A complete account of the synagogue at Dura, fully illustrated, is C. H. Kraeling and others, *The Synagogue: The Excavations at Dura-Europus, Final Report VIII, Part 1* (New Haven, 1956).

20. Frequently reproduced, e.g., Swindler, *Ancient Paintings*, Fig. 384.

21. See Kraeling and others, *The Synagogue*, p. 392.

22. These qualities may best be seen in the Buddha heads from Afghanistan;

see J. Barthoux, *Les Fouilles de Hadda*, Vols. III and IV, "Mémoires de la Délégation Archéologique Française en Afghanistan" (Paris, 1930, 1933).

23. For a brief discussion of the Arch, with bibliography, see S. B. Platner, *A Topographical Dictionary of Rome* (Oxford, 1929), pp. 36 ff.

XVIII: ROMAN EVANGELISTS

The material on the relationships between the Latin poets and the Sibylline Oracles in the first part of this chapter is adapted, with Professor Franz Dornseiff's generous permission, from his "Verschmähtes zu Vergil Horaz und Properz," *Berichte über die Verhandlungen der sächsischen Akademie der Wissenschaft zu Leipzig*, Philologische-Historische Klasse, Band XCVII, Heft 6 (Berlin, 1951), pp. 44 ff.

1. Trans. Charles Eliot Norton. 2. Lactantius *Divine Institutes* 7.24.11.

3. Trans. H. R. Fairclough, LCL.

4. The fullest account of the Sibylline Oracles is A. Rzach, in Pauly-Wissowa, Zweitex Reihe, II (1923), 2073–83. The newest text, trans., and commentary is A. Kurfess, *Sibyllinische Weissagungen* (Munich, 1951). Books 3–5, with trans. and commentary, appear in Charles, *Apocrypha and Pseudepigrapha of the Old Testament* (Oxford, 1913), II, 368 ff. The most convenient English trans. (from which the citations below are drawn) is H. N. Bates, *The Sibylline Oracles, Books III–V* (S.P.C.K., 1918).

5. Pointed out by Dornseiff, *op. cit.*, pp. 49 f.

6. One notable exception is E. Norden, *Das Geburt des Kindes* (Berlin, 1924). Norden holds that Vergil would have disdained to use a Jewish source, and has ransacked every corner of antiquity to find less convincing models. The Eclogue is the subject of an enormous literature; see e.g. H. Jeanmaire, *Le Messianisme de Virgile* (Paris, 1930); H. J. Rose, *The Eclogues of Vergil* (Berkeley, 1942).

7. N. W. DeWitt, "The Influence of the Saviour Sentiment upon Vergil," TAPA 54 (1923), 39–50.

8. Trans. J. P. Postgate, LCL.

9. So e.g. A. Kurfess, *Philologus* 91 (1937), 413, cited with approval by Dornseiff, *op. cit.*, p. 52.

10. Dornseiff, *op. cit.*, pp. 56 ff. This of course premises the priority of Vergil's poem, which a minority of scholars does not accept.

11. Trans. C. E. Bennett, LCL. 12. *Hermes* 73 (1938), 237 ff.

13. Passages pertaining to Jews and Judaism in all classical authors are collected in T. Reinach, *Textes d'auteurs grecs et romains relatifs au Judaisme* (Paris, 1895).

14. J. Handel, *Eos* 31 (1928), 501 ff.; K. Mras, *Wiener Studien* 54 (1936), 74 ff.

15. *Classical Philology* 37 (1942), 385 ff. 16. *Op. cit.*, p. 65, cf. pp. 64–104.

17. See Chap. 19, below. 18. See above, p. 113.

19. See W. R. Newbold, "Five Transliterated Aramaic Inscriptions," *American Journal of Archaeology* 30 (1926), 288–329.

20. See M. Hadas, "Oriental Elements in Petronius," *American Journal of Philology* 50 (1929), 378–85.

21. This is true of many examples in the useful collection in J. F. Hurst and H. C. Whiting, *L. Annaeus Seneca* (New York, 1877), pp. 40 ff.

22. It is interesting to note that when Hillel was asked to summarize the law "while standing on one foot" he made the identical reply (*bSabbath* 31a). Interesting too is the fact that *stans pede in uno*, otherwise unexampled in this sense, is used to express hasty composition in Horace *Satires* 1.4.10.

23. Tertullian *De anima* 20.

XIX: AN ELECT, WITH SOVEREIGNTY AND WITHOUT

1. Trans. G. Rawlinson.

2. The status of rulers in the ancient east, including Palestine, is dealt with at the opening of the next chapter.

3. See M. Hadas, "Aeneas and the Tradition of the National Hero," *American Journal of Philology* 69 (1948), 408 ff.

4. Trans. C. Day Lewis (New York, Anchor, 1953), and so the *Aeneid* passage below.

5. Chap. 18.

6. See M. Hadas, "Livy as Scripture," *American Journal of Philology* 61 (1940), 445 ff.; H. Hoch, *Die Darstellung des politischen Sendung Roms bie Livius* (Frankfurt, 1951); Iiro Kajanto, *God and Fate in Livy* (Turku, 1957).

7. See M. Hadas, "The Religion of Plutarch," *Review of Religion* 6 (1942), 270 ff.

8. *bGittin* 56b and parallels.

XX: AUTHORITY AND LAW

1. For the uses to which the contrast was put see F. Heinimann, *Nomos und Physis* (Basel, 1945).

2. An excellent conspectus is afforded by a symposium on "Authority and Law in the Ancient Orient," *Journal of the American Oriental Society*, Supplement 17 (1954).

3. *Ibid.*, p. 1.   4. E. A. Speiser in *ibid.*, pp. 8 f.

5. Cited by H. G. Güterbock in *ibid.*, p. 16.

6. D. H. H. Ingalls in *ibid.*, pp. 34 ff.   7. Derk Bodde in *ibid.*, pp. 46 ff.

8. *Ibid.*, p. 54.

9. For a succinct and authoritative account of political theory in ancient Israel see Baron I, 63 ff.

10. The reforms of Josiah and the influence of the Deuteronomist are dealt with in all Biblical handbooks; see e.g. J. A. Bewer, *The Literature of the Old Testament in its Historical Development* (New York, 1926), pp. 134, 147.

11. Cf. C. Hignett, *A History of the Athenian Constitution to the End of the Fifth Century* B.C. (Oxford, 1952).

12. Cf. H. Mitchell, *Sparta* (Cambridge, 1952).

13. *Klio* 12 (1912), 340.   14. Trans. H. G. Dakyns.

15. See M. Hadas, "The Social Revolution in Third Century Sparta," *Classical Weekly* 26 (1932–33), 41 ff., 49 ff.

16. A full and modern account of the period between Alexander the Great and the Roman conquest is Vol. I of M. Abel, *Histoire de la Palestine* (Paris, 1952). See also E. Bevan in CAH, VIII, 495 ff.

17. A convenient guide is R. H. Pfeiffer, *History of New Testament Times with an Introduction to the Apocrypha* (New York, 1949), which provides good bibliographies.

18. This view is common among students of Apocrypha and apocalyptic, as for example in R. H. Charles, *Apocrypha and Pseudepigrapha of the Old Testament* (Oxford, 1913); cf. R. H. Charles' *Religious Development between the Old and the New Testaments* (New York and London, 1914) in the Home University Library.

19. This view is common among students of rabbinics, e.g., G. F. Moore, *Judaism in the First Centuries of the Christian Era* (Cambridge, Mass., 1927).

20. See especially his *Jewish Symbols in the Greco-Roman Period* (New York, 1953), I, 132.

21. E. Bickerman has shown that Josephus *Antiquities* 12.138 ff. represents such a charter; see R. Marcus' summary of Bickerman's and other views in Appendix D of the LCL Josephus, VII, 763 f.

22. The class coloring of Pharisee legislation is demonstrated at length in L. Finkelstein, *The Pharisees: The Sociological Background of Their Faith* (Philadelphia, 1938).

23. A good general work is L. Homo, *Roman Political Institutions* (London, 1929).

24. Trans. W. R. Paton, LCL. 25. Trans. C. W. Keyes, LCL.

26. See M. Hadas, *History of Latin Literature* (New York, 1952), p. 70.

27. It is interesting to observe, in view of our theme that the *Monumentum Ancyranum* has no precedent in Latin epigraphy, but does have parallels in hellenistic and oriental inscriptions, which similarly glorify a ruler: see M. A. Levi, "La Composizione delle Res Gestae Divi Augusti," *Rivista di filologia classica* 25 (1947), 189–210.

28. Trans. C. W. Keyes, LCL.

29. See H. Wagenvoort, "Gravitas et Maiestas," *Mnemosyne* 5 (1952), 87 ff.

30. *American Journal of Philology* 65 (1944), 103. The Ulpian citation is from Digests 48.4.1: "proximum sacrilegio crimen est quod maiestatis dicitur."

31. See F. Dvornik, "The Emperor Julian's Reactionary Ideas on Kingship" in *Late Classical and Medieval Studies in Honor of A. M. Friend, Jr.* (Princeton, 1955), pp. 71 ff. The principal texts are in Julian's *Letter to Themistius* and Libanius' *Declamation* 5. Dvornik will soon publish a book on "Origins of Christian Political Philosophy."

32. For Roman connections with the Delphic Oracle see H. W. Parke and D. E. W. Wormell, *The Delphic Oracle* (Oxford, 1957), I, 265–91.

33. Cicero *De divinatione* 1.44.100; Livy 5.15.3; Plutarch, Camillus 3; et al.

34. Pliny *Historia naturalis* 36.26. 35. See above, p. 240.

INDEX